THE
DEEP
STATE
GOES VIRAL

ISBN Print: 9781630692995
ISBN Digital: 9781630692988

Published by Brownstone Institute 2025

Cover image: Anthony Freda

BROWNSTONE INSTITUTE
Austin, Texas | 2025

THE

DEEP STATE

GOES VIRAL

PANDEMIC PLANNING AND THE COVID COUP

DEBBIE LERMAN

BROWNSTONE
INSTITUTE

CONTENTS

FOREWORD

It was about a month into lockdowns, April 2020, and my phone rang with an unusual number. I picked up and the caller identified himself as Rajeev Venkayya, a name I knew from my writings on the 2005 pandemic scare. Now the head of a vaccine company, he once served as Special Assistant to the President for Biodefense, and claimed to be the inventor of pandemic planning.

Venkayya was a primary author of "A National Strategy for Pandemic Influenza" as issued by the George W. Bush administration in 2005. It was the first document that mapped out a nascent version of lockdowns, designed for global deployment. "A flu pandemic would have global consequences," said Bush, "so no nation can afford to ignore this threat, and every nation has responsibilities to detect and stop its spread."

It was always a strange document because it stood in constant contradiction to public health orthodoxies dating back decades and even a century. With it, there were two alternative paths in place in the event of a new virus: the normal path that everyone is taught in medical school (therapeutics for the sick, caution with social disturbances, calm and reason, quarantines only in extreme cases) and a biosecurity path that invoked totalitarian measures.

Those two paths existed side-by-side for a decade and a half before the lockdowns.

Now I found myself speaking with the guy who claims credit for having mapped out the biosecurity approach, which contradicted all public health wisdom and experience. His plan was finally being implemented. Not too many voices dissented, partially due to fear but also due to censorship, which was already very tight. He told me to stop objecting to the lockdowns because they have everything under control.

I asked a basic question. Let's say we all hunker down, hide under the sofa, eschew physical meetings with family and friends, stop all gatherings of all kinds, and keep businesses and schools closed. What, I asked, happens to the virus itself? Does it jump in a hole in the ground or head to Mars for fear of another press conference by Andrew Cuomo or Anthony Fauci?

After some fallacy-filled banter about the R-naught, I could tell he was getting exasperated with me, and finally, with some hesitation, he told me the plan. There would be a vaccine. I balked and said that no vaccine can sterilize against a fast-mutating respiratory pathogen with a zoonotic reservoir. Even if such a thing did appear, it would take 10 years of trials and testing before it was safe to release to the general population. Are we going to stay locked down for a decade?

"It will come much faster," he said. "You watch. You will be surprised."

Hanging up, I recall dismissing him as a crank, a has-been with nothing better to do than call up poor writers and bug them.

I had entirely misread the meaning, simply because I was not prepared to understand the sheer depth and vastness of the operation now in play. All that was taking place struck me as obviously destructive and fundamentally flawed but rooted in a kind of intellectual error: a loss of understanding of virology basics.

Around the same time, *The New York Times* posted without fanfare a new document called *PanCAP-A: Pandemic Crisis Action Plan - Adapted*. It was Venkayya's plan, only intensified, as released on March 13, 2020, three days before President Trump's press conference announcing the lockdowns. I read through it, reposted it, but had no idea what it meant. I hoped someone could come along to explain it, interpret it, and tease out its implications, all in the interest of getting to the bottom of the who, what, and why of this fundamental attack on civilization itself.

That person did come along. She is Debbie Lerman, intrepid author of this wonderful book that so beautifully presents the best thoughts on all the questions that had eluded me. She took the document apart and discovered a fundamental truth therein. The rule-making authority for the pandemic response was not vested in public-health agencies but the National Security Council.

This was stated as plain as day in the document; I had somehow missed that. This was not public health. It was national security. The antidote under development with the label vaccine was really a military countermeasure. In other words, this was Venkayya's plan times ten, and the idea was precisely to override all tradition and public health concerns and replace them with national security measures.

Realizing this fundamentally changes the structure of the story of the last five years. This is not a story of a world that mysteriously forgot about natural immunity and made some intellectual error in thinking that governments could shut down economies and turn them back on again, scaring a pathogen back to where it came from. What we experienced in a very real sense was quasi-martial law, a deep-state coup not only on a national but on an international level.

These are terrifying thoughts and hardly anyone is prepared to discuss them, which is why Lerman's book is so crucial. In terms of public debate about what happened to us, we are barely at the beginning. There is now a willingness to admit that the lockdowns did more overall harm than good. Even the legacy media has started venturing out to grant permission for such thoughts. But the role of the pharmaceuticals in driving the policy and the role of the national-security state in backing this grand industrial project is still taboo.

In 21st-century journalism and advocacy designed to influence the public mind, the overwhelming concern of all writers and institutions is professional survival. That means fitting into an approved ethos or paradigm regardless of the facts. This is why Lerman's thesis is not debated; it is hardly spoken of at all in polite society. That said, my work at Brownstone Institute has put me in close contact with many thinkers in high places. This much I can say: what Lerman has written in this book is not disputed but admitted in private.

Strange isn't it? We saw during the Covid years how professional aspiration incentivized silence even in the face of egregious violations of human rights, including mandatory school closures that robbed children of education, followed by face-covering requirements and forced injections for the whole population. The near-silence was deafening even if anyone with a brain and a conscience knew that all of this was wrong. Not even the excuse that "We didn't know" works anymore because we did know.

This same dynamic of social and cultural control is fully in operation now that we are through that stage and onto another one, which is precisely why Lerman's findings have not yet made their way to polite society, to say nothing of mainstream media. Will we get there? Maybe. This book can help; at least it is now available for everyone brave enough to confront the facts. You will find herein the most well-documented and coherent presentation of answers to the core questions (what, how, why) that all of us have been asking since this hell was first visited upon us.

Jeffrey Tucker

BROWNSTONE INSTITUTE
March 19, 2025

INTRODUCTION

For most of my adult life, I believed pretty much everything I read in *The New York Times* and heard on NPR. I thought there was a huge difference between Republicans and Democrats, right and left, conservative and liberal. And I was a proud, even self-righteous, liberal leftist Democrat.

Since March 2020, however, with the onset of the Covid lockdowns, all of those comfortable beliefs, and my former sense of belonging to a meaningful political and social movement, have evaporated. I find myself on the outside of the mainstream, attempting to construct a new worldview and find new people and institutions I can trust. One such newfound haven of sanity is Brownstone Institute – publisher of this book, and the website where most of the articles included here first appeared.

I'm lucky to be a pretty panic-proof type of person, so back at the beginning of 2020 I was not afraid. I did not think the virus posed a mortal threat to myself or my family. I knew it affected mostly elderly people with serious ailments. I also knew that there was never a pathogen in recorded history that was so transmissible and so deadly that it required locking down the entire world. And I found no evidence that the Wuhan virus, as it was called at the time, was such a pathogen.

Yet everyone else around me seemed to have completely lost their minds, first and foremost the media and public health experts. Instead of calming the public down and advocating common sense measures, they started screaming about "flattening the curve," masking, social distancing, and the necessity of depriving children of education and socialization to "protect grandma." Then they started bulldozing all of society into supporting not just untested and unregulated gene-based vaccines, but also coercive mandates of those vaccines.

It was utter madness.

Yet almost nobody else I knew saw things the way I did. Even when it became eminently clear that the virus posed little to no threat to children, they insisted that kids had to stay inside (the absolute worst thing I could imagine for a child) and wear masks. Then, when vaccine mandates were rolled out, even when it became indisputable that the vaccines did not stop infection or transmission, people turned vicious. "The unvaccinated" became a category of undesirable outcasts not allowed to participate in society. I found the irrational cruelty of people who considered themselves moral and compassionate to be downright terrifying.

The main cause of that irrational reaction was equally spine-chilling: a massive, global censorship and propaganda campaign undertaken by the entire online and traditional media apparatus. It was so gigantic that most people could not – and still do not – believe it could happen.

Due to that unprecedented narrative-control campaign, barely anyone was investigating what actually happened.

So I decided to do just that, and what I discovered was astonishing.

I discovered that the U.S. Covid pandemic response was not a public health response run by the HHS, CDC or any other public health body. Instead, it was a **biodefense/counter-terrorism response**, run by the Pentagon, National Security Council, and Department of Homeland Security.

When I continued to dig, I found that the same pattern was followed in many countries around the world. The pandemic response, according to all available evidence, was implemented according to globally planned and directed protocols.

None of this has been reported in the corporate media, and even in independent media spaces, very few have investigated or reported on these topics.

Why does it matter? You might ask. So what if the pandemic response was run by national security agencies according to a biodefense/counterterrorism playbook, rather than by public health agencies according to public health guidelines? And why is it surprising that most countries responded in similar ways?

Put simply, if it had been a regular public health response, Covid would not have differed from any of the viral epidemics or pandemics of the last century: The public would have been told to remain calm, wash hands frequently, and stay home if sick. Public health agencies would have tracked clusters of severe disease and treated them accordingly. This would have happened at different times, in different locations. Most people would barely have been aware that there was a novel virus circulating among them.

Instead, the response to Covid was the exact opposite: The media and public health agencies whipped the population into levels of panic massively disproportionate to the threat actually posed by the virus. Everyone was convinced that the only way to "beat the virus" was to lock down the whole world and wait for a never-before-tested or manufactured vaccine.

This book presents my attempt to understand why and how that switch happened: from a rational, medically, and ethically sound pandemic response to a global military-style lockdown-until-vaccine nightmare.

As you read the book, you will follow my understanding of what happened in reverse order: the first chapter is my analysis of the historical, economic, and political forces that converged to make the Covid pandemic response happen. Subsequent chapters delve into the details of the research that led to these conclusions.

What is "the deep state"?

Just a few words about what I mean by *The Deep State* in this book's title.

As explained by a generally unknown civil-servant-turned-author named Michael Lofgren who, according to an NPR report,[1] popularized the term "Deep State" in his 2014 "Anatomy of the Deep State,"[2] the Deep State can be understood as "a hybrid of corporate America and the national security state," which constitutes a "government within the government" that "operates according to no Constitutional rules or any constraint by the governed."

According to Lofgren's definition, which I adopt in this book, "the military-industrial complex, Wall Street – they're both about money,

....

1 Myre and Treisman, "The Man Who Popularized The 'Deep State' Doesn't Like The Way It's Used."

2 Lofgren, "Anatomy of the Deep State."

sucking as much money out of the country as they can, and control: corporate control and political control." Plus, I would add, this is now happening not just on a national, but on a global, level.

My hope for this book

I hope the research and analysis presented in these chapters will wake more people up to the crucial understanding that Covid was not a public health event. Rather, It was a demonstration of the crushing power exerted by an ever-expanding global deep state – in this case, the biodefense global public-private partnership – on us, the people of the world. And, hopefully, with fuller awareness and understanding, more people will resist the efforts continually exerted by these entities to agglomerate control over all of the world's wealth and resources.

For those who are skeptical, or who might consider such topics to be too conspiratorial, I hope this book can provide a new and interesting perspective.

ACKNOWLEDGEMENTS

Without the support of my family, I could not have survived, let alone thrived in the crazy investigative endeavors that culminated in the compilation of this book. My husband and daughter are the most exacting editors, letting me know when the first drafts of my articles inevitably sound like the "ravings of a lunatic" and helping me turn them into compelling pieces. My mother and son, and my dear friends Susan and Tamar, although they might not always agree with me, or even understand what the heck I'm going on about, are nevertheless supportive and proud of my work – which is all that matters.

Outside my family, more than anyone or anything else, Jeffrey Tucker and Brownstone Institute have helped me retain my sanity through these years of madness, and have made possible all my investigations, research, and writing that are included in this book. I cannot imagine my life without the support I have received from Brownstone, the collegiality and friendship of so many Brownstone scholars and contributors, and the ongoing community that Brownstone provides.

Rebekah Barnett, the fearless investigative journalist from Down Under, has provided invaluable editorial insight and advice. I am proud to have an image by the master graphic designer and artist Anthony Freda gracing the cover of this book.

To everyone mentioned here, and everyone else who has supported and encouraged me through these tumultuous times: Thank you. I am profoundly grateful.

PANDEMICS AND THE NEW WORLD ORDER

*I*n July 2022, I wrote an article entitled "The Catastrophic Covid Convergence,"[3] in which I attempted to explain the seemingly inexplicable cascade of events known as the Covid pandemic response (in this chapter shortened simply to "Covid") that began in early 2020.

After several years of researching and writing extensively[4] about this topic, I have come to realize that the Covid story is so much more complicated than I initially understood. It is not about a single public health event run by a few misguided or ill-intentioned individuals. It is not confined to any one government, and it is not a consequence of any one country's internal politics. It is, I now believe, a precautionary chapter in a much larger global saga.

The important questions to ask about Covid, given this understanding, are also very different from the ones I was asking at the beginning, such as: Was the virus an engineered bioweapon? Was it intentionally released? What were the names and motives of the people who ran the response?

Although, as of this book's publication in 2025, these continue to

3 Lerman, "The Catastrophic Covid Convergence."

4 *Debbie Lerman's Substack: debbielerman.substack.com*

be the focus of much public outcry and heated debate, they are actually secondary to the pandemic story I will tell in this chapter.

In Part 1, I will explain the convergence of global developments that led to Covid being predictable, if not inevitable.

In Part 2, I will look at how the globally uniform response to Covid was achieved.

I will include as few quotes and references as possible, because I want to tell a story based on my current knowledge and understanding, without a lot of distractions. The bibliography at the end of this chapter includes key books and articles that tell different parts of this story with hundreds of pages of references.

1.1 THE LEAD-UP TO COVID: RISE OF THE BIODEFENSE GLOBAL PUBLIC-PRIVATE PARTNERSHIP

Here I explain why Covid was a predictable outcome of the evolution of the U.S. national security state, and its convergence with global public-private partnerships, in the period since the end of the Cold War.

CONCOMITANT RISE OF WAR ON BIOTERROR AND UNCHECKED GLOBAL CORPORATISM

When the Cold War ended in the early 1990s, it was quickly replaced by the "War on Terror" as the income-generating, self-perpetuating-and-expanding mechanism for the U.S. military-industrial complex.

The war on terror generated decent returns for the national security apparatus when the 9/11 attacks were used as a pretext for Middle Eastern "regime changes," and when the terror threat was parlayed into the creation of DHS (Department of Homeland Security) – the U.S. Government's designated overseer of perpetual states of emergency and wrap-around internal surveillance.

The anthrax letters following 9/11 launched a less-noticed, but equally lucrative and long-term, budget-expanding war – this one on bioterror.

Biodefense experts mustered support for the war on bioterror with the terrifying claim that advances in biotechnology could enable random nutjobs to create deadly bioweapons in their garages. Major cities were vulnerable to bioterror attacks through their subways, water systems, etc. Loss of life could reach millions. Potential economic loss: trillions. Preventing such calamities was worth almost any price.

This increasingly lucrative war on bioterror developed simultaneously with another snowballing trend after the fall of Communism: a global march toward unchecked corporatism.

When the Eastern Bloc fell, no military, geographic, or ideological pushback remained against global corporatist forces. Wealth increasingly accrued to individuals and companies operating not within specific nations, but in a supranational sphere of deal-making and influence peddling. International banks and investment funds came to own more debt, and hold more wealth, than any national governments.

In this environment, enormous global conglomerates arose – referred to as global public-private partnerships, or GPPPs – loosely formed around various areas of activity and interest. One such GPPP was the biodefense/pandemic preparedness industrial complex – a globe-spanning, "too-big-to-fail" entity that ran the Covid pandemic response.

RISE OF THE BIODEFENSE/PANDEMIC PREPAREDNESS GLOBAL PUBLIC-PRIVATE PARTNERSHIP (GPPP)

To understand how the biodefense/pandemic preparedness GPPP coalesced, it is necessary to first look at the fields of biodefense and pandemic preparedness separately, and then at how they came to be yoked together into one rapidly metastasizing cartel – first as part of the U.S. security state, and then as an arm of the global governance structure dedicated to "global health security."

When Biodefense and Pandemic Preparedness Were Separate

Before the Anthrax attacks of 2001, the field of biodefense was mostly the purview of intelligence and military specialists. In secret labs, biowarfare scientists tried to concoct deadly bioweapons so they could then devise foolproof countermeasures against them. Intelligence agents tried to assess the biowarfare capabilities of enemy nations and rogue terrorists. They devised plans for how to quarantine a military base or a city in the case of an attack, and how to get countermeasures to soldiers/civilians as quickly as possible.

Because a bioterror attack would likely be localized to an area containing at most a few million people, the biodefense response of quarantine-until-countermeasure was a geographically, and temporally, limited plan. And because there were no bioweapons attacks on the U.S. after 2001, these plans remained entirely theoretical.

Similarly, before biodefense started attracting so much attention, pandemic preparedness was a quiet backwater of the public health realm. Epidemiologists and public health experts had come up with time-tested, non-dramatic plans to contain disease outbreaks: identify clusters of patients with serious/life-threatening symptoms, treat their symptoms with available medicines, isolate them from others if necessary, increase healthcare capacity on a local level as necessary, and let everyone else go on with their lives.

This type of disease outbreak preparedness is almost never front-page news and does not garner large budgets or public visibility. Yet it worked remarkably well to limit the number of deaths from even very deadly pathogens, like Ebola, MERS, and H1N1 influenza, to an average of no more than about 10,000 a year worldwide between 2000 and 2020.[5]

In summary, before the turn of the 21st century, both the biodefense and public health fields had relatively modest plans for dealing with deadly disease outbreaks – whether intentionally caused or naturally occurring. And neither type of outbreak ever happened on an unmanageable scale.

When Biodefense and Pandemic Preparedness Merged

The object of biodefense is to protect the military, and also civilian populations, from potential bioweapons attacks. But the pathogen/countermeasure research at the center of biodefense efforts can also be useful for pandemic preparedness, making it a "dual-use" endeavor.

Dual use refers to efforts that may serve both military and civilian objectives. In the case of biodefense/pandemic preparedness, it's easy to see: pathogens can be bioweapons, but they can also spread naturally and may cause destructive waves of disease; and countermeasures, including vaccines, can theoretically be used against both bioterror attacks and natural disease outbreaks.

In the decade after 9/11, as biodefense enjoyed an increasing portion of national security attention and spending, the field attracted many more scientists, academic institutions, and nonprofits to the study of pathogens and countermeasures. Naturally, many of these non-military entities came from fields including virology, immunology, and epidemiology, whose work is used – among other purposes – for pandemic preparedness. The civilian side of the research was mostly funded by public health agencies and mega-nonprofits interested primarily in vaccine development.

It was not long before the two fields merged into one "dual use" entity – conveniently defined as a crucial aspect of national security – called simply "biodefense" or "health security." In 2006, a new sub-agency was even

....

5 Re-Evaluating the Pandemic Preparedness And REsponse agenda (REPPARE), *Pandemic Risk Policy Brief: the evidence base of the pandemic preparedness agenda does not support the current urgency.*

created to cement the merger: ASPR – a military/intelligence-run entity within HHS – the umbrella civilian public health body. This symbiotic military/civilian enterprise could then attract a great deal more funding, and exert influence over a much vaster array of research institutions, nonprofits, and NGOs than either biodefense or pandemic preparedness could have done separately.

Another impetus for the merger of the two fields was their shared private partners: pharmaceutical companies, whose job it was to help design, research, and ultimately produce whatever countermeasures were deemed necessary for protection, either from bioweapons or naturally occurring pathogens. Ideally, the countermeasures for one type of disease outbreak would also work for the other.

This is why, in the decades after 2001, the biodefense field became obsessed with finding a "platform technology" that could provide protection from any conceivable bioweapon, while the public health/pandemic preparedness field pushed for a "universal flu vaccine" that could provide protection from any naturally occurring, respiratory-disease-causing virus. And, by 2019, both arms of the biodefense complex had invested a huge amount of funding and hype into a specific technology called "mRNA vaccine platforms" – thought to be the sought-after miracle countermeasure to all engineered viral bioweapons and all flu-causing viruses.

Biodefense/Pandemic Preparedness on a Global Scale

As discussed above, while all this merging of military and civilian research on bugs and drugs was happening on a national level, capital and political power were shifting away from nation-states and into global public-private partnerships, or GPPPs.

All of these gargantuan global entities share the following characteristics:

- Their backbone is the global banking system, whose interests they represent.
- Their agendas are usually aligned with the imperialist agenda of the United States – the world's only superpower – and its allies.
- Their power to impose their agendas on the world's population comes largely from the U.S. military-industrial complex and its partners and alliances (NATO, EU, Five Eyes, among others).

- They seek to enforce their agendas through advanced surveillance technology and AI, with the ultimate goal of gathering identity, health, and behavioral information about the entire world's population into centralized databases.
- They use international governance and networking bodies (UN, WHO, Atlantic Council, WEF, among others) to coordinate and disseminate their agendas to national governments.
- They use multinational consulting and management firms to help national governments implement their agendas.
- They include multinational corporations run by multibillionaires, who attain astronomical profits through their GPPP activities.
- They coalesce around various perceived existential crises, like climate change and "global health security" (another name for international biodefense/pandemic preparedness). These pursuits are marketed to the public not just as altruistic and life-saving, but as the only way to avoid complete global devastation.
- Their ability to convince the world's population to support their agendas derives from the global censorship and propaganda industrial complex – run through international intelligence alliances, partnering with marketing firms, academic institutions, and nonprofits – using "nudge" methods and the psychological warfare playbook (psychological operations, or psy-ops) originally designed for coups and counterinsurgencies.

With these characteristics in mind, we can list some of the main components of the biodefense/pandemic preparedness public-private partnership, to see just how enormous a complex it is. We can also see how the national biodefense complex scales up and merges with the global entity:

National Biodefense Complex	Global Biodefense Public-Private Partnership
Military/IC bioterror specialists, agencies and subcontractors, including among others: DARPA, BARDA, DTRA, Army Medical Research and Development Command installations (e.g. Ft. Dietrich), ASPR	International military and intelligence alliances, including NATO and Five Eyes, incorporating biodefense specialists, agencies and subcontractors in all member countries
Public health agencies and subcontractors, including among others: NIH, HHS, NIAID, CDC	International public health and governance bodies including EU, UN, WHO, WEF, with branches, representatives, and subcontractors in all member countries
U.S. scientists and research institutions, journals, and professional associations	Internationally based scientists and research institutions, journals, and professional associations
NGOs/nonprofits	International "philanthrocapitalists" and their organizations, including the Bill & Melinda Gates Foundation, the Wellcome Trust, and their many offshoots including GAVI and CEPI, with offices and representatives in numerous countries
Multinational pharmaceutical companies, subsidiaries, and subcontractors	
Multinational technology and surveillance companies, subsidiaries, and subcontractors	

The Biodefense GPPP Prepares for an Inevitable Catastrophe

Along with the backing of the international banks and the support of the censorship and propaganda industrial complex (shortened in this chapter to "psy-op complex") and multinational consulting firms, all of the components of the biodefense GPPP represent hundreds of billions of dollars in funding and financing, thousands of national and international companies, agencies, academic institutions, and NGOs in dozens of countries, and hundreds of thousands – if not millions – of jobs all over the world. Its sheer size and control over people and resources make this an entity that is "too big to fail."

Yet without a viable threat of a bioweapons attack or a catastrophic pandemic, this behemoth cannot continue to sustain and grow itself.

For that reason, as it ballooned in the two decades before Covid, the biodefense GPPP had to keep the threat of a catastrophic bioterror attack or global pandemic front and center. And it had to prepare all of its components to respond to the threat when it predictably, if not inevitably, occurred.

Tabletop Exercises

Preparations for the catastrophe included priming the world's governments for the inevitability of such an event, accomplished through "tabletop exercises" – simulations of what would happen in the event of a deadly bioattack or pandemic.

Between 2001 and 2019, regularly scheduled "tabletop exercises" carried out by representatives of the biodefense GPPP effectively promoted the story of catastrophic global threats posed by bioterror/pandemic events. The content of each exercise was less important than the overarching message: naturally emerging and engineered pathogens posed an existential threat to humanity, and nothing less than a global response would be necessary to avoid Armageddon.

Creating a New Business Model for Countermeasures

The most important component of a global response to such a catastrophe, in terms of accruing power and resources for the biodefense GPPP, is the manufacture and distribution of countermeasures to the entire global population, an effort spearheaded by pharmaceutical companies and their hundreds of subcontractors and subsidiaries.

But the traditional business model for private pharmaceutical companies does not lend itself to such a project. No private company can survive, let alone thrive, by devoting significant resources to building and maintaining manufacturing capacity for countermeasures against a hypothetical threat that might never happen.

Furthermore, the oversight and regulation of medical products will almost inevitably delay the availability of novel countermeasures until after an attack or outbreak is over. And, finally, even if the countermeasures can be manufactured and approved quickly enough, what if they cause unexpected outcomes (e.g., injury or death) for which the companies could be held liable?

All of these obstacles were overcome by the biodefense GPPP through under-the-radar legislative and legal maneuverings and regulatory capture in the decades leading up to Covid:

Regulatory Barriers Lowered to Zero or Near-Zero

Over several decades, important loopholes in countermeasure regulation were introduced into the legal code, most notably Emergency Use Authorization (EUA).[6] Internationally, defense treaties and biodefense agreements can lower regulatory barriers such that emergency authorization in one country could be applied to others. The WHO Emergency Use Listing (EUL) accomplishes this globally.[7] EUL was first used for the Covid vaccines.[8]

Liability Removed from Anyone Working on, Distributing, or Administering Countermeasures

The PREP Act[9] was a necessary additional legal measure to ensure that anyone who did anything with EUA products would not be liable in case the unregulated countermeasures went awry. The liability shield is extended by governments and regulatory bodies internationally along with EUA.

THE NOVEL CORONAVIRUS TRIGGER

By 2019 all of these preparations for a catastrophic global pandemic were in place, but the civilization-ending pathogen/bioterror attack had not yet materialized.

Then, in late 2019 a propitious public health emergency in Wuhan, China ended the very long dry spell in biodefense disasters: Clusters of

---

6 Lerman, "What is Emergency Use Authorization (EUA)?"

7 World Health Organization, "Emergency Use Listing Procedure."

8 World Health Organization, "WHO issues its first emergency use validation for a COVID-19 vaccine and emphasizes need for equitable global access."

9 42 U.S. Code § 247d–6d - Targeted liability protections for pandemic and epidemic products and security countermeasures.

patients exhibited severe symptoms of a respiratory disease that could not be attributed to any known pathogen. Analysis of the body fluids of the patients was performed, and a novel coronavirus was identified.

There are many unanswered questions about exactly how and when the novel coronavirus, subsequently called SARS-CoV-2, entered the human population, and how it turned into "the Covid-19 pandemic:" Was the virus engineered? When did the virus begin to circulate? Was the virus intentionally or accidentally released? Was it just one mutating virus, or several different ones?

Regardless of the answers to these questions, the important point to remember is that if it had not been SARS-CoV-2 in Wuhan, it would have been a different triggering event somewhere else – and the global pandemic response would have been the same.

1.2 THE GLOBAL COVID PANDEMIC RESPONSE AND ITS AFTERMATH

Here I delve into the specifics of the lockdown-until-vaccine Covid response, showing that the response was globally coordinated, and examining the global propaganda campaign with which populations were pummeled into compliance.

When the WHO declared a global Covid-19 pandemic on March 11, 2020, the biodefense global public-private partnership (GPPP) (discussed in Part 1) and its collaborators – most importantly, the censorship and propaganda industrial complex, which I refer to as the psy-op complex – had already been preparing the response rollout for several months (at least).

In order to show how the pandemic response was centrally coordinated, I will provide an overview of how it took place in different countries and how nearly identical each country's response was (see timeline in the following section). I will then delve into the actual goals and strategies of the pandemic planners, and show how they were implemented on a global scale.

RESPONSE ROLLOUT IN INDIVIDUAL COUNTRIES
Here's how the biodefense global pandemic response strategy materialized on the ground in most countries:

January – February 2020: Public health agencies seem to be in charge of responding to the outbreak. It is mostly confined to China, so there is not widespread panic. The public health plan is the same as always: monitor for local clusters of serious disease requiring treatment, and be prepared to scale up hospital capacity if needed. Guidelines are to wash your hands a lot, and stay home if you're sick.

End of February – Mid-March 2020: The media switches from criticizing China's draconian, anti-democratic lockdowns to praising them. Massive increase in panic propaganda and in calling on the public to play an active role in "flattening the curve" by wearing masks and "social distancing."

Mid-March – Mid-May 2020: States of Emergency intended for times of war/terrorism are declared everywhere, even where there are no cases of

Covid. Without telling the public, pandemic response is officially moved from public health agencies to military/intelligence-led bodies (US Task Force, UK Biosecurity Centre, among others) operating largely in secret. (Before mid-March these bodies were already in charge behind the scenes.) Public health agencies switch from traditional public health plans to nonstop lockdown-until-vaccine propaganda.

End of 2020 – End of 2022: Populations grow weary of lockdown measures, but new waves of panic propaganda focused on "cases" and "variants" lead to repeated lockdowns and a desperate desire for vaccines, followed by cult-like embrace of mandates, refusal to examine any evidence contradicting the "safe and effective" claims, and brutal ostracism of skeptics. The public accepts the necessity for repeated, endless vaccine boosters – contrary to everything it was initially told.

End of 2022 – today: Government commissions spend many months and many millions of dollars examining their countries' pandemic responses. Every commission in nearly every country finds that the public health agencies were woefully inadequate, that the public health response in January-February was catastrophically misguided, and that the lockdown-until-vaccine plan should have been implemented as soon as the first cases were discovered in China. Covid vaccines are now recommended along with seasonal flu vaccines. The mRNA platform is viewed as an unmitigated success, and tested against dozens of diseases and pathogens. Reports of injuries and deaths are ignored, obfuscated, and censored by every single government in the world.

The uniformity of this timeline across dozens of countries strongly suggests central coordination by the biodefense global public-private partnership. The way the timeline tracks with the GPPP's goals and strategies further strengthens the centralized response hypothesis.

Pandemic Goals: Sustaining and Growing the Biodefense GPPP

The overarching goal of the pandemic response, as discussed in part 1 of this story, was to sustain and expand the remit of the biodefense GPPP – including all of its globe-spanning public and private components. Two specific sub-goals were: 1) to get the much-fantasized-about universal vaccine – specifically the mRNA platform – out to the global market; and 2) to roll out global surveillance systems, including digital IDs (defined in the biodefense context as "vaccine passports") based on newly developed AI capabilities.

Pandemic Strategy: Lockdown-Until-Vaccine

The pandemic response strategy reflected the dual-use nature of the biodefense/pandemic preparedness endeavor: it was a biodefense response, which treated the entire world as a biowarfare zone, but it was presented to the public as an epidemiologically and scientifically based public health response.

If the Covid response had truly been based on public health (see Chapter 2 for a full discussion of this topic), the biodefense GPPP would have been mostly left out. People would have been able to judge the relative threat of the virus for themselves, most would get sick and recover, doctors would try various available treatments with different degrees of effectiveness until the vaccines became available, and by the time the vaccines appeared, nobody would be interested. This had happened before, with the H1N1 outbreak in 2009, when millions of vaccines were ordered, paid for, manufactured, and discarded. It was a case study for the opposite of what the biodefense complex wanted to achieve.

To avoid such a non-catastrophe this time around, the biodefense GPPP adopted the quarantine-until-countermeasure response from the biodefense playbook. Although it was intended for a relatively small geographic area, and the short timespan necessary to respond to a bioterror attack, this approach on a global scale was the most likely to achieve the GPPP's aims. It meant keeping billions of people in a state of panic and relative isolation for many months, in anticipation of the only allowable solution: vaccines.

(Note: I am using the word "vaccines" because that is what these products are commonly called. However, the mRNA Covid vaccines are a completely different category of treatment than any traditional vaccines used in the history of medicine.)[10]

There were three major obstacles at the outset of the pandemic to convincing everyone that lockdown-until-vaccine was the right course of action:

1. The plan could cause massive collateral damage in terms of economic, educational, psychological, and social devastation, which could make political and public health leaders balk.
2. The virus itself was potentially dangerous mostly for the elderly and infirm and could have been handled using traditional public health measures.
3. Professional epidemiologists, virologists, and non-biodefense pandemic planners would recognize these obvious facts and would tell the public that this was not, in fact, an accepted – or in any way valid – public health plan.

A fourth obstacle arose after the rollout of the miracle countermeasure that did not live up to its much-vaunted promise:

4. The mRNA platform didn't work. The mRNA products did not prevent infection or transmission. They did not have any other recognizable benefit. They caused a lot of injuries and deaths.

These obstacles would have been insurmountable, were it not for the enormous, globe-spanning network of the biodefense GPPP – and its reliance on the global power of the psy-op complex. With its representatives in every government's military/intelligence counterterrorism division and its deep ties to the global public health network, the biodefense complex disseminated the lockdown-until-vaccine plan to top levels of world governments. The psy-op complex, through its military/intelligence-academic-nonprofit networks in both broadcast and online media, controlled the narrative.

....

10 Steger and Henrion Caude, "Game Over for the mRNA-based "vaccine" technology," translated to English from German.

Here's how they convinced everyone that lockdown-until-vaccine was the only way to go. Part of this occurred behind the scenes, so this part of the story represents my best guess as to what exactly transpired:

1. First, world leaders had to be convinced that destroying their economies and severely restricting the freedoms of their entire populations was necessary. I believe biodefense leaders and their partners in global public health organizations, primarily the UN/ WHO, told political world leaders that the virus was an engineered potential bioweapon that leaked from a lab. They said it posed such an existential threat to humanity — like if you sprinkled anthrax over the whole world — that an unprecedented biodefense response was necessary. They created scary models based on grossly exaggerated threat estimates showing millions of deaths without draconian response measures. The silver lining: as long as regulatory barriers were eliminated, and funding flowed freely, a countermeasure could be produced that would save the world not just from this, but potentially from all deadly pathogens.

2. In every country, political and public health leaders told lower-level public health officials and the public – with the immense power of the psy-op complex behind them – that this was definitely not a bioweapon, but it was a naturally occurring virus the likes of which had never been seen before. And because it posed such an existential threat, wartime efforts were necessary to combat it. But those efforts, of course, were part of a widely accepted public health pandemic preparedness plan.

3. Through its control of research funding, medical journals, medical associations, and its tens of thousands of affiliated medical professionals, the biodefense GPPP flooded the zone with articles, interviews, and guidelines supporting the story that lockdown-until-vaccine was not just a valid public health plan, but the only "humane" one. Anyone disagreeing was said to be putting millions of lives at risk and thus deserving of professional ostracism: loss of funding, prestige, and employment. Those

professionals who spoke up were brutally attacked, silenced, and punished. This narrative control and bullying of dissenting medical professionals continues to this day.

4. The mRNA vaccines were deemed a priori "safe and effective," and a propaganda campaign, perhaps the biggest in the history of the world, was launched to ensure large swaths of the global population believed this message. This campaign is also ongoing.

Finally, there was one overarching requirement for getting the populations of nearly every country in the world to comply with the brutal lockdown-until-vaccine plan: unrelenting, unmitigated panic.

Fomenting Panic through Lies and Fake Public Health Measures

It is well documented that people in a state of fear will believe claims and submit to treatment that they would never accept under other circumstances. Sustained abridgment of fundamental rights like free speech, freedom of assembly, bodily autonomy, freedom to worship, freedom of movement, etc. can only work if entire populations are terrified – literally – out of their minds.

The panic during Covid was accomplished, sustained, and prolonged until the vaccine rollout, through the relentless propaganda and censorship campaign orchestrated by the psy-op complex on behalf of the biodefense GPPP.

Lies to Foment Panic

The following are the lies disseminated by the psy-op complex to scare global populations into compliance with the lockdown-until-vaccine response plan. It is extremely important to realize that in March 2020 all of these were known, based on scientific evidence and medical research and publications, to be false:

- Everyone is equally vulnerable: the virus kills young and old, healthy and ailing indiscriminately.
- Everyone who "tests positive" is equally contagious, even with no symptoms, so everyone needs to be treated as a threat.

- No natural immunity can be achieved: even if you get sick with the virus and recover, you will have no protection from future illness.
- Herd immunity is an immoral "strategy" for ending pandemics.
- There are no available treatments doctors can try to lower the risk of serious illness or death.
- Covid has uniquely long-lasting and debilitating aftereffects that can happen even if you have mild symptoms and can suddenly appear months or years after infection. [Note: this was not known to be true or false in March 2020, because not enough time had elapsed to even test this claim. But it went counter to everything we know about the sequelae (aftereffects) of viral infections.]
- Healthcare systems will completely collapse if the virus is allowed to take its natural course.
- Only vaccines can end the pandemic.

Believing these lies made the lockdown-until-vaccine plan seem like the only one that would prevent millions of deaths and debilitating cases of illness.

But what if people realized, after a few months, that a vast majority were getting infected but not getting very sick or dying? What if it became apparent that hospitals – except in rare occasional hot spots – were standing empty? What if those lies started to unravel before the vaccines were ready for rollout?

Treating Positive Test Results as Cases to Whip up More Panic

Probably the most important single tactic in sustaining and prolonging the pandemic (up to this very day) was the entirely novel, entirely non-scientific, non-medical, and counter to all common-sense way of measuring the impact of the virus.

In every past disease outbreak in history, the impact was measured based on the number of people who got sick and died. The number of people hospitalized was also an important metric. A "case" was considered someone who had symptoms requiring treatment.

But on February 2, 2020[11] [or earlier – that's the first date on which I have found a record of this], the WHO – the clearing house for biodefense

---

11 Lerman, "Covid Timeline Wiki Project: February 2, 2020."

pandemic edicts – updated their "confirmed case definition" to "A person with laboratory confirmation of infection, irrespective of clinical signs and symptoms." Based on this radically counter-medical definition, the Covid PCR test – rushed out one week before the change in case definition, and cranked up to a level of sensitivity that notoriously could yield a positive result on a pineapple – provided an endless torrential flood of new "cases."

Thereafter, all guidelines and recommendations were based nonsensically on case counts, not hospitalizations or deaths. Every new virus "variant" was presented as equally, if not more, devastating than the last – not based on how many people it sickened or killed, but based on how many positive test results it yielded.

No statistical or real-world correlation was ever made between rises or falls in "case counts" and the number of people who were actually getting hospitalized or dying. Even after many months of empty hospitals and decreasing death counts – the public was convinced that if case counts went up, bad things would happen.

Fake Public Health Measures to Sustain Panic

To sustain the public's belief in these bad things happening, despite all real-world evidence to the contrary, it was also necessary to convince everyone that lockdown-until-vaccine was a heroic endeavor requiring wartime levels of sacrifice and solidarity.

To this end, the psy-op complex inducted the public into a series of physical and social rituals that made citizens feel like soldiers in a high-stakes struggle against a fearsome enemy. Anyone objecting to the measures was deemed a selfish traitor against humanity.

Adherence to the measures guaranteed that people remained isolated for long periods of time – lowering the chances that they would notice the inconsistencies and lies in the messaging, and increasing their psychological investment in the lockdown-until-vaccine effort.

These measures included:

- Testing everyone all the time, regardless of symptoms
- Masking everyone everywhere, regardless of illness
- Social distancing to the point of complete, repeated self-quarantine, and never-ending lockdowns

Again, all of these measures were widely known to be medically and scientifically ineffectual, if not downright counterproductive, in combating rapidly spreading respiratory viruses. Most prominent public health bodies, including the WHO, CDC, and NIAID, had explicitly acknowledged before Covid that these were not effective pandemic response measures.

The most brilliant and insidious aspect of this "war on Covid" campaign was that vast swaths of the public, and of the public health and medical professions, became unwitting enforcers of the biodefense agenda – against the best interests of themselves, their loved ones, their communities, and their professional and ethical integrity. Snitching on non-compliers was encouraged. Shunning of dissenters was considered not just necessary, but righteous.

Proof of Vaccination as a Badge of Honor

After the rollout of the mRNA vaccines, the biodefense GPPP and psy-op complex extended not just the panic about variants and cases, but also the propaganda to convince the public that complying with vaccine mandates and showing proof of vaccination was a badge of honor in the noble all-of-society struggle against the diabolical virus.

Once it became incontrovertibly clear, several months after the rollout, that the mRNA vaccines did not stop infection or transmission, and that they could cause severe side effects in some people, this was an obviously counter-scientific, anti-epidemiological, and unethical requirement. Nevertheless, the more obviously absurd it became to require a potentially harmful intervention for those whose risk from Covid was near zero (e.g., pretty much anyone under 20), the more the psy-op complex doubled down on the nonsensical message that if you got vaccinated you were somehow protecting others.

This was a key message not just for convincing everyone to be good soldiers and take an increasing number of shots. It was also crucial to gaining widespread acceptance of the idea that one's willingness to sacrifice individual rights "for the greater good" could – and should – be tied to one's ability to travel freely, work, study, access goods and services, and be accepted as an "essential" member of society.

This, in turn, paved the way for society-wide digital ID systems, known in the Covid context as "vaccine passports" — an important enforcement and surveillance mechanism not just for biodefense purposes, but also for the shared agenda of all global public-private partnerships (as discussed in Part 1 of this story).

COVID AFTERMATH

I know the story I have told in this chapter might sound fantastical. One of the most ingenious aspects of the global Covid operation is that it was so brazen, so extreme, and so inconceivable – that it can actually hide behind its own implausibility.

Many people object that there cannot possibly be global coordinating mechanisms of the power and reach I have described. Not to mention such mechanisms displaying a total disregard for the well-being of the general population, in pursuit of their own power and control. It all sounds like a giant "conspiracy theory."

This is a reasonable and understandable objection. Because nothing of the magnitude of the global Covid response has ever been attempted before, we have no accessible framework or precedent for understanding how it happened.

And because many of the coordinating arms of global public-private partnerships involve secretive military and intelligence operations, it is very difficult to provide proof-positive documentation for every single claim in my story.

However, I believe that the way in which the Covid pandemic response unfolded cannot be satisfactorily explained in any other way. And when we look at the aftermath of Covid, and the global plans for what we are told are inevitable and frequent future pandemics – not just of the viral kind, but also cyber pandemics, racism pandemics, climate-related catastrophes, and so on – it becomes clear that Covid was not an end in itself, but a model for future globally managed catastrophic events.

Here is an excerpt from an April 16, 2024 document, entitled "U.S. Government Global Health Security Strategy"[12] that pretty much summarizes the biodefense GPPP Covid response, through its projection onto future pandemic planning.

Note how biodefense and pandemic planning have collapsed into

....

12 U.S. Government, *Global Health Security Strategy 2024.*

"global health security" and note the participants in developing and implementing this strategy – all the components of the biodefense GPPP.

> Over the last 3 years, we have more than doubled our global health partnerships—working directly with 50 countries to ensure they can more effectively prevent, detect, and control outbreaks. And we are working with partners to support an additional 50 countries to save even more lives and minimize economic losses. With strong bipartisan support from Congress, we also championed the creation of the Pandemic Fund, a new international body that has already catalyzed $2 billion in financing from 27 contributors, including countries, foundations, and philanthropies, to build stronger global health security capabilities.
>
> And we are leading efforts to ensure international financial institutions, such as the World Bank Group, scale up lending for pandemic prevention, preparedness, and response because health security, economic security, climate security, and national security are all related.
>
> This new Global Health Security Strategy lays out the actions the United States will take over the next 5 years...Through investments and cooperation with foreign partners, we will continue to build our capacity to prevent, detect, and respond to biological threats wherever they emerge. And we will rally greater support for these efforts from other countries, the private sector, and civil society to ensure long-term impact.

Here is an announcement about the EU digital IDs[13] going global, to ensure everyone's health security:

> On 1 July 2023, the WHO took up the EU system of digital COVID-19 certification to establish a global system that will help protect citizens across the world from on-going and future health threats, including pandemics. This is the first building block of the WHO Global Digital Health Certification Network that will

....

13 European Commission, "EU Digital COVID Certificate."

develop a system for global verification of health documents to deliver better health for all.

The WHO will facilitate this process globally under its own structure with the first use-case being the convergence of digital COVID-19 certificates.

The only way I know to push back against this colossal, ruthless machine is to expose it as much as possible. And convince as many people as possible to resist its edicts the next time it declares a "global health emergency."

BIBLIOGRAPHY

The following five sources contain pretty much all of the information and hundreds of pages of references that corroborate my pandemic story:

- Iain Davis, "*What Is the Global Public-Private Partnership?*," The Disillusioned Blogger, October 6, 2021.
- Toby Green and Thomas Fazi, *The Covid Consensus: The Global Assault on Democracy and The Poor – A Critique from the Left.* C. Hurst & Co. (Publishers) Ltd., 2023. [D. Lerman book review: https://debbielerman.substack.com/p/the-covid-consensus-to-understand]
- C.J. Hopkins. *The Rise of the New Normal Reich: Consent Factory Essays, Vol. III (2020-2021)*, Consent Factory Publishing, 2022.
- Robert F. Kennedy Jr., *The Wuhan Cover-Up and the Terrifying Bioweapons Arms Race*, Skyhorse Publishing, 2023. [D. Lerman book review: https://debbielerman.substack.com/p/rfk-jrs-new-book-the-wuhan-cover/.]
- Unlimited Hangout investigative series: "*Moderna's "Hail Mary,"* Unlimited Hangout, October 7, 2021; October 28, 2021; July 3, 2024.

These two books foreshadowed Covid (although their authors' pandemic-era writings reveal a surprising failure to make the connection):

- Mike Lofgren, *The Deep State: The Fall of the Constitution and the Rise of a Shadow Government*, Penguin Books, 2016.
- Naomi Klein, *The Shock Doctrine: The Rise of Disaster Capitalism*, Metropolitan Books, 2007.

IF COVID HAD BEEN A
PUBLIC HEALTH EVENT

*What would the pandemic response look like without global partnerships
or deep state coordination?*

When I explain the national security coup against public health (see
Chapter 3 for details) that took place during the Covid pandemic,
people often ask me: would it really have been so different if the NIH
and CDC had remained in charge of the pandemic response? What if
the Department of Defense, Department of Homeland Security, and the
National Security Council had never taken over?

Wouldn't the public health agencies have done basically the same things?

It is absolutely essential that everyone understand the answers to these
questions. They impact not just our awareness of what happened during Covid,
but also our assessment of how to handle all viral outbreaks in the future.

In this chapter, I will describe how the response to the pandemic would
have proceeded if normal public health guidelines had been followed, not
just in the U.S. but around the world, without interference from national
security authorities or covert biowarfare experts, and without the centralized control of the global public-private partnerships, described in
detail in Chapter 1.

Public health guidelines

Before Covid, the guidelines for dealing with a new outbreak of a flu-like virus were clear:

- avoid panic,
- search for cheap, widely available early treatments that may reduce the risk of serious illness,
- plan to increase healthcare capacity if necessary,
- help local and state medical personnel to identify and treat cases if and when the virus causes serious illness,
- and keep society functioning as normally as possible.

This was the approach used in all previous epidemics and pandemics. The guidelines are detailed in the planning documents of the WHO,[14] HHS,[15] and EU countries.[16]

When the military and national security agencies took over the response, these guidelines were replaced by a biowarfare paradigm: Quarantine until vaccine. In other words, keep everyone locked down while rapidly developing medical countermeasures. This is a response intended to counter biowarfare and bioterrorism attacks. It is not a public health response and is, in fact, in direct conflict with the scientific and ethical underpinnings[17] of established public health principles.

Had we adhered to the public health protocols that were initially followed in the early months of 2020, life in the United States and around the world would have looked like life in Sweden[18] during the pandemic,

....

14 World Health Organization, *Non-pharmaceutical public health measures for mitigating the risk and impact of epidemic and pandemic influenza.*

15 U.S. Department of Health and Human Services, *Pandemic Influenza Plan: 2017 Update.*

16 European Centre for Disease Prevention and Control, "Influenza pandemic preparedness plans."

17 Baker, "The Four Pillars of Medical Ethics Were Destroyed in the Covid Response."

18 Miltimore, "The New York Times Finally Warms to Sweden's Pandemic Response - Three Years Later."

with even less panic: no masks, no school closures, no lockdowns, very low excess deaths.

No panic

The reasons not to panic were apparent in early 2020 from the data we had gathered from China: the virus was deadly mainly to elderly people with multiple serious health conditions, did not cause life-threatening illness in children or in most people under 65, and did not seem poised to cause more of an increase in hospitalizations or deaths than a very bad flu season.

It can be difficult at this point – after years of unrelenting censorship and propaganda[19] – to remember that, at the beginning of 2020, the new virus emerging in China was not front and center in most people's minds. The U.S. media was busy covering election campaigns and economic issues, and the general attitude was that what was happening in China would not happen elsewhere.

Here are some examples of what medical and public health experts were saying in January, February and early March 2020:

January 30, 2020, CNBC: Dr. Ezekiel Emanuel, former President Obama's White House health advisor declared that "Americans are too worried about the new coronavirus that's spreading rapidly across China." He added: "Everyone in America should take a very big breath, slow down and stop panicking and being hysterical." And he explained: "I think we need to put it into context, the death rate is much lower than for SARS."[20]

February 27, 2020, CNN: The CNN website reported that CDC Director Dr. Robert Redfield "has a simple message for Americans: No, you shouldn't be afraid." The website also quoted NIH Director Dr. Alex Azar saying that "most people who get coronavirus will have mild to moderate symptoms and will be able to stay home, treating it like the

....

19 Betrus, "How the Media Fueled the Lockdowns."

20 Bursztynsky, "Ex-Obama health advisor: U.S. needs to 'stop panicking and being hysterical' about coronavirus."

severe flu or cold." And it reported that the CDC "does not recommend Americans wear surgical masks in public. Surgical masks are effective against respiratory infections but not airborne infections."[21]

February 28, 2020, *New England Journal of Medicine:* Drs. Anthony Fauci and Robert Redfield wrote that "the case fatality rate may be considerably less than 1%" and "the overall clinical consequences of Covid-19 may ultimately be more akin to those of a severe seasonal influenza (which has a case fatality rate of approximately 0.1%)." They cited Chinese data showing that "either children are less likely to become infected, or their symptoms were so mild that their infection escaped detection."[22]

March 4, 2020, *Slate:* Dr. Jeremy Samuel Faust, Harvard emergency physician, reassured readers that all the evidence available at the time "suggests that COVID-19 is a relatively benign disease for most young people, and a potentially devastating one for the old and chronically ill, albeit not nearly as risky as reported." He said the mortality rate was "zero in children 10 or younger among hundreds of cases in China" and that it was important to "divert our focus away from worrying about preventing systemic spread among healthy people—which is likely either inevitable, or out of our control."[23]

No censorship or propaganda

If we had continued down the road of a regular public health response, opinions like these from our national public health leaders would have continued to be published and discussed openly. There would have been open discussion of the virus's potential harms, and expert debates about various response measures. There would have been no need to censor any particular opinion or disseminate propaganda supporting any other.

If some experts thought we should shut down the entire country (or world), they would have debated this position with those experts who

21 Cable News Network (CNN), "February 27 coronavirus news."

22 Fauci et al., "Covid-19 - Navigating the Uncharted."

23 Faust, "COVID-19's Mortality Rate Isn't As High As We Think."

thought this was a gross and dangerous overreaction. The media would most likely have taken the side of the less draconian measures, because it would have been common knowledge that the virus was not lethal for most people, and that the infection fatality rate, or IFR (how many people died after getting infected) was, as Fauci and Redfield reported in February 2020, around 0.1 percent in the general population, and much lower for anyone under 65.

If anyone had published a model showing millions of potential deaths[24] based on a 2 or 3 percent or higher estimated fatality rate, their assumptions would have been openly questioned and debated, and most likely easily debunked using available data and observed fatality rates from the real world.

Here are other important topics the media would have been able to report on (as they were doing without censorship before the middle of March), had there been no intentional suppression of traditional public health guidelines, and no panic-fomenting propaganda (see Chapter 4 for censorship and propaganda details):

China

Scientific and medical data from China was never considered reliable before Covid, because in a totalitarian regime it is assumed that the data must always conform to the regime's agenda. Without censorship or propaganda, this would have remained true for everything related to Covid. The videos of people falling dead in the streets, the draconian lockdowns of millions of people, and the obviously absurd claims that the lockdowns in one area of the country had eradicated the virus everywhere for years on end, would all be openly questioned and debunked in the media.

Testing and quarantines

Without censorship or propaganda, the media would be able to invite top epidemiologists to explain to the public that once an airborne virus is widely disseminated in a population, you cannot stop it from spreading. You can use tests to help guide treatment. You can also use tests to figure

....

24 Malone, "Modelling Gone Bad."

out who has been exposed to the virus and is likely to have acquired immunity so they can interact safely with vulnerable populations. It would be common knowledge that it is not necessary or useful to test the entire population repeatedly or to quarantine healthy people.

Early spread
It would have been reassuring for people to know that the virus probably started spreading before December 2019.[25] This would mean that more people had already been exposed without getting sick or dying, which would support the low fatality estimates. It would also mean that since the virus was already widely disseminated, containment (using testing and quarantines) was not a viable or desirable objective, as experts were already stating (see Dr. Faust above).

Cases
Without unnecessary testing, the definition of a "case" would have remained what it had always been before Covid: someone who seeks medical care because they have serious symptoms. Thus, the media would report only on clusters of actual cases, if and when they emerged in different locations. There would be no ticker tapes with running numbers of asymptomatic people who tested positive. Instead of millions of positive "cases" (i.e., positive PCR tests), we would hear about hundreds or thousands of people who were hospitalized with serious symptoms, as in all previous epidemics and pandemics. This would happen in different places at different times, as the virus spread geographically. The vast majority of the population would never be counted as cases.

Natural immunity and herd immunity
Virologists and epidemiologists would be featured in the news, explaining that if you have been exposed to a virus you develop natural immunity. So, for example, if there were nurses at a hospital who had been sick with Covid, they could go back to work and not worry about getting seriously ill or spreading the virus. The public would also learn that the more people

25 Rice, "Evidence of Early Spread in the US: What We Know."

developed natural immunity, the closer we would get to herd immunity, which would mean the virus would have nowhere else to spread. Nobody would consider either of those terms a reckless strategy or a sociopathic plot to let the virus "rip" and kill large swaths of the population.

Early treatment

Doctors in China had several months' experience treating Covid before observable clusters of cases emerged in other countries. They had developed treatment protocols with available drugs[26] that they could have shared with the international medical community. The media would have reported on the efforts of researchers and doctors all over the world to find available treatments that could lower the risk of patients' hospitalization or death.

Vaccines

Without the lockdown-until-vaccine agenda, investments in vaccine development in 2020 would have been modest, and might have led to some clinical trials, although by the time they got to Phase III trials (on large numbers of patients), most people would already have natural immunity. The media would have been able to report in January 2020, as Anthony Fauci did in January 2023,[27] that "viruses that replicate in the human respiratory mucosa without infecting systemically, including influenza A, SARS-CoV-2, endemic coronaviruses, RSV, and many other 'common cold' viruses" have never been "effectively controlled by licensed or experimental vaccines."

With a focus on early treatments and keeping most people out of the hospital and in a normally functioning society, no one would have been holding their breath waiting for a "safe and effective" vaccine to emerge after only a few months' trials.

....

26 Qiu et al., "Chinese guidelines related to novel coronavirus pneumonia."

27 Morens et al., "Rethinking next-generation vaccines for coronaviruses, influenzaviruses, and other respiratory viruses."

Variants

Nobody would have cared about – or even heard of – variants. The discussion would have centered around who was getting seriously ill and dying, and how they could be treated to lower the numbers of hospitalizations and deaths. There would be no need to know whether someone was seriously ill with Alpha, Delta, or Omicron XBB1.16, because the variant would have no impact on treatment.

Long Covid

Every viral infection brings with it the potential for long-term symptoms, yet we've never talked about "long flu" or "long herpes." There was no data back in 2020 suggesting that Covid was radically different and was more likely to result in troublesome symptoms once the initial infection was resolved. Thus, the topic probably would not even have come up. If it had, experts would have explained that feeling fatigued or depressed many months after a viral infection is probably not related, and that if you did not have a serious case of the illness you were very unlikely to have any serious long-term symptoms.

Origins of the virus

If the biodefense experts had been honest with the public, they could have explained that the virus might have leaked from a lab, but that everything we knew about it – low fatality rate, steep fatality age gradient, no ill effects for children, etc. – was still true.

At this point, there could have been open and honest public debates about important topics relevant to the outbreak: What is gain-of-function research, why are we doing it, and should we continue?

There would have been no cover-ups or propaganda about the virus coming from an animal source. We would never know that pangolins or racoon dogs even existed.

Why this sounds like a fantasy

Once the global biodefense public-private partnership took over the pandemic response, there was only one objective: scare everyone as much as possible to gain compliance with lockdowns and make everyone desperate for vaccines. Public health experts, including the leaders of the

NIH, CDC, and NIAID, were no longer authorized to make their own pandemic policy decisions or public announcements. Everyone had to stick to the lockdown narrative.[28]

The forces of panic and propaganda, in the service of enormous profits[29] for pharmaceutical and media companies, once unleashed could not be contained.

It didn't have to be that way. The more people understand this, the less likely they are to go along with such devastating madness in the future.

....

28 Lerman, "Pandemic Leaders Were Biodefense Puppets and Profiteers."

29 Lerman, "Vaccine Harms Are Biodefense Plan's Collateral Damage."

UNCOVERING DEEP STATE CONTROL OF PANDEMIC RESPONSE

This chapter consists of 10 sections, chronicling the discoveries I made as I investigated the pandemic response. It started, pretty randomly, with an attempt to review Deborah Birx's book, Silent Invasion. Birx was an AIDS ambassador for USAID who became Coordinator of the U.S. Government's Covid Task Force. In her book, Birx describes what she claims was a massively botched response to a terrifying existential threat. As I read her story, a suspicion grew into near-certainty that this book, rather than revealing truths about what happened, was actually trying to cover up, distort, and distract from the actual facts of the matter. I now recognize it as a propaganda piece, like many other books and articles, including some analyzed in Chapter 4.

This discovery led me to start researching the government's pandemic response. And what I found was truly astonishing: the pandemic response was led by the security state, not the public health agencies. Further research revealed that the same was true in other countries as well.

All of this research led to the conclusions presented in Chapter 1 of this book. This chapter lays out the path I followed to reach those conclusions.

3.1 HOW DID DEBORAH BIRX GET THE JOB AS U.S. COVID TASK FORCE COORDINATOR?

This section exposes the questionable narrative behind the appointment of Deborah Birx as Coordinator of the U.S. Government's Pandemic Task Force. This is important, because it suggests the appointment was made for reasons other than public health. Why might the National Security Council be appointing the head of the country's pandemic response? Why was she not chosen by, and from among the ranks of, the nation's public health agencies?

● ● ●

Reading Deborah Birx's badly written, poorly edited *Silent Invasion*,[30] published at the end of April 2022, is not easy. In fact, it's mind-numbingly tedious, especially if you try to read every word and not skim over the myriad digressions, repetitions, and multi-paged meanderings.

Nevertheless, according to *The Atlantic*,[31] it is "the most revealing pandemic book yet," detailing how "Trump's team botched the pandemic."

I agree that this 521-page "excruciating story" (as *The New York Times*[32] calls it) is indeed revealing. However, it has little to do with Trump or what *The Atlantic* might consider pandemic botching.

The most revealing parts of the book are:

1) the claims about Birx herself that, upon close inspection, make little sense, contain strange inconsistencies, or contradict other claims made in the book and elsewhere; and

2) the absurd claims about epidemiology and public health generally, and SARS-CoV-2 specifically, endlessly repeated by Birx as scientific truths when in fact they are anything but.

....

30 Birx, *Silent Invasion.*

31 Tofel, "The Clearest Account Yet of How Trump's Team Botched the Pandemic."

32 Quammen, "Deborah Birx's Excruciating Story of Donald Trump's Covid Response."

Investigating these claims is important because they touch on crucial pandemic questions: Who made the terrible pandemic policy decisions and, perhaps most mysteriously and importantly, why?

Here I investigate the obfuscation surrounding Deborah Birx's appointment as White House Coronavirus Response Coordinator, and then the garbage science she so forcefully pushed once she got there.

How did she get the job?

I have not interviewed Dr. Birx in person, but I have read her book, as well as articles about her and interviews with her. Based on all of these, I put together a Q&A in which the questions are mine, and the answers are verbatim quotes from *Silent Invasion*, as well as Dr. Birx's testimony[33] before the Select Subcommittee on the Coronavirus Crisis in the U.S. House of Representatives on October 12, 2021, and other interviews.

Page numbers from the book and line numbers from the hearing transcript are in parentheses. Citations of other articles and interviews are also included.

Q: Dr. Birx, you were officially hired as White House Coronavirus Response Coordinator on February 27, 2020. Who offered you the job?

A: My friend Matt [Pottinger], the deputy national security advisor (p. 32)

Q: In the Congressional hearing on October 12, 2021, you said you did not know why Matt Pottinger[34] was the one to approach you for this job (lines 1505-1507). It does seem odd that Matt would be in charge of appointing a pandemic response coordinator, since public health and epidemiology were not at all part of his experience. As Lawrence Wright reports in *The New Yorker* in December 2020,[35] "in a very noisy Administration, he had

....

33 Birx, testimony to the U.S. House of Representatives, Select Subcommittee on the Coronavirus Crisis, October 12, 2021.

34 Senger, "The Talented Mr. Pottinger: The U.S. Intelligence Agent Who Pushed Lockdowns."

35 Wright, "The Plague Year."

quietly become one of the most influential people shaping American foreign policy." So why did he hire you again?

A: I've known him through his wife. I really knew his wife. I worked with her at the CDC. (lines 1507-1509)

Q: Matt's wife, Yen Pottinger, is a friend of yours?

A: A former colleague at the CDC and a trusted friend and neighbor (p. 32)

Q: So Matt Pottinger was not really a friend, it was his wife you were friends with?

A: I had known Matt through her eyes for the last three or four years. (lines 1526-1529)

Q: What did you say in your Face the Nation interview on January 24, 2021[36] about your relationship with Matt and Yen Pottinger?

A: I've known him and I've known his wife for a very long time. We've worked on pandemics together. Both of us were in Asia during SARS. And so we understood how serious this can go.

Follow-up questions:

- Matt and Yen married in 2014. Did you know Matt before that?

[ANSWER NOT FOUND]

- When you say you've worked on pandemics together, you do not mean you and Matt Pottinger. You mean you and Yen Pottinger worked on AIDS research at the CDC at some point while you were there, between 2007 and 2014. Correct?

....

36 *CBS News*, "Transcript: Dr. Deborah Birx on 'Face the Nation,' January 24, 2021."

Yes[37]

- As far as you and Matt, when you say both of you were in Asia during SARS – you mean back in 2002-2003, you were in Thailand doing research on an AIDS vaccine that never came to fruition, and Matt was a reporter for Reuters and the *Wall Street Journal* in China?

Yes[38, 39]

Q: You were Yen Pottinger's boss at the CDC when you worked at the Division of Global HIV/AIDS, a position you left in 2014. What can you tell us about your friendship with Yen from the time you left that job until Matt offered you the Covid Task Force position?

A: In our three years working together at the CDC, I had marveled at her abilities in the lab. (p. 32)

As early as mid-January, Yen and I had been in communication about the outbreak in China. As events unfolded, we shared whatever insights, information, and anxiety we had. (p. 32)

Q: You and Yen were communicating about your anxieties starting in mid-January. You say you were communicating with Matt even earlier than that?

A: Off and on in early January 2020, I'd share my thoughts with Matt: about the larger picture, about how the virus response in the United States should go, and about how the White House could better manage its messaging around the virus (p. 33)

Q: How did you communicate with Matt?

....

37 Wright, "The Plague Year."

38 George W. Bush Presidential Center, Deborah Birx profile.

39 U.S.-China Economic and Security Review Commission, Matt Pottinger biography.

A: In my back-channel communications with Matt, I pulled together all the publicly available data I'd been compiling and analyzing, connecting the dots to create a concerning picture, and sent it to Yen to forward to him. (p. 34)

Q: So were you communicating with Yen as a friend or as someone who conveyed your concerns, through her husband, to the White House?

A: In communicating with Matt, I had ensured they would have everything I was seeing, to use during White House meetings. I let Yen know that the earliest data available showed that the Wuhan outbreak and subsequent spread would be, at a minimum, ten times what SARS had been. (p. 34-35)

Q: Why were you communicating with a deputy national security advisor through his wife?

A: For privacy and security reasons, I wasn't ready to use official White House email. I trusted that Matt would share the information with those who needed it and not reveal that I was his source. (p. 34)

Q: When you say "privacy and security reasons," what do you mean?

A: Fearing blowback for stepping outside my area of responsibility, I asked him not to use my name when discussing the opinions and data I was providing. (p. 60)

Q: You were sending Matt Pottinger, a deputy national security advisor with high security clearance, data that you say was publicly available, through his wife's private email, to pass on to the White House without revealing you as his source?

A: I had access to more unreported, real-time global data (p. 57)

Through her work, Irum [Zaidi, my PEPFAR chief epidemiologist and data person] knew another "data person," who had access to figures about the novel coronavirus from around the world and very specific data from China. This individual was taking a great risk in passing it along to Irum, and his courage serves as an example for all of us. (p. 59)

Q: So now you're saying you were getting secret data (not publicly available) from China that was unavailable to Matt Pottinger (although he was the Deputy National Security Advisor for Asia), and passing it along to him through personal communications with his wife, in the hopes of influencing White House policy?

A: What I wanted to do was define the actions being taken on the emerging virus based on the data. In my years of working with high-level leaders around the world, I had wielded metrics to move minds and formulate policies, standing behind data to justify the changes (p. 34) I communicated to Matt that we needed to break this chain linking the novel coronavirus to SARS and the seasonal flu and reprioritize testing, full mitigation, mask wearing, improved hygiene, and more social isolation. (p. 38)

Q: So you felt it was your job to give Matt Pottinger very specific public health policy recommendations for the White House long before you were hired for the task force position. But he had offered you a job as early as November 2019, correct?

A: In November 2019, shortly after settling into his new role, Matt had communicated to me that he wanted me to work at the White House in some capacity as a public health security advisor. (p. 33)

Q: Were you aware that the timing of Matt's offer reportedly coincided with an intelligence report (denied by the Pentagon)[40] from the National Center for Medical Intelligence (NCMI) about a potentially dangerous virus already circulating in China in November 2019?

[ANSWER NOT FOUND]

....

40 Margolin and Meek, "Intelligence report warned of coronavirus crisis as early as November: Sources."

Q: What is a public health security advisor? Is that related to the National Security Council (NSC) which, in your book, you say hired you through Matt?

A: The NSC had seen the early reports out of China and Asia before my arrival. Indeed, through Matt Pottinger, it was they who had recruited me to the White House to reinforce their warnings. (p. 169)

Q: The NSC and Matt Pottinger had already seen the early data from China that you said you were passing along to Matt through Yen?

A: The NSC had seen the early reports out of China and Asia before my arrival. (p. 169)

Q: When you recount how Matt called to offer you the task force job on February 23rd and 24th, you state that he had access to information you did not, correct?

A: Matt's urgency represented another degree of concern: the unknown. If he was this concerned, what else was happening? What else would happen? With one of the highest security clearances, Matt had access to all kinds of information that I did not. (p. 61)

Q: So was Matt Pottinger, Deputy National Security Advisor for Asia and a top influencer on foreign policy, with one of the highest security clearances, depending on you for information unavailable to him otherwise, or not?

[SEE ABOVE ANSWERS]

Q: At the Congressional hearing in October 2021, what did you say about your communications with Matt and Yen Pottinger regarding the pandemic?

A: [They] reached out to me about what I was seeing globally, what I thought this was going to become, and we were communicating primarily around what we were seeing globally on the pandemic. And more about the global response than specifically the White House response. (lines 308-309)

Q: As mentioned earlier, you received a White House job offer from Matt Pottinger back in November 2019. At the Congressional hearing you were asked when your conversations with Yen and Matt shifted into the possibility of you "taking on a role." (line 318) What was your answer to the Committee?

A: The end of January, they were looking for someone to talk to the American people about the pandemic and what was being done. (lines 319-321)

Q: In your book you describe that offer, on January 28th, as being arranged through Yen, Matt's wife. Correct?

A: On January 28th... I received a text from Yen Pottinger. (p. 32) Yen knew I would be on the White House complex for my meeting with Erin Walsh, and the text she sent me said that Matt had a "proposition" for me. She didn't know any of the details, but Matt had apologized for the short notice and said he hoped we could meet face-to-face. Yen arranged so that I could meet him in the West Wing, and once we were both there, Matt got to the point quickly. He offered me the position of White House spokesperson on the virus. (p. 33)

Q: Let's recap: You're saying the offer of a job as White House spokesperson on the coronavirus came from Matt Pottinger, a high-level national security advisor whose wife, a senior technical advisor for laboratory surveillance at Columbia University, arranged your meeting in the West Wing. Why was Yen involved in this hiring process? How did Yen have the authority or connections to arrange such a meeting?

[ANSWERS NOT FOUND]

Q: After you refused the spokesperson job several times, Matt Pottinger came back with a different offer: White House Coronavirus Response Coordinator. According to Lawrence Wright's *New Yorker* article,[41] it was Yen's idea to offer you the position. The article also makes it sound like this was the first time Matt considered you for a job:

At home, Pottinger fumed to Yen that eight hundred million dollars was half the sum needed just to support vaccine development through Phase III trials.

"Call Debi," Yen suggested.

Debi was Deborah Birx, the U.S. global AIDS coördinator.

From 2005 to 2014, she led the C.D.C.'s Division of Global H.I.V./AIDS (making her Yen Pottinger's boss). Birx was known to be effective and data-driven, but also autocratic. Yen described her as "super dedicated," adding, "She has stamina and she's demanding, and that pisses people off." That's exactly the person Pottinger was looking for.

What are other reasons you've given for why you were the right person for the Task Force job?

A: As early as February 13, the day before I left for South Africa, Yen and I exchanged texts. Matt had told her that there was a lack of leadership and direction in the CDC and the White House Coronavirus Task Force. (p. 54)

[from Yen's text:] He thinks you should take over Azar, Fauci, and Redfield's jobs, because you're such a better leader than they are. He has been underwhelmed thus far. (p. 38)

....

41 Wright, "The Plague Year."

On February 26, Matt called me expressing greater worry. He told me that every moment I delayed making my decision, I could potentially be costing American lives. (p. 62)

Matt seemed certain I was the missing piece. He knew I had worked on RNA viruses like SARS-CoV-2, from the laboratory bench to the community, developing tests, therapeutics, and vaccines. (p. 65)

Q: More specifically, what epidemics or pandemics have you dealt with?

A: I've also seen the devastation that viruses mete out. HIV, SARS-CoV-1, MERS-CoV, Ebolavirus—I've been on the front lines and have worked with many other experts in the field as the world navigated these public health crises. (p. 3)

Q: But in your work you actually dealt with...?

A: HIV, TB and malaria (p. 26)

Q: What did your family think about the White House job offer?

A: Yen and I had a bit of a laugh when she asked me what my husband thought of my taking on a new role. I'd told her that, given that I was still in South Africa and he was in the United States, I hadn't yet told him (not to mention my adult daughters) about the possible White House move. (p. 63)

Q: How long had you been married?

A: I'd married only a few months before (p. 202)

Q: You did not tell your brand new husband that you were offered a top level position at the White House?

A: I was that concerned about information being leaked. Who knew who was monitoring our communications? (p. 63)

• • •

EXECUTIVE SUMMARY: HOW SHE GOT THE JOB

Deborah Birx, an immunologist and Army Colonel who worked for the Department of Defense and U.S. Military on AIDS research, served as Directory of the CDC's Division of Global HIV/AIDS and as the U.S. Global AIDS Coordinator[42], was appointed White House Coronavirus Response Coordinator on February 27th, 2020.

She had no training or experience in epidemiology, novel pathogen pandemic response, (unless you consider combating well-established and known diseases like AIDS, tuberculosis, and malaria in developing countries such response), or airborne respiratory viruses like the coronavirus.

She was offered the position by Matt Pottinger, Deputy National Security Advisor for China, who told Birx that if she did not take the job American lives could be lost. According to Yen Pottinger (Matt's wife) Matt thought Birx was a better leader than the heads of NIAID, the CDC, and other senior public health officials. The basis for Matt's very high opinion of Birx's leadership capabilities and the importance of her appointment to saving American lives is unknown.

Yen Pottinger was a researcher who had worked in Dr. Birx's CDC lab. Yen and Deborah may or may not have been good friends who kept in touch after Birx left her job at that lab in 2014, the year Matt and Yen married. Birx may or may not have been friends with Matt independently of Yen. Yen may or may not have been the person to suggest Birx for the Task Force Coordinator job.

Before the Coordinator job, way back in November 2019 when nobody was talking about a potential coronavirus pandemic, Matt Pottinger had offered Birx a public health security advisor job. This may or may not have actually been a job offer from The National Security Council, which may or may not have known at the time of a potentially dangerous virus circulating in China.

At the end of January 2020, Matt offered Birx a different job, as White

....

42 George W. Bush Presidential Center, Deborah Birx profile.

House coronavirus spokesperson. Birx first learned of this through a text from Yen Pottinger, who claimed not to know what Matt wanted to propose, and then proceeded – through unknown security clearances and connections – to coordinate a meeting in the West Wing where the job offer was made. Birx declined.

Starting in mid-January 2020, or maybe earlier, weeks before that spokesperson job offer, Birx communicated with Yen and Matt about the novel coronavirus that she supposedly learned about on January 3rd from the news (*Silent Invasion*, p. 3). Birx was mostly communicating with Yen about her fears and anxieties and/or she was communicating with Yen and Matt about her global observations. Or maybe she was giving Matt specific advice through Yen regarding pandemic policies that she wanted him to transmit to the White House.

Birx was basing her public health policy recommendations, which she may or may not have been sending to Matt through Yen in early or mid-January 2020 (when she was officially working on AIDS in Africa) on publicly available data. Or she may have had access to secret data from China.

Matt had access to secret data that Birx did not have and seemed very concerned about the situation, possibly due to that secret data.

Throughout her communications with Matt and Yen Pottinger, Birx was very worried about security and secrecy, which is why she was using personal emails and texts rather than Matt's official White House email. She did not even tell her grown daughters or her husband about the big White House job offer, because she thought this was such sensitive information and who knew who was monitoring her communications.

It is unknown when Birx's new husband learned of his wife's big White House appointment.

3.2 FAKE SCIENCE OF PANDEMIC RESPONSE REVEALED IN DEBORAH BIRX'S WORDS

This section exposes the contradictory and ultimately nonsensical "scientific" claims used to support the lockdown-until-vaccine biodefense pandemic response plan. The section addresses the claims made specifically in Deborah Birx's book, but these were the same claims made by the entire public health propaganda machine. Understanding how utterly non-scientific they are is a key to understanding that the response had nothing to do with public health.

• • •

In the previous section, I examined the murky circumstances behind the appointment of Dr. Deborah Birx as Coordinator of the White House Coronavirus Response Task Force on February 27, 2020. (Note: this was an important date for the global pandemic response planners, as detailed in Chapter 4.2)

Based on that examination, I surmised that Dr. Birx did not get the job due to her medical or public health experience. Rather, as Birx herself tells it, the National Security Council recruited and appointed her to the job, through Deputy National Security Advisor for Asia, Matt Pottinger.[43]

But why? Why would someone with no relevant medical or scientific background be appointed to a top pandemic-response position? The answer, I believe, is that Birx was installed in that position in order to impose the untested, unscientific, totalitarian pandemic mitigation measures chosen by the biosecurity community.

Taking a step back, before the speculative why, let's examine a more concrete what: What were the predictably ineffectual and disastrous pandemic management measures imposed on us by the Task Force, coordinated by Dr. Deborah Birx, and what was her rationale for imposing them?

---

43 Senger, "The Talented Mr. Pottinger: The U.S. Intelligence Agent Who Pushed Lockdowns."

The Dreaded Silent Spread

Everything Birx claims about the Covid pandemic, and all of her prescriptions for mitigating it, are based on a single idea, expressed repeatedly in her book, *Silent Invasion*:

"The distribution and spread of the virus would be far greater and far quicker [than the 2002/3 SARS virus] due to the undetected silent invasion I fundamentally believed was taking place across the globe." (p. 28)

In other words, as Birx explains, the SARS-CoV-2 virus was different from other flu-like viruses and previous pandemics because it was spreading faster, and it was less detectable as it was spreading. Why was it less detectable? Because most people who were infected had "a mild disease – another way to describe silent spread" (p. 92).

Let's take another second to consider the words of Dr. Deborah Birx herself: silent spread means mild disease. The more silent spread, the more people are getting infected but experiencing mild to undetectable symptoms.

Transmissibility and fatality

If silent spread means most people have mild disease, why does Birx think SARS-CoV-2 is so dangerous that it merits shutting down the entire world and imposing unprecedented mitigation measures?

As she explains (p. 18), when we want to know how dangerous a virus is, we have to consider how easily and quickly it spreads, and how many people who are infected end up dying. But instead of looking at each of those factors separately, Birx conveniently conflates them:

"More exposure meant more infections, which meant a greater frequency of serious illness and death." (p. 56)

In other words, the more people are infected, the more people will get seriously ill or die. But we just learned from Birx that most people who were infected with SARS-CoV-2 through silent spread had mild or no symptoms. So, by her own account, more infection does not necessarily mean more serious illness or death.

It's not rocket science. It's not even Epidemiology 101. It's just plain logic.

The Diamond Princess

Now let's say we don't want to resort to mere logic to refute Birx's baseless implication that silent spread makes SARS-CoV-2 exceptionally dangerous. Suppose we look at what a world-renowned epidemiologist had to say in March 2020 about what silent spread means in terms of the overall danger posed by a novel coronavirus.

John Ioannidis[44] is a Stanford professor and leading world expert in epidemiology, statistics and biomedical data, with hundreds of publications and expertise in precisely those areas that are crucial for understanding an emerging pandemic. He's just the type of person you'd want advising you on how to evaluate the threat posed by a novel virus.

In an article published March 17, 2020,[45] Ioannidis explained that to figure out how dangerous a pathogen is, you need to calculate approximately how many people who get infected are going to die.

Ioannidis used the Diamond Princess cruise ship to calculate an approximate fatality rate (the number of people who get infected and die) for SARS-CoV-2. He used the cruise ship because the passengers were quarantined for long enough to allow the virus to spread among them, and those with symptoms were tested for Covid. Seven people of the 700 who tested positive died. That's a fatality rate of 1% (7/700).

However, as Birx herself notes: "The documented spread was intense, going from 1 to 691 confirmed positives in only three weeks—and those were just the people with symptoms. If they had been testing more widely, among asymptomatic people, the real number could be two to three times greater: 1,200 to 1,800 infections." (p. 46)

Ioannidis also thought that many untested people might have been infected. In which case, let's say for example there were 1,400 untested but infected people, the fatality rate would go down to 0.33% (7/2,100). And if there were 2,800 untested but infected people, the fatality rate would be 0.2% (7/3,500). And so on.

That's what silent spread means for the fatality rate: the more the

....

44 Stanford Medicine, John Ioannidis biography.

45 Ioannidis, "A fiasco in the making? As the coronavirus pandemic takes hold, we are making decisions without reliable data."

virus infects people without killing them, the less lethal it is. Which, in a rational world, would presumably mean we would need less drastic mitigation measures.

Birx, however, in one of her many feats of illogical counterfactual obfuscation, concludes that, because the measures she thinks are key to stopping the spread (masks and distancing) are actually not working to stop the spread, the virus is obviously spreading silently, which means we need to impose more of those measures:

"Despite the measures the Japanese health ministry had put in place, this explosive growth was clear evidence of silent spread." (p. 46)

Again, it sounds too absurd to be the basis for all the crazy Covid policies, but there it is. And, of course, Birx never follows her argument to its logical conclusions which are:

1. If masking and distancing are not preventing silent spread, why are we imposing them?
2. If most people are getting mild disease, why do we need universal mitigation measures in the first place?

Testing

Birx's illogical insistence that silent spread makes the virus more dangerous leads her to an even more illogical monomaniacal focus on testing and case numbers.

Because, according to Birx, if silent spread is an evil in and of itself, the only way it can be combatted is to make it less silent through testing. And the more cases there are, no matter how mild or asymptomatic, the more danger the virus supposedly poses.

Apparently, Birx is unaware that the World Health Organization, in its guidelines[46] for nonpharmaceutical interventions (NPIs) for pandemic influenza, states clearly that:

....

46 World Health Organization Writing Group, "Nonpharmaceutical Interventions for Pandemic Influenza, National and Community Measures."

Evidence and experience suggest that in pandemic phase 6 (increased and sustained transmission in the general population), aggressive interventions to isolate patients and quarantine contacts, even if they are the first patients detected in a community, would probably be ineffective, not a good use of limited health resources, and socially disruptive.

In other words, testing asymptomatic people and isolating them in order to stop or slow the spread of a pandemic respiratory virus that has already spread to the general population is not only pointless, but potentially harmful. Moreover, the faster and more silently the virus has spread, the less useful testing and isolation become, because the virus is that much more widespread in the population already.

And, as Birx herself was frantic to warn everyone, including President Trump, in March 2020 when she started advocating for massive testing, "the virus is undoubtedly already circulating widely, below the radar, in the United States" (p. 3)

Masking and social distancing

So what about other measures? As discussed above, the Diamond Princess revealed to Birx that masking and social distancing cannot stop the "silent spread." Yet somehow these are among her top mitigation strategies.

Birx says her certainty as to the effectiveness of masking and distancing came from her time in Asia during the 2002-2004 SARS epidemic.

"I was doing work in Asia back in 2002 when the sudden acute respiratory syndrome (SARS) outbreak began" (p. 9), she recalls. [NOTE: SARS actually stands for Severe Acute Respiratory Syndrome, but here Birx replaces "severe" with "sudden" – just another tiny clue that scientific credibility is not a primary focus of the book.]

What she conveniently fails to tell us is that she was not in China, where that outbreak originated, nor was she in any of the highly impacted Asian countries. Rather, she was in Thailand, working on an AIDS vaccine. She also omits the fun fact that there were 9 infections and 2 deaths in all of

Thailand[47] from that SARS virus.

Nevertheless, however far removed she actually was from the epicenter of the 2002-2004 outbreak, Birx confidently asserts:

> One of the things that had kept the SARS case fatality rate from being worse was that, in Asia, the population (young and old alike) adopted the wearing of masks routinely.... Masking was a normal behavior. Masks saved lives. Masks were good. (p. 36)

[ANOTHER NOTE ON ERRONEOUS SCIENTIFIC TERMINOL-OGY: masks are not and have never been associated with lowering the case fatality rate (CFR) of any disease. CFR is how many people die once they are infected and fall ill. CFR is lowered by treatments that prevent ill people from dying. Masks, theoretically, may prevent people from getting infected. They cannot prevent death in the already ill.]

Birx displays the same certainty regarding social distancing:

> Another strategy that suppressed the 2003 SARS outbreak was social distancing guidelines—limiting how close you got to other people, especially indoors...Along with wearing masks, these behavioral changes had the greatest effect on mitigating the SARS epidemic by limiting community spread and not letting the virus claim more lives. (p. 37)

Birx provides no footnotes, citations, or any scientific evidence at all for these assertions or, for that matter, for any of her pseudo-scientific claims. As noted in Jeffrey Tucker's astute review[48] of *Silent Invasion*, there is not a single footnote in the entire book.

Yet, if we look at the scientific literature, we find that those who studied NPIs during the time of the 2002-2004 SARS outbreak came to the exact opposite conclusion. The WHO Working Group on International and

----

47 Wikipedia, "2002-2004 SARS outbreak." Accessed February 12, 2024.

48 Tucker, "Dr. Birx Praises Herself While Revealing Ignorance, Treachery, and Deceit."

Community Transmission of SARS concluded[49] that:

> The 2003 outbreak of severe acute respiratory syndrome (SARS) was contained largely through traditional public health interventions, such as finding and isolating case-patients, quarantining close contacts, and enhanced infection control. The independent effectiveness of measures to 'increase social distance' and wearing masks in public places requires further evaluation.

In other words, masking and social distancing were the interventions least proven to affect the spread or outcome of the SARS epidemic on which Birx claims to base her policies.

Strengthening this conclusion, in the WHO's 2006 review of NPIs for flu pandemics, the recommendations state explicitly that:

> Mask wearing by the general population is not expected to have an appreciable impact on transmission, but should be permitted, as this is likely to occur spontaneously.[50]

Whatever justifications were found or invented for masking during Covid subsequent to Birx's appointment to the White House Task Force, the ones on which she claims to have based her policies were bogus from the get-go.

This is clearly of no concern to Birx, whose purpose in *Silent Invasion* is apparently not to convey sound scientific or public health principles. She's much more concerned with showing how she and her co-lockdown-conspirator, Deputy National Security Advisor Matt Pottinger, were in total agreement about all the non-scientific mitigation measures independently of one another:

> Independently from me, Matt became the self-appointed White House prophet of mask wearing," Birx proclaims. But, to her

---

49 Bell, "Public health interventions and SARS spread, 2003."

50 World Health Organization Writing Group, "Nonpharmaceutical Interventions for Pandemic Influenza, National and Community Measures."

distress, "at the White House, Matt's message about wearing masks to prevent silent spread had fallen on deaf ears." (p. 36)

Which leads one to wonder: where did Pottinger, a journalist-turned-intelligence agent, get his very strong opinions on the utility of masking to mitigate respiratory viral pandemics in general, and the Covid pandemic in particular?

According to Lawrence Wright's non-scientific, largely anecdotal article in *The New Yorker* in December 2020, Pottinger got the idea while driving a stick-shift car, talking to a doctor in China, and scribbling notes on the back of an envelope (all at the same time!):

> On March 4th, as Matt Pottinger was driving to the White House, he was on the phone with a doctor in China. Taking notes on the back of an envelope while navigating traffic, he was hearing valuable new information about how the virus was being contained in China. The doctor...emphasized that masks were extremely effective with COVID, more so than with influenza. 'It's great to carry around your own hand sanitizer,' the doctor said. 'But masks are going to win the day.'[51]

Then, after getting this incredibly new and valuable information from an unnamed "doctor in China," even as his parked car was sliding backward into a tree (he apparently forgot the emergency brake), Pottinger "kept thinking about masks." Apparently, he was mesmerized by the idea. Why? Because he "thought it was evident that, wherever a large majority of people wore masks, contagion was stopped 'dead in its tracks.'"

That's pretty much it. Matt thought it was evident that masks had stopped the contagion in Hong Kong and Taiwan – based on what evidence we'll probably never know – and therefore must be implemented everywhere.

....

51 Wright, "The Plague Year."

CONCLUSION & UNRESOLVED ISSUES

In *Silent Invasion* – a book I value as a prime exemplar of pandemic propaganda – Deborah Birx does not even try to make coherent scientific or public health policy arguments in favor of the Chinese-style total-itarian measures she advocated. Instead, she provides nonsensical, self-contradictory assertions – some downright false and others long disproven in the scientific literature.

I doubt Birx believes any of the fake science claims made in her book. Rather, as with the issue of how she was appointed in the first place (explored in the previous section), the entire narrative is a smoke screen or diversion, intended to draw attention away from who actually appointed her and why.

If we knew the answers to those two questions (by whom and why Birx was appointed), I believe we would find that:

– All of the devastating Chinese-style lockdown measures were imposed on the U.S. and the world by government officials with no pandemic experience but lots of military and national security connections, more specifically biosecurity involvement.

– It was not the SARS-CoV-2 virus and its effects in the real world that concerned Birx, Pottinger, and their bosses and counterparts in other countries. It was the goals of the biodefense public-private partnership, as discussed in Chapter 1, that they were pursuing.

3.3 BIRX WAS PUT ON THE TASK FORCE TO ENACT THE BIODEFENSE PROGRAM

This section delves deeply into the question of who Deborah Birx, and by extension the entire White House Task Force, was actually working for. It exposes the pretense that she was working in tandem with the public health leaders, and suggests that she was leading the response on behalf of entirely different entities – namely, the National Security Council and, by extension, the biodefense global public-private partnership, as discussed in Chapter 1.

• • •

In the two previous sections, I looked into the shady circumstances surrounding Deborah Birx's appointment to the White House Coronavirus Response Task Force and the laughable lack of actual science behind the claims she used to justify her testing, masking, distancing and lockdown policies.

Considering all that, the questions arise: Who was actually in charge of Deborah Birx and whom was she working with?

But first: Who cares?

Here's why I think it's important: If we can show that Birx and the others who imposed totalitarian anti-scientific testing, masking, social distancing, and lockdown policies knew from the get-go that these policies would not work against an airborne respiratory virus, and nevertheless they imposed them FOR REASONS OTHER THAN PUBLIC HEALTH, then there is no longer acceptable justification for any of those measures.

Furthermore, whatever mountains of post-facto bad science were concocted to rationalize these measures are also completely bunk. Instead of having to go through each ridiculous pseudo-study to demonstrate its scientific worthlessness, we can throw the whole steaming pile in the garbage heap of history, where it belongs, and move on with our lives.

In my admittedly somewhat naive optimism, I also hope that by exposing the non-scientific, anti-public-health origins of the Covid catastrophe, we may lower the chances of its happening again.

And now, back to Birx.

She did not work for or with Trump

We know Birx was definitely not working with President Trump, although she was on a task force ostensibly representing the White House. Trump did not appoint her, nor did the leaders of the Task Force, as Scott Atlas recounts in his revelatory book on White House pandemic lunacy, *A Plague Upon Our House.*[52] When Atlas asked Task Force members how Birx was appointed, he was surprised to find that "no one seemed to know." (Atlas, p. 82)

Yet, somehow, Deborah Birx – a former military AIDS researcher and government AIDS ambassador with no training, experience or publications in epidemiology or public health policy – found herself leading a White House Task Force on which she had the power to literally subvert the policy prescriptions of the President of the United States.

As she describes in *Silent Invasion,*[53] Birx was shocked when "at the halfway point of our 15 Days to Slow the Spread campaign, President Trump stated that he hoped to lift all restrictions by Easter Sunday." (Birx, p. 142) She was even more dismayed when "mere days after the president had announced the thirty-day extension of the Slow the Spread campaign to the American public" he became enraged and told her, "'We will never shut down the country again. Never.'" (Birx, p. 152)

Clearly, Trump was not on board with the lockdowns, and every time he was forced to go along with them, he became enraged and lashed out at Birx – the person he believed was forcing him.

Birx laments that "from here on out, everything I worked toward would be harder—in some cases, impossible," and goes on to say she would basically have to work behind the scenes against the President, having "to adapt to effectively protect the country from the virus that had already silently invaded it." (Birx, pp. 153-4)

Which brings us back to the question: Where did Birx get the nerve and, more mysteriously, the authority to so blithely act in direct opposition to the President she was supposed to serve, on matters affecting the lives of the entire population of the United States?

....

52 Atlas, *A Plague Upon Our House.*

53 Birx, *Silent Invasion.*

Atlas regrets what he thinks was President Trump's "massive error in judgment." He argues that Trump acted "against his own gut feeling" and "delegated authority to medical bureaucrats, and then he failed to correct that mistake." (Atlas, p. 308)

Although I believe massive errors in judgment were not unusual for President Trump, I disagree with Atlas on this one. In the case of the Coronavirus Response Task Force, I actually think there was something much more insidious at play.

Trump had no power over Birx or pandemic response

After lamenting Trump's delegation of authority to "medical bureaucrats," Scott Atlas unwittingly hints at forces beyond Trump's control. "The Task Force was called 'the White House Coronavirus Task Force,'" Atlas notes, "but it was not in sync with President Trump. It was directed by Vice President Pence." (Atlas, p. 306) Yet, whenever Atlas tried to raise questions about Birx's policies, he was directed to speak with Pence, who then failed to ever address anything with Birx:

> Given that the VP was in charge of the Task Force, shouldn't the bottom-line advice emanating from it comport with the policies of the administration? But he would never speak with Dr. Birx at all. In fact, (Marc) Short [Pence's chief of staff], clearly representing the VP's interests above all else, would do the opposite, telephoning others in the West Wing, imploring friends of mine to tell me to avoid alienating Dr. Birx. (Atlas, p. 165-6)

Recall that Pence replaced Alex Azar as Task Force director on February 26, 2020 and Birx's appointment as coordinator, at the instigation of Asst. National Security Advisor Matt Pottinger,[54] came on February 27th. Subsequent to those two appointments, it was Birx who was effectively in charge of United States coronavirus policy.

What was driving that policy, once she took over? As Birx writes, it was

---

54 Senger, "The Talented Mr. Pottinger: The U.S. Intelligence Agent Who Pushed Lockdowns."

the NSC (National Security Council) that appointed her, through Pottinger, and it was her job to "reinforce their warnings" – which probably entailed secretly telling the president that the virus was a potential bioweapon that had escaped from a US-funded lab in Wuhan.

Trump was probably issued this warning, as evidenced not just by his repeated mentions, but by what *Time Magazine* called[55] his uncharacteristic refusal to explain why he believed it. The magazine quotes Trump saying "I can't tell you that," when asked about his belief in the lab leak. And he repeats, "I'm not allowed to tell you that."

Why in the world was the President of the United States not allowed to override AIDS researcher/diplomat Birx on lockdown policies nor explain to the public why he believed there was a lab leak?

The answer, I believe, is that Trump was uncharacteristically holding back because he was told (by Birx, Pottinger and the military/intelligence/biosecurity interests for whom they worked) that if he did not go along with their policies and proclamations, millions of Americans would die.

As Dr. Atlas repeatedly notes with great dismay: "the Task Force doctors were fixated on a single-minded view that all cases of COVID must be stopped or millions of Americans would die." (Atlas, p. 155-6)

That was the key message, wielded with great force and success against Trump, his administration, the press, the states, and the public, to suppress any opposition to lockdown policies.

She dictated policy to the entire Trump administration

In his book, Atlas observes with puzzlement and consternation that, although Vice President Pence was the nominal director of the Task Force, Deborah Birx was the person in charge: "Birx's policies were enacted throughout the country, in almost every single state, for the entire pandemic—this cannot be denied; it cannot be deflected." (Atlas, p. 222)

Atlas is "dumbstruck at the lack of leadership in the White House," in which, "the president was saying one thing while the White House Task Force representative was saying something entirely different, indeed

---

55 Elliott, "How Distrust of Donald Trump Muddled the COVID-19 'Lab Leak' Debate."

contradictory" and, as he notes, "no one ever set her [Birx] straight on her role." (Atlas, p. 222-223)

Not only that, but no matter how much Trump, or anyone in the administration, disagreed with Birx, "the White House was held hostage to the anticipated reaction of Dr. Birx" and she "was not to be touched, period." (Atlas, p. 223)

One explanation for her untouchableness, Atlas suggests, is that Birx and her policies became so popular with the press and public that the administration did not want to "rock the boat" by replacing her before the election. This explanation, however, as Atlas himself realizes, crumbles in the face of what we know about Trump and the media's hostility towards him:

> They [Trump's advisors] had convinced him to do exactly the opposite of what he would naturally do in any other circumstance—to disregard his own common sense and allow grossly incorrect policy advice to prevail. ... This president, widely known for his signature 'You're fired!' declaration, was misled by his closest political intimates. All for fear of what was inevitable anyway—skewering from an already hostile media. (Atlas, p. 300-301)

I would suggest, again, that the reason for the seemingly inexplicable lack of gumption on Trump's part to get rid of Birx was not politics, but behind-the-scenes machinations of the biodefense cabal.

Who else was part of this cabal with its hidden agendas and oversized policy influence? Our attention naturally turns to the other members of the Task Force who were presumably co-engineering lockdown policies with Birx. Surprising revelations emerge.

There was no troika. No Birx-Fauci lockdown plan. It was all Birx.
It is universally assumed, by both those in favor and those opposed to the Task Force's policy prescriptions, that Drs. Deborah Birx, Tony Fauci (head of NIAID at the time) and Bob Redfield (then director of the CDC) worked together to formulate those policies.

Yet the stories told by Birx herself, and the reports by Task Force infiltrator Scott Atlas suggest otherwise.

Like everyone else, at the onset of his book, Atlas asserts: "The architects of the American lockdown strategy were Dr. Anthony Fauci and Dr. Deborah Birx. With Dr. Robert Redfield… they were the most influential medical members of the White House Coronavirus Task Force." (Atlas, p. 22)

But as Atlas's story unfolds, he presents a more nuanced understanding of the power dynamics on the Task Force:

> Fauci's role surprised me the most. Most of the country, indeed the entire world, assumed that Fauci occupied a directorial role in the Trump administration's Task Force. I had also thought that from viewing the news," Atlas admits. However, he continues, "The public presumption of Dr. Fauci's leadership role on the Task Force itself…could not have been more incorrect. Fauci held massive sway with the public, but he was not in charge of anything specific on the Task Force. He served mainly as a channel for updates on the trials of vaccines and drugs. (p. 98)

By the end of the book, Atlas fully revises his initial assessment, strongly emphasizing that, in fact, it was primarily and predominantly Birx who designed and disseminated the lockdown policies:

> Dr. Fauci held court in the public eye on a daily basis, so frequently that many misconstrue his role as being in charge. However, it was really Dr. Birx who articulated Task Force policy. All the advice from the Task Force to the states came from Dr. Birx. All written recommendations about their on-the-ground policies were from Dr. Birx. Dr. Birx conducted almost all the visits to states on behalf of the Task Force. (Atlas, p. 309-10)

It may sound jarring and unlikely, given the public perception of Fauci, as Atlas notes. But in Birx's book the same unexpected picture emerges.

Methinks the lady doth protest too much

As with her bizarrely self-contradictory statements about how she got hired, and her blatantly bogus scientific claims, Birx's story about her mind-melded closeness with Fauci and Redfield falls apart upon closer examination.

In her book, Birx repeatedly claims she trusts Redfield and Fauci "implicitly to help shape America's response to the novel coronavirus." (Birx, p. 31) She says she has "every confidence, based on past performance, that whatever path the virus took, the United States and the CDC would be on top of the situation." (Birx, p. 32)

Then, almost immediately, she undermines the credibility of those she supposedly trusts, quoting Matt Pottinger as saying she "'should take over Azar, Fauci, and Redfield's jobs, because you're such a better leader than they are.'" (Birx, p. 38-9)

Perhaps she was just giving herself a little pat on the back, one might innocently suggest. But wait. There's so much more.

Birx claims that in a meeting on January 31, "everything Drs. Fauci and Redfield said about their approach made sense based on the information available to me at that point," even though "neither of them spoke" about the two issues she was most obsessed with: "asymptomatic silent spread [and] the role testing should play in the response." (Birx, p. 39)

Then, although she says she "didn't read too much into this omission," (p. 39) just two weeks later, "as early as February 13" Birx again mentions "a lack of leadership and direction in the CDC and the White House Coronavirus Task Force." (p. 54)

So does Debi trust Tony and Bob's leadership or does she not? The only answer is more self-contradictory obfuscation.

Birx is horrified that nobody is taking the virus as seriously as they should: "then I saw Tony and Bob repeating that the risk to Americans was low," she reports. "On February 8, Tony said that the chances of contracting the virus were 'minuscule.'" And, "on February 29, he said, 'Right now, at this moment, there is no need to change anything you're doing on a day-to-day basis.'" (Birx, p. 57)

This does not seem like the kind of leader Birx can trust. She half-heartedly tries to excuse Redfield and Fauci, saying "I now believe that Bob and Tony's words had spoken to the limited data they had access to from the CDC," and then, in another whiplash moment, "maybe they had data in the United States that I did not."

Did Tony and Bob provide less dire warnings because they had insufficient data or because they had more data than Birx did? She never clarifies, but regardless, she assures us that she "trusted them" and "felt reassured every day with them on the task force." (Birx, p. 57)

If I was worried that the virus was not being taken seriously enough, Birx's reports on Bob and Tony would not be very reassuring, to say the least.

Apparently, Birx herself felt that way too. "I was somewhat disappointed that Bob and Tony weren't seeing the situation as I was," she says, when they disagreed with her alarmist assessments of asymptomatic spread. But, she adds, "at least their number supported my belief that this new disease was far more asymptomatic than the flu. I wouldn't have to push them as far as I needed to push the CDC." (Birx, p. 78)

Is someone who disagrees with your assessment to the point that you need to push them in your direction also someone you "implicitly trust" to lead the U.S. through the pandemic?

Apparently, not so much.

Although she supposedly trusts Redfield and sleeps well at night knowing he's on the Task Force, Birx has nothing but disdain and criticism for the CDC – the organization Redfield leads.

"On aggressive testing I planned to have Tom Frieden [CDC director under Obama] help bring the CDC along," she recounts. "Like me, the CDC wanted to do everything to stop the virus, but the agency needed to align with us on aggressive testing and silent spread." (p. 122) Which makes one wonder: If she was so closely aligned with Redfield, the head of the CDC, why did Birx need to bring in a former director – in a direct challenge to the sitting one – to "bring the CDC along?" Who is "us" if not Birx, Fauci and Redfield?

Masks were another issue of apparent contention. Birx is frustrated because the CDC, led by her "We've-got-each-other's-back" bestie, Bob Redfield (Birx, p. 31), will not issue strict enough masking guidelines. In fact, she repeatedly throws Bob's organization under the bus, basically accusing them of causing American deaths: "For many weeks and months to come," she writes, "I fretted over how many lives could have been saved if the CDC had trusted the public to understand that...masks would do no harm and could potentially do a great deal of good." (Birx, p. 86)

Apparently, Fauci was not on board with the masking either, as Birx says that "getting the doctors, including Tom [Frieden] and Tony, to be in complete agreement with me about asymptomatic spread was slightly less of a priority. As with masks, I knew I could return to that issue as soon as I got their buy-in on our recommendations." (Birx, p. 123)

Who is making "our recommendations" if not Birx, Fauci and Redfield?

The myth of the troika

Whether or not she trusted them (and it's hard to believe, based on her own accounts, that she did), it was apparently very important to Birx that she, Fauci, and Redfield appear as a single entity with no disagreements whatsoever.

When Scott Atlas, an outsider not privy to whatever power plays were happening on the Task Force, came in, his presence apparently rattled Birx (Atlas, p. 83-4), and for good reason. Atlas immediately noticed strange goings-on. In his book, he repeatedly uses words like "bizarre," "odd," and "uncanny" to describe how Fauci, Redfield, and Birx behaved. Most notably, they never ever questioned or disagreed with one another in Task Force meetings. Not ever.

"They shared thought processes and views to an uncanny level," Atlas writes, then reiterates that "there was virtually no disagreement among them." What he saw "was an amazing consistency, as though there were an agreed-upon complicity" (Atlas, pp. 99-100). They "virtually always agreed, literally never challenging one another." (p. 101)

An agreed-upon complicity? Uncanny agreement? Based on all of the disagreements reported by Birx and her repeated questioning and under-mining of Bob and Tony's authority, how can this be explained?

I would contend that in order to obscure the extent to which Birx alone was in charge of Task Force policy, the other doctors were compelled to present a facade of complete agreement. Otherwise, as with any opposition to, or even discussion of, potential harms of lockdown policies, "millions of Amercans would die."

This assessment is strengthened by Atlas's ongoing bafflement and distress at how the Task Force – and particularly the doctors/scientists who were presumably formulating policy based on data and research – functioned:

> I never saw them act like scientists, digging into the numbers to verify the very trends that formed the basis of their reactive policy pronouncements. They did not act like researchers, using critical thinking to dissect the published science or differentiate a correlation from a cause. They certainly did not show a physician's clinical perspective. With their single-minded focus, they did not even act like public health experts. (Atlas, p. 176)

Atlas was surprised, indeed stunned, that "No one on the Task Force presented any data" to justify lockdowns or to contradict the evidence on lockdown harms that Atlas presented. (Atlas, p. 206) More specifically, no data or research was ever presented (except by Atlas) to contradict or question anything Birx said. "Until I arrived," Atlas observes, "no one had challenged anything she said during her six months as the Task Force Coordinator." (Atlas, p. 234)

Atlas cannot explain what he's witnessing. "That was all part of the puzzle of the Task Force doctors," he states. "There was a lack of scientific rigor in meetings I attended. I never saw them question the data. The striking uniformity of opinion by Birx, Redfield, Fauci, and (Brett) Giroir [former Admiral and Task Force "testing czar"] was not anything like what I had seen in my career in academic medicine." (Atlas, p. 244)

How can we explain the puzzle of this uncanny apparent complicity by the Task Force troika?

Methinks the intelligence agent also doth protest too much

An interesting hint comes from the string of anecdotes comprising Lawrence Wright's *New Yorker* article "The Plague Year."[56] Wright writes that Matt Pottinger (the NSC liaison to Birx) tried to convince Task Force members that masking could stop the virus "'dead in its tracks'" but his views "stirred up surprisingly rigid responses from the public-health contingent."

....

56 Wright, "The Plague Year."

Wright continues to report that "In Pottinger's opinion, when Redfield, Fauci, Birx, and (Stephen) Hahn spoke, it could sound like groupthink," implying that those were the members of the "public-health contingent" who did not agree with Pottinger's masking ideas.

But wait. We just noted Birx's frustration, indeed deep regret, that the CDC led by Redfield, as well as Fauci (and even Frieden) did not agree with her ideas on asymptomatic spread and masking. So why does Pottinger imply that she and the "public-health contingent" of the Task Force were group-thinking this issue, against him?

I would suggest that the only way to make sense of these contradictions within Birx's narrative and between her, Atlas, and Pottinger's stories, is if we understand "align with us" and "our recommendations" to refer not to the perceived Birx-Fauci-Redfield troika, but to the Birx-Pottinger-biodefense cabal that was actually running the show.

In fact, Birx and Pottinger put so much effort into insisting on the solidarity of the troika, even when it contradicts their own statements, that the question inevitably arises: what do they have to gain from it? The benefit of insisting that Birx was allied with Fauci, Redfield, and the "public-health contingent" on the Task Force, I would argue, is that this deflects attention from the Birx-Pottinger-cabal non-public-health alliance.

Her authority and policies emanated from a hidden source

The explanation of Atlas's perceived "puzzle of the Task Force doctors" that makes the most sense to me is that Deborah Birx, in contrast and often in opposition to the other doctors on the Task Force, represented the interests of the biodefense cabal: those not just in the U.S. but in the international intelligence/biosecurity community who imposed the lockdown-until-vaccine pandemic response on behalf of the global biodefense GPPP (see chapter 1).

Once we separate Birx from Trump, from the rest of the administration, and from the others on the Task Force, we can see clearly that her single-minded and scientifically nonsensical emphasis on silent spread and asymptomatic testing was geared toward a single goal: to scare everyone so much that lockdowns would appear to be a sensible policy. This is the same strategy that was, uncannily in my opinion, implemented almost to the letter in nearly every other country around the world.

I'll close this chapter of the Birx riddle wrapped in a mystery inside an enigma, with Scott Atlas's report of his parting conversation with President Trump:

> 'You were right about everything, all along the way,' Trump said to Atlas. 'And you know what? You were also right about something else. Fauci wasn't the biggest problem of all of them. It really wasn't him. You were right about that.' I found myself nodding as I held the phone in my hand. I knew exactly whom he was talking about. (Atlas, p. 300)

And now, so do we.

3.4 HOW TO MAKE THE WORLD COMPLY WITH LOCKDOWN-UNTIL-VACCINE

This section is a deep dive into the tactics used by the U.S. Government's Covid Task Force, and by most governments around the world, to gain the public's compliance with the non-scientific, anti-public health, lockdown-until-vaccine pandemic response.

• • •

In his scathing account of his time on the Task Force, *A Plague Upon Our House*,[57] Dr. Scott Atlas – the only outsider I'm aware of who managed to penetrate even the outer reaches of the U.S. Covid Response Task Force – uses phrases like "Kafkaesque absurdity," "incomprehensible error," and "frankly immoral" to describe what he witnessed. Indeed, if the Task Force had actually been trying to apply best practices to pandemic mitigation, then everything they did would seem incomprehensibly misguided and obviously terrible – as it did to Atlas.

However, if you believe (as I do) that Birx was imposing the biodefense cabal's agenda on the Task Force and the country (and, by extension, the world), then everything they did suddenly makes perfect sense: All the policies that seemed ridiculous when examined separately worked splendidly together to whip up massive panic, which in turn induced global compliance with draconian lockdowns.

In other words, each anti-scientific, non-public-health measure in itself – e.g., universal cloth masking, testing and quarantining after the virus was widespread, focusing on cases instead of hospitalizations or deaths – was not intended to achieve anything, except the singular goal of fomenting massive fear. And the purpose of the fear was to ensure maximum compliance with lockdowns.

Which brings us back to Scott Atlas, who inadvertently, in decrying the Task Force's terrible policies and behaviors, managed to reveal the

----

57 Tucker, "A President Betrayed by Bureaucrats: Scott Atlas's Masterpiece on the Covid Disaster."

outline of their hidden agenda.

Based on Atlas's astute observations of Birx and Co.'s worst practices, I have compiled a ten-step list of instructions for how to get the world to comply with totalitarian lockdown policies in response to a not-very-devastating pandemic.

[ALL QUOTES ARE FROM ATLAS'S BOOK, KINDLE VERSION]

1. Whip up as much fear as possible. If you want entire populations to agree to prolonged draconian lockdowns that have never been used or tested before, then people have to be really, really, really scared.

[ATLAS REPORTING A CONVERSATION WITH DR. ANTHONY FAUCI:]

I challenged him to clarify his point, because I couldn't believe my ears. 'So you think people aren't frightened enough?' He said, 'Yes, they need to be more afraid.' To me, this was another moment of Kafkaesque absurdity. I replied, 'I totally disagree. People are paralyzed with fear. Fear is one of the main problems at this point.' Inside, I was also shocked at his thought process, as such an influential face of the pandemic. Instilling fear in the public is absolutely counter to what a leader in public health should do. To me, it is frankly immoral. (p. 186)

All internal meetings involving Birx were filled with warnings and exhortations advocating locking society down, although never using those words. (p. 131)

2. Insist that the virus is unlike any other. The unknown is always scarier than what we know. Plus, if we cannot apply anything we know about any other viruses, then we can justify any untested, unprecedented response we choose.

Perhaps the most fundamental error that went unchallenged was the World Health Organization's initial characterization of this virus as entirely new. Even its name—novel coronavirus—implied that we knew nothing about it in terms of its causes, effects, and management protocols. That 'novelty' also implied that no one would have any immune-system protection from it. (p. 32)

That mischaracterization helped incite panic and was fundamental to prompting the ensuing draconian lockdowns. (pp. 32-33)

2a. Insist that natural immunity does not apply. If this virus is unlike any other, then maybe exposure to it does not confer immunity as exposure to every other virus does.

Today, as the world still struggles with the biological truth of the importance of natural immunity as part of herd immunity, I contemplate why it was viewed as some sort of diabolical term. But it's clear to see why it was employed by those clinging to lockdowns at all costs. Casting herd immunity as reckless and dangerous was unethical, but ultimately even more effective than simple character assassination for a political purpose. Of all the cynical ways to manipulate people, fear was their best way to maintain lockdowns, despite the massive destruction from lockdowns that regular people saw before their own eyes. (p. 374)

3. Emphasize how little we know and how uncertain we are about the virus. Neither past experiences nor real-time data can allay fears, because we know nothing about this virus and will continue to know nothing until we somehow manage to crush it.

There was no articulation of what we knew, what the scientific studies and the world's evidence had shown. On the contrary, Fauci repeatedly emphasized in his occasional Task Force comments, as he did in his frequent media interviews, what we did not know with certainty, just as a layman without any medical perspective would do. For instance, the issue of risk to children, or spread from children to adults, was always, 'Well, we don't know for sure,' despite repeated studies from all over the world elucidating that we did know.

That pattern of highlighting uncertainties while minimizing decades of fundamental immunology and virology was alarmist and contrary to the expected behavior of a public health leader. It created massive fear inside and outside the White House, and it drove on-the-ground lockdowns and mandates. (pp. 167-168)

3a. Use only worst-case scenario models to determine policy.

Suddenly, computer modelers and people without any perspective about clinical illnesses were dominating the airwaves. Along with millions of Americans, I began witnessing unprecedented responses from those in power and nonscientific recommendations by public health spokespeople...These recommendations were not just based on panic; they were responsible for generating even more panic. (p. 25)

Regardless of the obvious and continual failures of statistical models, the prominent display of those same models in the media continued... The discussion about models represents one of the early displays of groupthink in this pandemic. The repetition of misinformation from many voices became accepted as truth. Media outlets and prominent policymakers clung to those same failed models, and they kept inciting panic. (p. 319)

4. Ignore all previous medical, scientific, and public health knowledge and guidelines.

The more I studied the data and the literature, the more obvious it became that basic biology and simple logic were missing from the discussion. Instead, fear had seemingly displaced critical thinking about the data already at hand. No one seemed to remember many fundamentals of science taught in college and medical school. (p. 26)

4a. Impose medically and scientifically bunk mandates that serve only to signal a never-ending state of emergency.

Masks were already proven to be ineffective for influenza, a virus of similar size. That had been reviewed by the CDC in May 2020 and by Oxford University's Centre for Evidence-Based Medicine in July 2020. The empirical evidence from the U.S. and all over the world already had shown masks failed to stop COVID-19 cases from surging. (pp. 331-2)

Relying on masks would be dangerous, implying protection for those at risk to die, like the vulnerable elderly, when legitimate protection was not conferred. Requiring masks would also increase the fear, as a visible public reminder of the 'extreme danger.' (p. 332)

5. Do not consult anyone who applies traditional pandemic response standards, including world experts who conduct scientific, medical, and ethical/economic/social risk-benefit analyses.

It was baffling to me, an incomprehensible error of whoever assembled the Task Force, that there were zero public health policy experts and no experts with medical knowledge who also analyzed economic, social, and other broad public health impacts other than the infection itself. Shockingly, the broad public health perspective was never part of the discussion among the Task Force health advisors other than when I brought it up. Even more bizarre was that no one seemed to notice. (p. 107)

In the end, the most egregious failure of the Task Force was its complete and utter disregard for the harmful impact of its recommended policies. This was outright immoral, an inexplicable betrayal of their most fundamental duty. (p. 151)

6. Insist on testing everyone all the time regardless of symptoms and regardless of how much the virus has already spread.

Testing for this virus had turned into a national, indeed, international obsession. (p. 103)

This was diagnostic testing, with broad-reaching policy aims. In this pandemic, a positive test was a major driver of the policy of quarantining and isolating healthy people with low-risk profiles—shuttering businesses, closing schools—in short, a key to locking down the country. (p. 107)

Mass testing of low-risk people in low-risk environments was the inevitable pathway to lockdowns, and lockdowns were destructive. (p. 116)

6a. Crank up the tests to diagnostically useless levels, so the numbers of seemingly positive cases are always sky-high.

PCR tests were the basis of defining cases, and the basis for quarantines, but most were misleading. Using a PCR 'cycle threshold' of thirty-five—even lower than the thirty-seven to forty cycles used routinely to detect the virus—fewer than 3 percent of "positives" contain live, contagious virus, as reported by Clinical Infectious Diseases. Even *The New York Times* wrote in August that 90 percent or more of positive PCR tests falsely implied that someone was contagious. Sadly, during my entire time at the White House, this crucial fact would never even be addressed by anyone other than me... (pp. 113-114)

7. Insist that the only relevant metric is case counts. The more cases you count, the worse the pandemic is, the more scared people are, the longer lockdowns continue.

Their strange shift from flattening the curve to maintaining that we must stop all cases of COVID-19, at all costs, was firmly set in stone. (p. 160)

Of the first 11,000 'cases' as defined by positive tests, zero were hospitalized. Soon over 25,000 cases—positive tests in mostly asymptomatic students—had been registered. Yet with all those 'cases,' zero hospitalizations—no illnesses requiring significant medical care. My view was that there was an alarming disconnect between the data on risk to college-age individuals and the policies being implemented. (p. 204)

8. Insist that the virus is very dangerous for everyone. If you admit that certain demographic groups have a lower risk, people will not be scared enough.

Even allowing for a non-expert level of knowledge, the Task Force doctors somehow ignored the evidence indicating the very low risk from this infection for the overwhelming majority of people. Birx even emphasized at the Task Force that this infection was extremely dangerous exactly because it was so commonly asymptomatic. (p. 167)

The medical science was consistent from the early days of the pandemic that even seasonal influenza is more dangerous to young children than this coronavirus. This perspective would have been enormously reassuring to parents, yet it was never put forth by those dominating the public narrative. (p. 321)

9. Treat politicians and the general population as children requiring your guidance. Once they're scared enough, you become the trustworthy authority figure who tells them what to do.

It was my impression that most governors sincerely wanted assistance on designing their states' response; instead, they were receiving basic admonitions and unscientific rules, as though they were children. (p. 180)

10. Never admit your policies cause any harm. Insist to everyone (including yourself) that without them millions would have died.

I never fully understood why there was no admission, even internally by the Task Force, that the Birx-Fauci strategy did not work. (p. 237)

To this day, I cannot understand why the human cost of the lockdowns never mattered to anyone else on the Task Force. It was never brought up while I was there, not a single doctor ever spoke of it. The media continues to ignore perhaps the most remarkable insight in the Fauci email trove discovered under FOIA in June 2021—the total lack of mention of harms from the lockdown throughout the pandemic. (pp. 240-241)

CONCLUSION

Dr. Scott Atlas was appalled at what he considered gross errors and unethical behavior on the part of the White House Coronavirus Task Force doctors, led by Dr. Deborah Birx. He could not comprehend how medical professionals, like himself, could impose such disastrous policies.

The questions Atlas raises are ones with which I, too, struggled for much of the pandemic:

- Why was the public not told about the steep age gradient of the virus?
- Why were parents not reassured that their children were at lower risk from this virus than from the flu?
- Why was natural immunity not just dismissed but suddenly considered an immoral "policy?"
- Why were we testing and quarantining long after it was clearly useless in terms of slowing the spread?
- Why were case counts, based on obviously bogus positive test results, considered a more important metric than hospitalizations and deaths?

I am deeply grateful to Atlas for his insights and inside reporting from the Task Force, because in raising these questions, he also inadvertently helped me come up with an answer: Everything Birx and the Task Force (and the biodefense GPPP behind them) did was meant to foment fear, leading to compliance with unprecedented, untested, and predictably unsuccessful – not to mention enormously destructive – global lockdowns.

Atlas knew that fear was the tool they were using, but he could not understand how they could do so in good conscience. Nor can I.

> Using emotional distress as a tool to ensure greater adherence to government policy is immoral in public health, yet fear was consciously leveraged by those most influencing the citizenry. (p. 348)

> Of all the cynical ways to manipulate people, fear was their best way to maintain lockdowns, despite the massive destruction from lockdowns that regular people saw before their own eyes. (p.374)

It is only through exposing the real motives behind this egregiously immoral behavior by global "public health" leaders that we can delegitimize their entire panic/lockdown enterprise, thereby hopefully lowering the chances of it happening again.

<u>3.5</u> U.S. COVID RESPONSE WAS LED BY THE SECURITY STATE, NOT PUBLIC HEALTH AGENCIES

Following my revelations about Deborah Birx and the White House Task Force, I decided to look into the actual pandemic plans that Birx and the Task Force were supposedly following. This led to the revelation – previously unreported anywhere, as far as I know – that the U.S. government's Covid response policy was dictated not by any public health body, but by the National Security Council. And the policy was carried out not by public health agencies, but by FEMA, a sub-agency of the Department of Homeland Security. In short, while public health leaders were the face of the pandemic, telling people that they represented "science," what they actually represented were the policies of the biodefense global public-private partnership, as discussed in Chapter 1.

The documents I uncovered show that:

- *As of March 13, 2020 the National Security Council (NSC) was officially in charge of the U.S. government's Covid policy.*
- *Starting on March 18, 2020, The Federal Emergency Management Agency (FEMA), under the Department of Homeland Security (DHS), was officially in charge of the U.S. government's Covid response.*

• • •

THE NATIONAL SECURITY COUNCIL WAS IN CHARGE OF U.S. COVID POLICY

An astonishing government document dated March 13, 2020 entitled: "PanCAP Adapted U.S. Government COVID-19 Response Plan" (*PanCAP-A*)[58] reveals that United States policy in response to SARS-CoV-2 was set not by the public health agencies designated in pandemic

----

58 U.S. Department of Health and Human Services, *PanCAP Adapted U.S. Government COVID-19 Response Plan*, March 13, 2020.

preparedness protocols (Pandemic and All Hazards Preparedness Act,[59] PPD-44,[60] BIA), but rather by the National Security Council, or NSC.

This is the pandemic response org chart, from p. 9 of *PanCAP-A*, showing the NSC solely responsible for Covid policy:

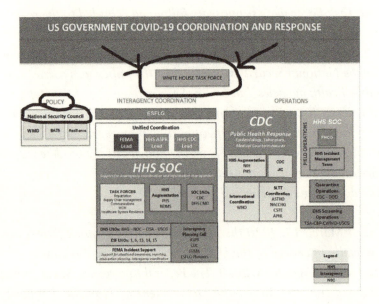

What is the National Security Council?

According to its website, the NSC "is the President's principal forum for considering national security and foreign policy matters with his or her senior advisors and cabinet officials."

In February 2020, the website listed the following as attendees:

> Its regular attendees (both statutory and non-statutory) are the Vice President, the Secretary of State, the Secretary of the Treasury, the Secretary of Defense, and the Assistant to the President for National Security Affairs. The Chairman of the Joint Chiefs of Staff

....

59 Pandemic and All-Hazards Preparedness Act, Pub. L. No. 109-417, 120 Stat. 2831.

60 Federal Emergency Management Agency, *FEMA Support to Coronavirus Response Fact Sheet*, March 4, 2020.

is the statutory military advisor to the Council, and the Director of National Intelligence is the intelligence advisor. The Chief of Staff to the President, Counsel to the President, and the Assistant to the President for Economic Policy are invited to attend any NSC meeting. The Attorney General and the Director of the Office of Management and Budget are invited to attend meetings pertaining to their responsibilities. The heads of other executive departments and agencies, as well as other senior officials, are invited to attend meetings of the NSC when appropriate.[61]

Some time after that, the page changed, reflecting how Covid had altered the very way the NSC defined itself.[62] A new paragraph was been added to the description of the NSC, as follows:

Today's challenges demand a new and broader understanding of national security–one that facilitates coordination between domestic and foreign policy as well as among traditional national security, economic security, health security, and environmental security. The Biden-Harris NSC recognizes and reflects this reality.

And new language was added regarding the attendees:

The heads of other executive departments and agencies, as well as other senior officials, including the COVID-19 Response Coordinator and the Special Presidential Envoy for Climate, are invited to attend meetings of the NSC when appropriate to address the cross-cutting nature of many critical national security issues, such as homeland security, global public health, international economics, climate, science and technology, cybersecurity, migration, and others.

....

61 U.S.Government, National Security Council website landing page, archived February 15, 2020.

62 U.S.Government, National Security Council website landing page, archived May 31, 2024.

The President's National Security Advisor, who heads the NSC, is "the President's most important source of policy advice on foreign and national security policy," according to the White House Transition Project's document for The National Security Advisor and Staff.[63] "In some administrations," according to this document, "foreign and national security policy making is essentially centralized in the hands of the NSC advisor with minimal input from cabinet-level departments such as State or Defense." Furthermore, "there is little statutory or legal constraint (beyond budgetary limits) in how the role of NSC advisor is defined or how the NSC staff is organized and operates." (pp. 1-2)

In other words, if the NSC is in charge of Covid response, it can pretty much decide and impose anything it wants without any constraints or oversight, as long as the President agrees, or at least lets them take the lead.

But what exactly is *PanCAP-A*, in which the NSC appears in such a surprising Covid-response leadership role?

PanCAP-A is the closest we have to a national Covid response plan
PanCAP-A stands for *Pandemic Crisis Action Plan – Adapted*. It was "adapted" from the 2018 Pandemic Crisis Action Plan, the most recent government plan prior to Covid.

Neither of these plans is readily available on any government website. In fact, *Pan-CAP-A* is only available as a leaked document in a *New York Times* online archive.

The difficulty of finding the U.S. government's pandemic plan is noted in a statement on "Preparedness for COVID-19"[64] presented to the U.S. Senate Committee on Homeland Security and Government Affairs on April 14, 2021.

In this statement, Elizabeth Zimmerman, a former FEMA Administrator, who is sharing with the Senate Committee her findings on "The Initial Pandemic Response and Lessons Learned," says she had trouble finding the government's plan for the U.S. response to Covid-19:

....

63 The White House Transition Project, *The National Security Advisor and Staff,* Report 2017-24.

64 Zimmerman, Written statement for U.S. Senate Committee on Homeland Security and Government Affairs, *Preparedness for COVID-19: The Initial Pandemic Response and Lessons Learned,* April 14, 2021.

In researching disaster response plans to refresh my memory for this hearing, I found several detailed plans that were publicly available and saw mention of plans and directives that were not publicly available. The time spent searching for these plans and directives was frustrating for an experienced emergency manager...

Then, in reference to the plans she was able to find, or knew about but may not have actually seen, she says:

Following the Anthrax attacks in 2001, the federal government invested a lot of money on processes and plans centered on public health response – bioterrorism and pandemics in particular. ... One of the latest plans, January 2017, is the Biological Incident Annex (BIA) to the Response and Recovery Federal Interagency Operational Plans (FIOPs). The BIA is the federal organizing framework for responding and recovering from a range of biological threats, including pandemics.

However, **it was not publicly seen that these plans were being used during the onset of COVID-19 nor does it seem that there was a national COVID-19 response plan.**
[boldface added]

Finally, she references the *2018 PanCAP*, the adapted *PanCAP*, and then makes another surprising statement:

Also, there was a 2018 Pandemic Crisis Action Plan (PanCAP) that was customized for COVID-19 specifically and adopted in March 2020 by HHS and FEMA; the plan identified the U.S. Department of Health and Human Services (HHS) as the Lead Federal Agency (LFA) with FEMA supporting for coordination. However, **a mere five days after the national COVID-19 emergency was announced, FEMA became the LFA.**"
[boldface added]

FEMA REPLACED HHS AS THE LEAD FEDERAL AGENCY, WITH NO WARNING OR PREPARATION

What Zimmerman is saying here is that, in the *PanCAP-A* org chart, where the NSC is in charge of policy and the HHS is in charge of almost everything else – actually, FEMA is in charge of everything else.

This means that, in effect, **starting on March 18, 2020, the HHS – which comprises the CDC, NIAID, NIH, and other public-health-related agencies – had NO OFFICIAL LEADERSHIP ROLE in pandemic response – not in determining policy and not in implementing policy.**

This is a staggering piece of information, considering that all pandemic preparedness plans, as Zimmerman notes, placed the Health and Human Services Agency (HHS) at the helm of pandemic response.

How was FEMA put in charge?

According to the Stafford Act, which "constitutes the statutory authority for most Federal disaster response activities especially as they pertain to FEMA and FEMA programs," the disasters to which FEMA is empowered to respond include:

> ...any natural catastrophe (including any hurricane, tornado, storm, high water, winddriven water, tidal wave, tsunami, earthquake, volcanic eruption, landslide, mudslide, snowstorm, or drought), or, regardless of cause, any fire, flood, or explosion, in any part of the United States, which in the determination of the President causes damage of sufficient severity and magnitude to warrant major disaster assistance under this Act to supplement the efforts and available resources of States, local governments, and disaster relief organizations in alleviating the damage, loss, hardship, or suffering caused thereby.[65]

Very clearly, FEMA is an agency neither designed nor intended to lead public health initiatives or the country's response to disease outbreaks.

Yet, as Zimmerman reported, on March 18, 2020, just five days after

---

65 Robert T. Stafford Disaster Relief and Emergency Assistance Act, Pub. L. No. 93-28, 102 Stat. 4689.

the official date of *PanCAP-A*, the Department of Health and Human Services (HHS) was removed from its lead role in pandemic response, and FEMA was (at least operationally if not policy-wise) put in charge.

In a Congressional Research Service report from February 2022, entitled "FEMA's Role in the COVID-19 Federal Pandemic Response," the opening paragraph states:

> On March 13, 2020, President Donald J. Trump declared a nationwide emergency under the Robert T. Stafford Disaster Relief and Emergency Assistance Act (the Stafford Act, P.L. 93-288 as amended), authorizing assistance administered by the Federal Emergency Management Agency (FEMA). Five days later, the President notified then-FEMA Administrator Peter Gaynor that the agency would assume leadership of the federal pandemic response effort—the first known instance of FEMA serving in such a role for a public health incident.[66]

FEMA's January 2021 COVID-19 Initial Assessment Report emphasizes how unusual this chain of events was:

> The agency's response to COVID-19 has been unprecedented. When the White House directed FEMA to lead operations, COVID-19 became the first national pandemic response that FEMA has led since the agency was established in 1979. It was also the first time in U.S. history the President has declared a nationwide emergency under Section 501b of the Stafford Act and authorized Major Disaster Declarations for all states and territories for the same incident.[67] (p. 5)

....

66 U.S.Congressional Research Service, *FEMA's Role in the COVID-19 Federal Pandemic Response*, February 10, 2022.

67 Federal Emergency Management Agency, *Pandemic Response to Coronavirus Disease 2019, (COVID-19): Initial Assessment Report*, January 2021.

A FEMA fact sheet from March 4, 2020 reveals that the agency was not given advanced warning of the enormous new responsibilities that would be thrust upon it just two weeks later:

> At this time, FEMA is not preparing an emergency declaration in addition to the Public Health Emergency declared by HHS on January 31, 2020.[68] (p. 2)

The table below is from a September 2021 report from the Office of Inspector General (OIG) of the Department of Homeland Security, "Lessons Learned from FEMA's Initial Response to COVID-19."[69] This document stresses that "The *PanCAP-A* did not address the changes that ensued when FEMA was designated the LFA. Furthermore, FEMA (and HHS) did not update the *PanCAP-A* or issue interim guidance addressing the changes in critical roles and responsibilities for each agency." (p. 11)

Table 1. Strategic Guidance vs. Federal Response Activities for Pandemic

Strategic Guidance	Federal Response Activities
HHS will serve as LFA. (As described in the Biological Incident Annex (BIA), PanCAP and PanCAP-A)	FEMA serves as LFA.
HHS ASPR Regions are responsible for processing resource requests and HHS Assistant Secretary for Preparedness and Response headquarters determines the sourcing. (PanCAP-A)	FEMA serves as lead in the resource request process and determines the sourcing.
FEMA is responsible for managing non-medical supply resourcing. (BIA)	FEMA is managing medical supply resourcing for critical lifesaving resources such as PPE and ventilators.

Source: DHS OIG analysis of strategic guidance and Federal response

BIA=Biological Incident Annex to the Response and Recovery Federal Interagency Operational Plans, January 2017

....

68 Federal Emergency Management Agency, *FEMA Support to Coronavirus Response Fact Sheet,* March 4, 2020.

69 U.S. Department of Homeland Security, *Lessons Learned from FEMA's Initial Response to COVID-19,* September 21, 2021.

In other words, HHS – the agency designated by statute and experience to handle public health crises – was removed, and FEMA – the agency designated by statute and experience to "help people before, during and after disasters"[70] like earthquakes and fires – was put in charge. But the pandemic planning document was not updated to reflect that change or how that change would affect the Covid response.

Why was FEMA suddenly and unexpectedly given this lead role? I would argue that the NSC wanted to ensure that no policy or response initiative emanating from the public health departments would play any role in the Covid response. Since FEMA had no planning documents or policies regarding disease or pandemic outbreaks, there would be nothing in the way of whatever the NSC wanted to do.

Furthermore, the Department of Homeland Security (DHS) is the parent agency of FEMA. Thus, when FEMA became the Lead Federal Agency for pandemic response, it was essentially the DHS that was in charge.

So what did the NSC want to do? *PanCAP-A*, in which the NSC takes the lead role in setting Covid policy, does not give a detailed answer, but does clearly place NSC policy above anything else that might contradict it.

What does PanCAP-A say?

On p. 1, under "Purpose" it states:

> This plan outlines the United States Government (USG) coordinated federal response activities for COVID-19 in the United States (U.S.). The President appointed the Vice President to lead the USG effort with the Department of Health and Human Services (HHS) serving as the Lead Federal Agency (LFA) consistent with the Pandemic and All Hazards Preparedness Act (PAHPA) and Presidential Policy Directive (PPD).

In other words, in accordance with a bunch of pandemic preparedness laws and directives, the HHS is the Lead Federal Agency in charge of pandemic response.

....

70 Federal Emergency Management Agency, "About Us."

As we move through the document, however, the roles and responsibilities of the HHS become increasingly muddled and diminished.

On p. 6 under "Senior Leader Intent" it says:

> The National Security Council (NSC) requested adaptation of the PanCAP to address the ongoing threat posed by COVID-19 in support of the Administration's efforts to monitor, contain, and mitigate the spread of the virus. The plan builds on objectives that prepare the USG to implement broader community and healthcare-based mitigation measures...

In other words, everything the *Pan-CAP-A* says about how the HHS is planning to address the pandemic is "adapted" in favor of "objectives" that prepare the government to implement "broader measures."

On the next page, we get the exact same vague language under "Strategic Objectives," which include implementing "broader community and healthcare-based mitigation measures." A footnote tells us "These objectives were directed by the NSC Resilience DRG PCC on February 24, 2020."

What is the NSC Resilience DRG PCC? There is no explanation, appendix, or addendum, nor anything in the entire *PanCAP-A* to answer this question – a noteworthy omission, since it apparently defines the objectives upon which the entire U.S. pandemic response is based.

Similarly, on p. 8 under "Concept of Operations," we read:

> This concept of operations aligns interagency triggers to the CDC intervals for each phase and groups key federal actions according to response phase. It also layers in the COVID-19 Containment and Mitigation Strategy developed by the NSC.

There is no explanation or description of what the "Containment and Mitigation Strategy developed by the NSC" is referring to.

Where is there a record of what the "NSC Resilience DRG PCC" directed on February 24, 2020? *PanCAP-A* does not contain this record, nor did an exhaustive Google search turn it up. DRG PCC probably stands for the National Security Council's Domestic Resilience Group (DRG)

Policy Coordination Committee (PCC), but that's about all we know.

Under "Concept of Operations" the *PanCAP-A* says it "layers in the COVID-19 Containment and Mitigation Strategy developed by the NSC." The words "Containment," "Mitigation," and "Strategy" are capitalized, suggesting they may be the title of an actual document. But such a document, if it exists, is nowhere to be found.

To summarize: the *PanCAP-A*, the closest document we have to a national Covid response plan, does not actually tell us what the basis for the "strategic objectives" of the plan are, nor does it present the strategy developed by the NSC to attain those objectives.

So we have a pandemic planning document whose objectives and strategy are hidden.

CONCLUSION

Everything we thought we knew about the U.S. government's Covid response is upended in the *Pandemic Crisis Action Plan – Adapted (PanCAP-A)*, which gave the NSC sole authority over policy, and the simultaneous Stafford Act declaration, which resulted in FEMA/DHS taking the lead role in its implementation.

This means the doctors on the White House Task Force who headed HHS departments – including Fauci, Redfield, and Collins, the heads of the CDC, NIAID, and NIH – had no authority over determining or implementing Covid policy and were following the lead of the NSC and the DHS (Department of National Security), which is the department under which FEMA operates.

It means our response to the Covid pandemic was led by groups and agencies that are in the business of responding to wars and terrorist threats, not public health crises or disease outbreaks.

I believe that the national security authorities took control of the Covid pandemic response not just in the U.S. but in many of our allied countries (the UK, Australia, Germany, Israel, and others) in order to impose strict lockdowns in anticipation of Warp Speed vaccine development.

Furthermore, all of the seemingly nonsensical and unscientific policies – including mask mandates, mass testing and quarantines, using case counts to determine severity – were imposed in the service of the singular goal of fomenting fear in order to induce public acquiescence with the lockdown-until-vaccines policy.

And once the national security authorities were in charge, the biodefense GPPP, consisting of national security and intelligence operatives, propaganda/psy-op (psychological operations) departments, pharmaceutical companies, and affiliated government officials and NGOs assumed leadership roles.

3.6 PUBLIC HEALTH VS. BIODEFENSE PANDEMIC RESPONSE PLANS

In this section, I compare the planning documents for public health responses to naturally occurring pandemics to biodefense plans for responding to bioterrorism. It becomes clear that the Covid response was not based on any public health protocols. The lockdown-until-vaccine plan was from the biodefense playbook.

• • •

As discussed in previous sections, in the United States, the Covid pandemic response was designed and led by the national security branches of government, not by any public health agency or official.

Furthermore, we do not have a public record of what the national security pandemic plan actually stated.

So what? You might ask. Why should we care if Covid policy was determined by the National Security Council (NSC) instead of the Centers for Disease Control and Prevention (CDC)? What's so bad about the Federal Emergency Management Agency (FEMA) taking over as lead federal agency for pandemic response, replacing Health and Human Services (HHS)?

National security is about protecting us from threats of war and terrorism

The answer to these questions is, in short, that the national security pandemic response plans, devised under the rubric of biodefense,[71] are aimed at countering bioterrorism attacks.[72] They focus on[73] preventing hostile actors from obtaining bioweapons, surveilling for potential bioweapons use, and developing medical countermeasures.

....

71 The White House, Press Release, "Biodefense for the 21st Century," April 28, 2004.

72 Berger et al., *Roadmap for Biosecurity and Biodefense Policy in the United States.*

73 Poulin, *A U.S. Biodefense Strategy Primer.*

According to the World Health Organization,[74] "biological and toxin weapons are either microorganisms like virus, bacteria or fungi, or toxic substances produced by living organisms that are produced and released deliberately to cause disease and death in humans, animals or plants."

In the rare event of an actual bioweapons attack – the biodefense strategy can be summarized as quarantine-until-vaccine: keep individuals as isolated from the bioweapon as possible, for as long as necessary, until you have an effective medical countermeasure (medicine/vaccine).

Bioterrorism response plans – under the broader umbrella of counter-terrorism[75] – are not designed to incorporate the complicated nuances of public health principles,[76] which balance the need to protect individuals from a pathogen with the need to keep society as functional as possible to maintain overall well-being.

If counterterrorism measures are deployed against a public health threat, it is thus not surprising to witness massive disruptions to society,[77] and harms to public health[78] – as we have seen with the Covid-19 pandemic response.

Counterterrorism measures are not commensurate with public health

A good example of the gap between biodefense and public health policies in the context of the Covid response is the Model State Emergency Health Powers Act (MSEHP)[79] – an act invoked by state governors[80] to initiate

....

74 World Health Organization, "Health Topics: Biological Weapons."

75 U.S. Government, *Interagency Domestic Terrorism Concept of Operations Plan (CONPLAN)*, January 2001.

76 Inglesby et al., "Disease mitigation measures in the control of pandemic influenza."

77 Thakur, "Governments Were Given Credible Warnings about Lockdown Harms but Didn't Listen."

78 Bell, "Global health and the Art of Really Big Lies."

79 The Center for Law and the Public's Health at Georgetown and Johns Hopkins Universities, *The Model State Emergency Health Powers Act, as of December 21, 2001.*

80 Lesher, "COVID-19 and the Left: an Ignored Civil Rights Crisis; a Missed Opportunity."

and perpetuate lockdowns. This act was specifically designed to give states a legal framework for responding to bioterrorism. As William Martin reported in the *American Journal of Public Health* in 2004,

> In late 2001, during the aftermath of the anthrax letter attacks, model legislation was proposed to relevant state agencies to update their states' public health laws to meet the threat of bioterrorism. This legislation was the Model State Emergency Health Powers Act.[81]

A Columbia Law Review article from October 2021, analyzing the emergency acts invoked by states during the Covid pandemic – including the original MSEHP and more modern, revised versions of it – concluded that these acts were not intended as frameworks for responding to naturally occurring, long-lasting viral pandemics like Covid:

> It is clear that even the more modern statutes were not intended to apply to chronic emergencies such as COVID-19, with unilateral decision-making going on for over a year, or to responses such as social distancing regulations or mass lockdowns.[82]

In other words, laws intended to protect us from bioterrorism are not appropriate in situations that involve "chronic emergencies," like viral pandemics.

What happened when counterterrorism measures replaced public health policy?

We may not have a record of what the National Security Council's Covid-19 policy was, or what measures they came up with to implement that policy. However, everything that was blatantly anti-public health, unscientific, or downright insane in our lived Covid experience can be explained, if we assume the Covid response was based not on public health

....

81 Martin, "Legal and public policy responses of states to bioterrorism."

82 Weiss, "Binding the Bound: State Executive Emergency Powers and Democratic Legitimacy in the Pandemic."

but on a counterterrorism, lockdown-until-vaccine, policy.

Here are some of the seemingly inexplicable phenomena that become painfully clear when we assume biodefense/counterterrorism replaced public health policy in the U.S. government's Covid-19 reponse:

The justification for mitigation measures stemmed not from their ability to promote or preserve public health, but from their ability to achieve counterterrorism objectives (lockdown-until-vaccine).

- *Masking:* pre-Covid public health pandemic plans recognized no scientific evidence[83] for universal mask mandates. But masks instilled fear[84] which promoted compliance with lockdowns and vaccine mandates.
- *Testing:* pre-Covid public health pandemic plans recognized no scientific basis[85] for testing and isolating once a virus is widespread. But the more you test and isolate, the more people are effectively quarantined, and the more desperate they are for an exit strategy (vaccines).
- *Lockdowns:* pre-Covid public health plans, ironically including *PanCAP-A* called for, at most, shutdowns limited in time (during a big surge of serious illness) and geography (places with big surges). Country-wide, extended lockdowns regardless of waves or local variations were implemented for the first time in history after the National Security Council took over[86] Covid policy, following the example[87] of the totalitarian Chinese regime.

....

83 World Health Organization, *Non-pharmacuetical public health measures for mitigating the risk and impact of epidemic and pandemic flu influenza.*

84 Senger, "The Point of Masks: To Cause Alarm."

85 World Health Organization, *Non-pharmacuetical public health measures for mitigating the risk and impact of epidemic and pandemic flu influenza.*

86 Brownstone Institute, "Donald Trump's March 16, 2020, Press Conference that Kicked Off This Catastrophe, Transcribed."

87 Senger, "Why Did Intellectuals and Officials Celebrate and Copy China's Lockdown Model?"

This is a crucial concept: Arguing about whether mask mandates, testing and isolating, social distancing, lockdowns etc. are good public health policies or bad public health policies is a moot point. They are not public health policies at all.

All of these measures were devised solely in the service of gaining compliance with the biodefense/counterterrorism plan of lockdown-until-vaccine. Once mass formation[88] happened, the enforcement and implementation of these measures was eagerly taken up by public health officials not in the know about the counterterrorism agenda.

Government messaging preserved a public health veneer, while camouflaging the biodefense GPPP agenda.

The officials who announced the National Security Council's policies to the public were top public health leaders like Drs. Fauci, Redfield, and Collins ("the experts"). These public health officials did not design the policy they were publicly advocating. However, their advocacy fooled the public into accepting counterterrorism policy as a manifestation of actual epidemiologic knowledge and public health doctrine ("the science").

Note: Dr. Deborah Birx was presented as a public health official, but was in fact brought in by the Department of Homeland Security to serve as the "scientific" and "expert" front for the counterterrorism agenda (as discussed in sections 1-3 of this chapter).

The massive effort to cloak lockdown-until-vaccine measures in public health legitimacy was the root of pandemic propaganda.

This was not a campaign of public health officials who were too dumb to understand basic principles of epidemiology or too ignorant to know core tenets of public health (at least at the federal level – lower down the chain it became a phenomenon of mass formation).[89] It was a campaign of national security operatives who did not care about principles of epidemiology and had no interest in basic tenets of public health.

----

88 Frijters et al., "Crowd Creation: A New Political Tool."

89 Foster et al., "Covid and the Madness of Crowds."

Attempts to depict lockdowns as pillars of pre-Covid public health policy were deliberate propaganda.
They were intended to "nudge"[90] the public to accept counterterrorism measures as legitimate public health policy. Examples include: articles[91,92] falsely claiming lockdowns were well-established and/or potentially effective U.S. public health pandemic policy; Michael Lewis' *The Premonition*[93] which expounded the same false narrative (see Chapter 4.1 for a discussion of this particular piece of pandemic propaganda); and the publication of the Red Dawn emails[94] by *The New York Times* – an email chain championing lockdowns, in which many government health officials were copied but nearly none actually participated.

Counterterrorism measures designed to suppress and vanquish enemies of the state were deployed against U.S. citizens.
This occurred not just in the realm of propaganda and censorship, aptly described by Dr. Robert Malone[95] as "military-grade information warfare capability and technology that was designed for our opponents outside the U.S. and has been turned on American citizens." Such tactics were also employed in concerted attacks on individuals and organizations opposed to mandates and lockdowns. Just a few select examples include:

- FBI harassment of Ecohealth Alliance whistleblower Dr. Andrew Huff (*The Truth About Wuhan*,[96] Chapter 20)

- Vicious attacks on family members of world-class epidemiologists who opposed lockdowns, including false rumors that Dr. John

....

90 Sidley, "The Nudge: Ethically Dubious and Ineffective."

91 Lipton and Steinhauer, "The Untold Story of the Birth of Social Distancing."

92 McNeil, "To Take On the Coronavirus, Go Medieval on It."

93 Lewis, *The Premonition*.

94 Brownstone Institute, "The Red Dawn Email Dump: February-March 2020."

95 Malone, "Lies My Government Told Me," *RFK Jr Podcast*.

96 Huff, *The Truth About Wuhan*.

Ioannidis'[97] mother died of Covid-19 – rumors which caused her to suffer a heart attack[98]; and sophisticated, multi-pronged attacks on Dr. Ioannidis, Dr. Jay Bhattacharya,[99] and his wife[100, 101,102] for legitimate scientific work. These attacks were not just nasty Twitter comments or professional takedowns. It is highly unlikely that a single scientific opponent or angry member of the public would engage in them. (Interestingly, Michael Lewis – whose *Premonition* is a prime example of biodefense-as-public-health propaganda – is also a prominent promulgator of attacks on these scientists. Coincidence? I find it highly unlikely.)

- Strange, inexplicable interventions by security agencies in the lives of lockdown opponents, including *Brownstone Journal* contributor Robin Koerner, who tells the following startling story:

> As I was walking down the jet-bridge onto my plane at Heathrow airport, I was pulled back by an officer with a metal detection wand. She gave me the full frisk and emptied all my bags. I asked her what was going on. I told her that I'd never been pulled aside just feet from the plane having gone through security and all the final checks.
>
> 'It's something the Americans asked us to do,' she responded.[103]

....

97 Ioannidis, "A fiasco in the making? As the coronavirus pandemic takes hold, we are making decisions without reliable data."

98 Jamison, "A top scientist questioned virus lockdowns on Fox News. The backlash was fierce."

99 Brownstone Institute, Jayanta Bhattacharya profile.

100 Lee, "JetBlue's Founder Helped Fund A Stanford Study That Said The Coronavirus Wasn't That Deadly."

101 Lewis, "The Person Who Knows," *Against the Rules Podcast.*

102 Bhattacharya and Kulldorff, "The Collins and Fauci Attack on Traditional Public Health."

103 Koerner, "Do You Really Have Nothing to Hide?"

Nothing was found on his person or in his luggage and he was allowed to travel normally, but upon his return to the US, Koerner's Global Entry status was revoked. Global Entry[104] is a program that "allows expedited clearance for pre-approved, low-risk travelers," according to the U.S. Customs and Border Protection (CBP) website.[105] The CBP is charged with "keeping terrorists and their weapons out of the U.S. while facilitating lawful international travel and trade" and is an arm of the Department of Homeland Security (DHS).

Koerner has yet to learn why he was turned from a low-risk traveler into a potential terrorist.

• Eerie warning calls to prominent lockdown opponents, including Brownstone founder Jeffrey Tucker. As Tucker describes it,[106] Dr. Rajeev Venkayya, who headed a bioterrorism study group in George W. Bush's White House (and who stars in none other than *The Premonition*, by Michael Lewis), called to urge Tucker to stop opposing lockdowns. "He said it was our only choice because we had to wait for a vaccine," Tucker recalls.

Why would Venkayya – someone with no personal or professional ties to Tucker – bother to call with this exhortation? It would make no sense if he were a public health official trying to mitigate the effects of a viral pandemic. It makes terrifying sense when we know he was a biodefense expert advocating a counterterrorism, lockdown-until-vaccine policy.

• Sophisticated social media visual aids aimed at demonizing organizations and individuals opposed to lockdowns. What person acting alone would have the tools or resources to produce a scary spider web like this and disseminate it online?

....

104 U.S. Customs and Border Protection, "Global Entry."

105 U.S. Customs and Border Protection, "About CBP."

106 Tucker, "How Fanatics Took Over the World."

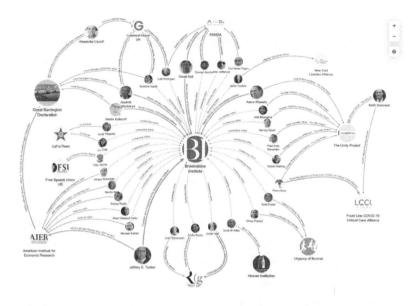

Prominent epidemiologists and public health specialists were deliberately excluded from the government's pandemic planning. In a public health crisis like the Covid-19 pandemic, you'd think the world's top epidemiologists and specialists in pandemic management and public health, including Dr. Scott Atlas, Dr. John Ioannidis, Dr. Jay Bhattacharya, among many others, would be consulted. But if a counterterrorism agenda is secretly being implemented, such specialists would pose a serious threat by exposing the public health harms.

This is why those scientists were so viciously attacked when they came out with public statements like the Great Barrington Declaration.[107] It's also why Deborah Birx was so vehemently opposed to Dr. Atlas joining the Task Force. Thankfully, in *A Plague Upon Our House*, Dr. Atlas managed to do precisely what Birx and the biodefense cabal wanted to prevent. Without knowing why it was happening, he revealed the total lack of actual public health knowledge in the Task Force's policy:

> It was baffling to me, an incomprehensible error of whoever assembled the Task Force, that there were zero public health policy

....

107 Brownstone Institute, "A Short History of the Great Barrington Declaration."

experts and no experts with medical knowledge who also analyzed economic, social, and other broad public health impacts other than the infection itself. Shockingly, the broad public health perspective was never part of the discussion among the Task Force health advisors other than when I brought it up. Even more bizarre was that no one seemed to notice. (p. 107)

The secrecy of national security and intelligence operations was applied to what was supposed to be a public health response.
When we look for who was responsible for U.S. Covid-19 response policy, we hit a wall. The National Security Council classified pandemic response meetings,[108] starting in January 2020, in direct contrast to what is expected during a public health crisis.

The result is that anyone who knows what our Covid response policy truly was is theoretically barred from revealing it. We do know, as discussed in the previous section, that the public health agencies were not in charge of the policy, and we know they were pushed out of their leadership role in coordinating and implementing the response. So Fauci et al. are technically correct if they claim no responsibility – although how they could in good conscience advocate such policies is another matter.

We probably need a whistleblower with top security clearance to get around this giant hurdle.
The beneficiaries of the national security pandemic response include a web of intersecting military and national security agencies, private corporations, and non-governmental global health organizations.

All of these entities are eager to amass ever more funding and power by perpetuating this type of non-public health response.[109] Epidemiologic knowledge, public health principles, medical ethics and the well-being of the general population have nothing to do with what these entities have in mind.

Thus, the most important question emerging from the Covid response

....

108 Lerman, "What to Ask a Covid Task Force Member Under Oath."

109 Lerman, "Why the Pandemic-Industrial Complex Won't Go Away."

is: Can we stop them? Judging by the installation of biodefense global public-private partnership (as discussed in Chapter 1), members in the highest seats[110] of public health power, and President Biden's 2022 National Biodefense Strategy,[111] it's going to be an uphill battle.

---

110 Senger, "Lead Lockdown Advisor Jeremy Farrar Promoted to be WHO's Chief Scientist."

111 Bhattacharya, "The Dangers of the Biden Pandemic Plan."

3.7 THE ROLE OF mRNA PRODUCTS IN THE BIODEFENSE PLAN

In this section, I document the history of the efforts of the biodefense industrial complex to develop rapid, universally applicable countermeasure platforms, based on biotech methods that never produced a safe or viable product before Covid.

• • •

Understanding vaccines in the context of biodefense planning

Ever since 9/11 and the anthrax attacks of 2001, the development of medical countermeasures against potential biological weapons has been a major part of the U.S. government's overall counterterrorism efforts.

As explained in a 2021 *Lancet* paper, "Biodefense Research Two Decades Later: Worth the Investment?":

> Factors such as sustained government and private funding resources driven by the looming threat of bioterrorism and the recent occurrence of natural outbreaks of bioterror-related pathogens including Coxiella burnetii, Ebola virus (EBOV), SARS-CoV-1, SARS-CoV-2, influenza, and Lassa virus are likely major contributors to the ever-expanding global biodefense market.[112]

When we understand the Covid response in this biodefense framework, SARS-CoV-2 is a "bioterror-related pathogen" and the antiviral medicines and vaccines developed to control it are medical countermeasures. These definitions are important, because they unlock "Warp Speed" development tracks that are not available when you try to develop a vaccine or medicine against just any old pathogen.

....

112 Long and Marzi, "Biodefense Research Two Decades Later: Worth the Investment?"

Medical countermeasures are worth billions (and many more billions!)

Starting in 2001, the budget for researching and developing medical countermeasures ballooned exponentially, as described in the above mentioned *Lancet* paper:

> Total U.S. biodefense funding dramatically increased from ~$700,000,000 in 2001 to ~$4,000,000,000 spent in 2002; the peak of funding in 2005 was worth nearly $8,000,000,000 and continued with steady average spending around $5,000,000,000.

That's over $100 billion devoted to biodefense in two decades.

And what were those billions devoted to? In a 2003 abstract entitled "Expanded Biodefense Role for the National Institutes of Health"[113] Dr. Anthony Fauci articulates his biodefense vision:

> …the goal within the next 20 years is to have 'bug to drug' within 24 hours. This would meet the challenge of genetically engineered bioagents.

In other words, Fauci envisions the enormous increase in biodefense spending going toward the research and development of platforms that – by 2023 – will be able to magically generate medical countermeasures for any bioweapon in a single day.

Fifteen years later, with no such fantastical platform in sight, DARPA (Defense Advanced Research Projects Agency) published an updated medical countermeasure plan in 2017 entitled "Removing the Viral Threat: Two Months to Stop Pandemic X from Taking Hold."[114] Instead of Fauci's 24 hours from bug to drug, this plan tells us "DARPA aims to develop an integrated end-to-end platform that uses nucleic acid sequences to halt the spread of viral infections in sixty days or less."

....

113 Fauci, "Expanded Biodefense Role for the National Institutes of Health."

114 Defense Advanced Research Projects Agency, "Removing the Viral Threat: Two Months to Stop Pandemic X from Taking Hold."

Before Covid, this 60-day plan in no way encompassed a global vaccine rollout involving billions of doses. It was limited to developing countermeasures that could protect U.S. troops in cases of bioweapons attacks – even if just temporarily. As reported in March 2020 by the IEEE, a nonprofit professional organization for engineering and technology:

When DARPA launched its Pandemic Preparedness Platform (P3) program two years ago, the pandemic was theoretical. It seemed like a prudent idea to develop a quick response to emerging infectious diseases. Researchers working under the program sought ways to confer instant (but short-term) protection from a dangerous virus or bacteria.

On March 11, 2020, when COVID-19 was declared a global pandemic, the DARPA program had yet to produce any safe or effective countermeasures against anything – not even short-term.[115]

As a July 2020 *Washington Post* article noted:

Established years before the current pandemic, the program was halfway done when the first case of the novel coronavirus arrived in the United States early this year. But everyone involved in the effort by the Defense Advanced Research Projects Agency (DARPA) knew their time had come ahead of schedule.

Thus, when Covid came along, the platforms that use nucleic acid sequences (DNA and mRNA), having never produced a single usable product, were thrust into Warp Speed to produce, among others, Moderna and BioNTech/Pfizer's Covid vaccines.[116]

---

115 Strickland, "DARPA Races To Create a "Firebreak" Treatment for the Coronavirus."

116 Sonne, "How a secretive Pentagon agency seeded the ground for a rapid coronavirus cure."

Medical countermeasures bypass regulatory barriers

The problem with developing vaccines, if you expect them to be truly safe and effective, is that it takes a long, long time. The research process, including three phases that evaluate multiple parameters of safety and efficacy, requires years of careful experimentation and analysis.

Then, by the time you have a safe and effective vaccine, the threat of the virus is probably over. Which means no pharmaceutical company wants to invest in such a risky proposition. For anyone who believes they have a promising vaccine candidate or platform, these hurdles can seem unnecessarily cumbersome and counterproductive.

One solution, ingeniously utilized by the Covid vaccine developers, is to define the vaccine as a medical countermeasure in a war against a "bioterror-related pathogen" after declaring a Public Health Emergency that opens the way for Emergency Use Authorization.

Chapter 5.1 describes the process of bypassing regulatory oversight for the Covid mRNA vaccines.

3.8 THE ROLE OF PUBLIC HEALTH LEADERS IN THE BIODEFENSE PANDEMIC RESPONSE

As discussed in previous sections, the destructive pandemic response policies were drawn up by the national security arms of the government, not the public health agencies. Yet public health leaders were the ones advocating these policies in the media and pushing compliance by the public. This section examines whether the public health leaders who advocated terrible pandemic response policies were intentionally deceitful, acting in good faith, or just plain dumb.

• • •

Scandalous incompetence. Profound stupidity. Astounding errors. This is how many analysts – including Dr. Vinay Prasad,[117] Dr. Scott Atlas,[118] and popular Substack commentator eugyppius[119] – explain how leading public health experts could prescribe so many terrible pandemic response policies.

And it's true: the so-called experts certainly made themselves look foolish over the course of Covid. Public health leaders like Rochelle Walensky[120] and Anthony Fauci[121] made false claims,[122] or contradicted themselves[123] repeatedly, on subjects related to the pandemic response,

....

117 Prasad, "Heart attacks and strokes after a COVID diagnosis."

118 Lerman, "Debi Does Lockdowns."

119 eugyppius, "Rainmaking and Mask Mandates, or: The dumb chain of coincidences that brought community masking tyranny to the West."

120 *Reason TV*, "The CDC's changing vaccine story (Vinay Prasad analyzes Walensky statements)."

121 One America News Network, "Dr. Fauci caught on camera contradicting himself about severity of coronavirus."

122 Senger, "Rochelle Walenskey's Terrible Testimony."

123 Felix, "Dr Fauci contradicts himself on wearing a mask during Covid 19 pandemic."

while leading scientists, like Peter Hotez[124] in the US, and Christian Drosten[125] in Germany, were equally susceptible to such flip-flops and lies. Then there were the internationally renowned medical researchers, like Eric Topol,[126] who repeatedly committed obvious errors in interpreting Covid-related research studies.

All of these figures publicly and aggressively promoted anti-public health policies, including universal masking, social distancing, mass testing and quarantining of healthy people, lockdowns, and vaccine mandates.

It seems like an open-and-shut case: Dumb policies, dumb people in charge of those policies.

This might be true in a few individual cases of public health or medical leaders who really are incapable of understanding even high school-level science. However, if we look at leading pandemic public health and medical experts as a group – a group consisting of the most powerful, widely published, and well-paid researchers and scientists in the world – that simple explanation sounds much less convincing.

Even if you believe that most medical researchers are shills for pharmaceutical companies and that scientists rarely break new ground anymore, I think you'd be hard-pressed to claim that they lack basic analytical skills or a solid educational background in the areas they've studied. Most doctors and scientists with advanced degrees know how to analyze simple scientific documents and understand basic data.

Additionally, those doctors and public health professionals who were deemed experts during the pandemic were also clever enough to have climbed the academic, scientific, and/or government ladders to the highest levels.

They might be unscrupulous, sycophantic, greedy, or power-mongering. You might think they make bad moral or ethical decisions. But it defies logic to say that every single one of them understands simple scientific data less than, say, someone like me or you. In fact, I find that to be a facile, superficial judgment that does not get to the root cause of their seemingly stupid, incompetent behavior.

....

124 Orfalea, "Peter Hotez - Vaccine Expert."

125 Goddek, "Christian Drosten: his lies exposed."

126 Prasad, "What happens when doctors don't read papers well?"

Returning to some specific examples, I would argue that it is irrational to conclude, as Dr. Prasad did,[127] that someone like Dr. Topol, Founder and Director of the Scripps Research Translational Institute, who has published over 1,300 peer-reviewed articles and is one of the top 10 most cited researchers in medicine [128] cannot read research papers "at a high level." And it is equally unlikely that Anthony Fauci, who managed to ascend and remain atop the highest scientific perch in the federal government for many decades, controlling billions of dollars in research grants[129], was too dumb to know that masks don't stop viruses.

There must, therefore, be a different reason why all the top pro-lockdown scientists and public health experts – in perfect lockstep – suddenly started (and continue to this day) to misread studies and advocate policies that they had claimed in the past were unnecessary, making themselves look like fools.

Public health experts were messengers for the biodefense response

The most crucial single fact to know and remember when trying to understand the craziness of Covid times is this:

The public health experts were not responsible for pandemic response policy. The military-intelligence-biodefense leadership was in charge.

In previous sections, I examined in great detail the government documents that show how standard tenets of public health pandemic management were abruptly and secretly thrown out during Covid. The most startling switch was the replacement of the public health agencies by the National Security Council and Department of Homeland Security at the helm of pandemic policy and planning.

As part of the secret switch, all communications – defined in every previous pandemic planning document as the responsibility of the CDC – were taken over by the National Security Council under the auspices of the White House Task Force. The CDC was not even allowed to hold its own press conferences!

....

127 Prasad, "Heart attacks and strokes after a COVID diagnosis."

128 Scripps Research, Eric Topol profile.

129 National Institute of Allergy and Infectious Diseases, "NIAID Budget Data Comparison."

As a Senate report from December 2022 notes:

From March through June 2020, CDC was not permitted to conduct public briefings, despite multiple requests by the agency and CDC media requests were 'rarely cleared.' HHS stated that by early April 2020, 'after several attempts to get approvals,' its Office of Assistant Secretary for Public Affairs 'stopped asking' the White House 'for a while.' (p. 8)[130]

When public health and medical experts blanketed the airwaves and Internet with "recommendations" urging universal masking, mass testing and quarantining of asymptomatic people, vaccine mandates, and other anti-public health policies – or when they promoted obviously flawed studies that supported the lockdown-until-vaccine biodefense agenda – they were not doing so because they were dumb, incompetent, or misguided.

They were performing the role that the leaders of the national security/biodefense response gave them: to be the trusted public face that made people believe lockdown-until-vaccine was a legitimate public health response.

Why did public health leaders go along with the biodefense agenda?

We have to imagine ourselves in the position of public health and medical experts at top government positions when the intelligence-military-biodefense network took over the pandemic response.

What would you do if you were a government employee, or a scientist dependent on government grants, and you were told that the lockdown-until-vaccine policy was actually the only way to deal with this particular engineered potential bioweapon?

How would you behave if an unprecedented event in human history happened on your watch: an engineered virus designed as a potential bioweapon was spreading around the world, and the people who designed it told you that terrifying the entire population into locking down and waiting

130 U.S. Senate Committee on Homeland Security and Governmental Affairs, *Historically Unprepared: Examination of the federal Governments Pandemic Preparedness and Initial COVID-19 Response*, December 2022.

for a vaccine was the only way to stop it from killing many millions?

More mundanely, if your position and power depended on going along with whatever the powers-that-be in the NSC and DHS told you to do – if your job and livelihood were on the line – would you go against the narrative and risk losing it all?

And, finally, in a more venal vain: what if you stood to gain a lot more money and/or power by advocating for policies that might not be the gold standard of public health, but that you told yourself could bring about major innovations (vaccines/countermeasures) that would save humanity from future pandemics?

We know how the most prominent Covid "experts" answered those questions. Not because they were dumb, but because they had a lot to lose and/or a lot to gain by going along with the biodefense narrative – and they were told millions would die if they failed to do so.

Why understanding the motives of public health leaders during Covid is so important

Paradoxically, deeming public health experts stupid and incompetent actually reinforces the consensus narrative: that lockdowns and vaccines were part of a public health plan. In this reading, the response may have been terrible, or it may have gone awry, but it was still just a stupid public health plan designed by incompetent public health leaders.

Such a conclusion leads to calls for misguided and necessarily ineffectual solutions: Even if we replaced every single HHS employee or defunded the HHS or even the WHO altogether, we would not solve the problem and would be poised to repeat the entire pandemic fiasco all over again.

The only way to avoid such repetition is to recognize the Covid catastrophe for what it was: an international biodefense campaign focused maniacally on lockdowns and vaccines, to the exclusion of all traditional and time-tested public health protocols.

We need to wake up to the fact that, since the terrorist attacks of 9/11 (if not earlier), we have ceded control of the agencies that are supposed to be in charge of public health to an international military-intelligence-pharmaceutical cartel.

This "public-private partnership" of bioterrorism experts and vaccine developers is not interested in public health at all, except as a cover for their very secret and very lucrative biowarfare research and countermeasure development.

Public health was shunted aside during the Covid pandemic, and the public health leaders were used as trusted "experts" to convey biowarfare edicts to the population. Their cooperation does not reflect stupidity or incompetence. Making such claims contributes to the coverup of the much more sinister and dangerous transfer of power that their seemingly foolish behavior was meant to hide.

3.9 IT WAS BIODEFENSE, NOT PUBLIC HEALTH: UK EDITION

In previous sections, I analyzed government documents showing that the Covid pandemic response in the U.S. was not designed or led by public health agencies. Rather, it was a biodefense response, led by the National Security Council and FEMA/Department of Homeland Security.

In addition to military/intelligence agencies, the biodefense global public-private partnership that ran the Covid response (discussed in detail in Chapter 1) encompassed global pharmaceutical companies, government agencies, and global NGOs – most notably, the Bill & Melinda Gates Foundation and the Wellcome Trust[131] – who invest in and benefit from all the activities related to pandemic preparedness, first and foremost: vaccines.

The same thing happened in many countries:

- Between January and mid-March 2020, the public health agencies were handling the coronavirus outbreak as they would any other. They monitored for local outbreaks where people were getting sick with symptoms, told people not to panic, and gave scientifically and epidemiologically sound advice: no masks necessary, wash your hands, and stay home if you're sick.
- In mid-March there was a complete reversal on everything: suddenly both the political and the public health officials were saying millions would die if we did not shut everything down and wait for vaccines.

In this section I will discuss how this pattern was repeated in the British Covid pandemic response: the national public health agency was replaced at the helm of the response by military/intelligence entities, and the response switched from public health to lockdown-until-vaccine – specifically, as a top UK minister testified – the mRNA vaccines.

....

131 Banco et al., "How Bill Gates and partners used their clout to control the global Covid response - with little oversight."

Initial UK Public Health Response

Wikipedia describes in detail how in the first months of 2020, the pandemic response in the UK followed standard epidemiological and scientific guidelines:

> Even as late as March 11th, the authorities were eschewing face masks and explaining that herd immunity would be the inevitable endpoint:
>
> On 11 March, the Deputy Chief Medical Officer for England Jenny Harries said that the government was 'following the science' by not banning mass gatherings. She also said, on face masks, 'If a healthcare professional hasn't advised you to wear a face mask… it's really not a good idea and doesn't help.' She added that masks could 'actually trap the virus in the mask and start breathing it in.'
>
> On 13 March, British government Chief Scientific Adviser Patrick Vallance told BBC Radio 4 one of 'the key things we need to do' is to 'build up some kind of herd immunity so more people are immune to this disease and we reduce the transmission.'[132]

These are all standard public health procedures in dealing with a respiratory virus that is spreading in the population.

Accordingly, in the *UK Coronavirus Action Plan*[133] dated March 3, 2020, there is no mention of masks, social distancing, or asymptomatic testing; and the plan provides reassurance that most people will have mild flu-like disease.

Under "Responsibilities for Preparedness and Response" the Plan states: "DHSC [Department of Health and Social Care] is the lead U.K. government department with responsibility for responding to the risk posed by a future pandemic."

Then, the response took a sudden and extreme turn from public health management to a wartime stance with police enforcement:

....

132 Wikipedia, "British government response to the COVID-19 pandemic," accessed February 12, 2025.

133 U.K Department of Health and Social Care, *Coronavirus action plan: a guide to what you can expect across the UK,* March 3, 2020.

On 17 March 2020, [Prime Minister Boris] Johnson announced in a daily news conference that the government 'must act like any wartime government and do whatever it takes to support our economy.'

Six days later,

Johnson announced the first national lockdown on 23 March 2020 and Parliament introduced the Coronavirus Act 2020, which granted the devolved governments emergency powers and empowered the police to enforce public health measures.

Was the Coronavirus Act 2020[134] an updated public health plan to deal with a circulating respiratory virus? Not at all. It was a 138-page emergency act, delegating unprecedented powers to UK governments (England, Scotland, Ireland, and Wales) to lock down and quarantine citizens. As Wikipedia summarizes:

The provisions of the Coronavirus Act enabled the government to restrict or prohibit public gatherings, control or suspend public transport, order businesses such as shops and restaurants to close, temporarily detain people suspected of COVID-19 infection, suspend the operation of ports and airports, temporarily close educational institutions and childcare premises, enroll medical students and retired healthcare workers in the health services, relax regulations to ease the burden on healthcare services, and assume control of death management in particular local areas. The government stated that these powers may be 'switched on and off according to the medical advice it receives.'

Thus, by the end of March 2020, the Coronavirus Act, introduced in Parliament on March 19, 2020 and passed through an expedited process

---

134 Coronavirus Act 2020, c.7

in just a few days, despite its 138 pages of unprecedented emergency powers, replaced the DHSC's March 3 Coronavirus Plan.

Effectively, the UK had transitioned from the public health plan to the lockdown plan or, as Dominic Cummings – Chief Advisor to Prime Minister Johnson in 2020 – testified to Parliament, "from Plan A to Plan B." (Oral evidence: Coronavirus: Lessons learnt, HC 95, p. 29)[135]

At the same time, as Cummings reported, the DHSC was removed from its lead role in the pandemic response, and a new agency was put in charge: the Joint Biosecurity Centre, or JBC.

Here's what Cummings said when asked about the JBC (p. 56):

> Q1079 **Dawn Butler:** Yes, just a quick couple of questions. Can you tell us a little about the Joint Biosecurity Centre, because we do not know that much about it, like who attends? Have you ever attended a meeting? Who is on it?
>
> *Dominic Cummings:* Yes. It was created partly as an attempt to, as Jeremy said—"How do we make this transition from plan A to plan Bill?" A

Note that the transcript says "from plan A to plan Bill." Listening to the actual hearing,[136] it is clear that Cummings says "Plan B" not "Plan Bill," but the typo is amazingly apt, as will become apparent in the final part of this section.

Also note that MP [Member of Parliament] Butler says not much is known about the JBC, including who is on it. When pressed, Cummings does not answer that question and says: "Just senior officials." (p. 57)

Joint Biosecurity Centre

So what exactly was this new body in charge of the UK pandemic response – which even members of Parliament knew little about – once the response switched from the public health guidelines of Plan A to the wartime footing of Plan B?

....

135 Cummings, testimony to the U.K. House of Commons, Health and Social Care Committee and Science and Technology Committee, *Coronavirus: Lessons learnt*, May 26, 2021.

136 *ITV News*, "In full: Dominic Cummings' evidence on UK government's handling of Covid crisis."

As reported by the Greyzone:

> In May 2020... London rolled out an initiative called the Joint Bios-
> ecurity Centre (JBC). The JBC was advertised as a state-of-the-art
> system that provided 'evidence-based, objective analysis to inform
> local and national decision-making in response to COVID19
> outbreaks.' Purportedly tracking the virus' spread in real-time, its
> coronavirus 'alert level' was directly modeled on the Joint Terrorism
> Analysis Centre's 'traffic light' system, established in 2003.
>
> JBC was first led by Tom Hurd, a veteran intelligence official who
> months earlier had been put forward as the likely next MI6 chief.
> Hurd soon returned to running counter-terrorism for the Home
> Office, however, and was replaced by senior GCHQ [the UK's
> 'intelligence, security and cyber agency'] operative Clare Gardiner.
> Her appointment reportedly came at the behest of Cabinet Secretary
> Simon Case, GCHQ's former Director of Strategy.
>
> At the time, concerns were rising about the growing role of intel-
> ligence service personnel in managing the pandemic.[137]

The *Financial Times* reported on the JBC on June 5, 2020:

> Downing Street has appointed a senior spy to lead the UK's joint
> biosecurity centre, which will monitor the spread of coronavirus
> across the country and suppress new outbreaks. Clare Gardiner,
> head of cyber resilience and strategy at the National Cyber Security
> Centre — a branch of signals intelligence agency GCHQ — will
> become the centre's first director-general, responsible for advising
> ministers on the 'alert level' for the virus; which is similar to assessing
> the terror threat.
>
> The decision to put a security official in charge is likely to cause
> consternation among public health experts, who have questioned
> whether the template of a terror analysis centre is appropriate for

---

137 Klarenberg, "The journalist-run, intelligence-linked operation that warped
British pandemic policy."

managing a viral pandemic.[138]

Moreover, just as in the US, the intelligence/counterterrorism agency that took over the response operated in secrecy and with no public scrutiny or oversight.[139]

The Greyzone continues:

Despite the body's [JBC's] enormous and constantly expanding power, the opaque JBC has entirely eluded scrutiny from British media since its launch. Its membership, the minutes of its meetings, data, analysis, and arguments all remain a secret, while it maintains the power to impose restrictions if not outright lockdowns without explanation or warning at any time.

To summarize: The British government's response to the Covid pandemic switched from "Plan A" – a public health response led by the Department of Health, to "Plan B" – a surveillance and lockdown response, modeled on responses to terrorist attacks, led by intelligence operatives, and operating in secrecy.

What prompted the switch?

This is the million dollar question – not just in the UK, but in the U.S. and all over the world, where the same pattern was followed.

Any documents directly stating the reason for the switch, and who actually ordered it, are not in the public domain, because "Plan B" was carried out by secretive government agencies (the NSC in the US, the JBC in Britain), whose proceedings are not publicly available.

Nevertheless, in his testimony to Parliament, Dominic Cummings offered some unsurprising clues.

....

138 Warrell and Neville, "Senior spy appointed to lead UK's joint biosecurity centre."

139 Lerman, "CDC Was NOT in Charge of Covid Communications. The National Security Council Was."

Dominic Cummings: "How Do We Make This Transition from Plan A to Plan B [Plan Bill]?"

In the May 2021 hearings,[140] Cummings testified that in March 2020 he was being told by "people like Bill Gates and that kind of network" that the "new mRNA vaccines could smash the conventional wisdom," which should "not necessarily" be followed. (p. 79)

> The conventional wisdom was that we were not going to be able to have any vaccines in 2020. In March, I started getting calls from various people saying, "These new MRNA vaccines could well smash the conventional wisdom, and don't necessarily stick to it." People like Bill Gates and that kind of network were saying that.

It's significant to note that in March 2020, Operation Warp Speed – which encompassed different types of vaccines, not just mRNA-based products – had not even officially launched yet. There was no way to know whether mRNA or any other vaccines could be successfully tested, approved, and manufactured in time to impact the course of Covid. Yet "Bill Gates and that kind of network" were already saying conventional wisdom would be smashed by them.

The same network, according to Cummings, said he needed to think of developing vaccines for Covid as "the Manhattan Project in World War II or the Apollo program." This is the exact same language used by career bioweapons expert and Operation Warp Speed creator, Robert Kadlec.[141]

Cummings said they told him "the actual expected return on this is so high that even if it does turn out to be all wasted billions, it is still a good gamble in the end."

....

140 Cummings, testimony to the U.K. House of Commons, Health and Social Care Committee and Science and Technology Committee, *Coronavirus: Lessons learnt*, May 26, 2021.

141 Lerman, "How Awesome is the Deep State, Really?"

Essentially, what happened is that there was a network of Bill Gates-type people who were saying, "Completely re-think the whole paradigm of how you do this. Build in parallel—here is the science thing; here is the manufacturing thing; here's the distribution; here's the supply; here's the logistics; here's the data."

The normal thing is that you do those sequentially. What Bill Gates and people like that said to me and others at No. 10 was, "You need to think of this much more like some of the classic programmes of the past—the Manhattan project in world war two or the Apollo programme—and build it all in parallel. In normal Government accounting terms, that is completely crazy, because if nothing works out you have spent literally billions building all these things up, and the end result is nothing—you get zero for it, it's all waste.

What Bill Gates and people and Patrick Vallance and his team were saying was that the actual expected return on this is so high that even if it does turn out to be all wasted billions, it is still a good gamble in the end. All the conventional Whitehall accountancy systems for that cannot basically cope with it, and you have to throw them all down the toilet. That is, essentially, what we did.

As a result of these conversations with "Bill Gates and people like that," Cummings reported, he and Chief Scientific Advisor Patrick Vallance decided they "must take it out of the Department of Health." (p. 79)

What exactly is "it?" At the very least, the whole vaccine development, manufacturing, and procurement process. More broadly, the inference of his testimony is that "it" was the entire pandemic response, which Cummings described as "PPE, testing, shielding" and "all the problems the DH [Department of Health] had."

Plan B, based on Cummings' testimony, was to wait for the vaccines. And how do you do that? Use the surveillance of the JBC, the emergency powers of the government, and the enforcement of the police to lockdown until the vaccines become available. But not just any vaccines. The Bill Gates-promised mRNA vaccines.

CONCLUSION

In the UK, as in the US, the Covid pandemic response switched abruptly in mid-March 2020 from long-established public health protocols to an unprecedented totalitarian lockdown-until-vaccine plan. The apparent impetus was the anticipation for the astronomical "return" on mRNA vaccines, which had yet to be developed, tested, or approved.

I believe the same pattern happened in all Five Eyes (US, UK, Canada, Australia, NZ) and NATO countries.

The result was, as Reuters reported in December 2021, the biggest upward wealth shift in history,[142] devastation of poor communities and countries,[143] destruction of small businesses worldwide, and a massive concentration of wealth and power in the hands of global corporations, NGOs, and the military/intelligence alliances that provided enforcement and cover for their efforts.

This is not a conspiracy theory. It is a description of what happened.

ACKNOWLEDGMENTS

Investigative journalist Paula Jardine[144] contributed research to this section. *Daily Sceptic*'s Will Jones published some of this information in his excellent August 2022 article: "Where Lockdowns and Fast-Tracked Vaccines Came From."[145]

---

142 John, "Pandemic boosts super-rich share of global wealth."

143 Lerman, "The Covid Consensus: To Understand the Global Pandemic Disaster, Read This Book."

144 *The Conservative Woman*, Paula Jardine profile.

145 Jones, " Where Lockdowns and Fast-Tracked Vaccines Came From."

3.10 IT WAS BIODEFENSE, NOT PUBLIC HEALTH: HOLLAND AND GERMANY EDITION

In previous sections, I analyzed government documents showing that the Covid pandemic response in the U.S. was not designed or led by the public health agencies. Rather, it was a biodefense lockdown-until-vaccine response, led by the National Security Council and FEMA/Department of Homeland Security.

I showed that the same pattern was repeated in the UK.

And I posited that this was a globally planned and executed response – overseen by what I call the Biodefense Global Public-Private Partnership (GPPP). The lockstep in which nearly all Western countries responded to the "novel coronavirus" in early 2020 suggested that national governments were not in charge. Rather, a global plan was being executed on behalf of a larger and more powerful entity, or entities.

This table, also discussed in Chapter 1, describes the entity I believe was in charge – the Biodefense GPPP – including its numerous, world-encompassing components. The table shows how the biodefense complex scales up from national to international components. This is true not just in the U.S., but also in the many countries that responded in a nearly identical fashion to the Covid event.

National Biodefense Complex	Global Biodefense Public-Private Partnership
Military/IC bioterror specialists, agencies and subcontractors, including among others: DARPA, BARDA, DTRA, Army Medical Research and Development Command installations (e.g. Ft. Dietrich), ASPR	International military and intelligence alliances, including NATO and Five Eyes, incorporating biodefense specialists, agencies, and subcontractors in all member countries
Public health agencies and subcontractors, including among others: NIH, HHS, NIAID, CDC	International public health and governance bodies including EU, UN, WHO, WEF, with branches, representatives, and subcontractors in all member countries
U.S. scientists and research institutions, journals, and professional associations	Internationally based scientists and research institutions, journals, and professional associations
NGOs/nonprofits	International "philanthrocapitalists" and their organizations, including the Bill & Melinda Gates Foundation, the Wellcome Trust, and their many offshoots including GAVI and CEPI, with offices and representatives in numerous countries
Multinational pharmaceutical companies, subsidiaries, and subcontractors	
Multinational technology and surveillance companies, subsidiaries, and subcontractors (for outbreaks and compliance with measures	

The Covid Coup in Holland

As mentioned in the description of the Biodefense GPPP above, it was most likely through military and intelligence alliances, including NATO and the Five Eyes, that the Covid pandemic response was coordinated.

This has recently been confirmed by the Dutch Minister of Health, as reported by the Centre for Research on Globalization (globalresearch. ca) on November 8, 2024:

> Dutch Health Minister Fleur Agema has acknowledged in parliament
> that the Dutch pandemic policy is taking place 'under the direction
> of National Coordinator for Security and Counterterrorism (NCTV)

and Defense" and must comply with "NATO obligations.'[146]

Dutch researcher Cees van den Bos, who contributed directly to this section, notes that "during the Covid pandemic, Fleur Agema was an opposition leader who was critical of the Covid response in the Netherlands, which makes her statements all the more explosive." He explains that "she was opposed to vaccine mandates and lockdowns, with a loud voice in the Dutch parliament. But since she became the Minister of Health back in July 2024, she clearly changed her mind, saying that she follows orders from the NCTV based on NATO obligations."

As noted by GlobalResearch, van den Bos was already reporting on this situation at the end of 2022, when he "accused the NCTV of having committed a 'coup d'etat.'"[147] The article continues:

> The crisis management was almost everywhere in the hands of the military and intelligence services, and in our country it rested with the NCTV.

Van den Bos reports that "the NCTV, which is the Dutch version of the U.S. Department of Homeland Security (DHS), took the lead in every democratic process." He elaborates:

> They centralized power structures by taking away the mandate from local mayors and shifted them to 25 regional key points of contact. The NCTV also founded a military unit of special forces that specialized in the Behavioural Dynamics Methodology (BDM), which is an evolution of Cambridge Analitica (sic).
>
> The Army unit was called Land Information Manouvre Centre (LIMC) and was tasked with surveillance of citizens on the internet. When word got out to the public about the existence of the LIMC,

....

146 Centre for Research on Globalization, "Dutch Minister of Health Acknowledges that The Pandemic Policy is a Military Operation. "The Ministry of Health Oberys NATO and NCTV"."

147 Van den Bos, "The orchestration of a coup by the NCTV," translated to English from Dutch.

the Dutch Minister of Defence terminated the unit instantly, because the activities were against the law. The same thing happened in Canada with their Precision Information Team (PIT).

According to van den Bos, "the NCTV also founded a Parliamentary Team for harmonizing the parliamentary process. They controlled the debate in the Dutch parliament and made sure political parties 'would not surprise each other' with difficult questions."

In addition, he reports that although the Dutch government chose not to activate martial law, the NCTV "introduced a Temporary Covid-19 Law (TWM), which gave the government martial powers without the possibility for the parliament to discuss or object to the Covid response and measures."

The Dutch Government's National Crisis Communication Taskforce (NKC), says van den Bos, "was also a team of the NCTV that coordinated all the public communications and the narratives surrounding the pandemic. All media campaigns, fact checks, narratives and nudging campaigns were coordinated in the NKC with the help of behavioural scientists."

As reported in a previous section, the same thing happened in the U.S., when the National Security Council took control of all Covid communications.

FOIA documents supporting all of van den Bos' claims are available on his Substack.[148] Most are in Dutch – right click for the English translate function. This article is in English: https://treesandforest.substack.com/p/corona-policy-set-by-the-european.[149]

In his research, van den Bos notes that the Dutch pandemic response seemed to be following traditional pandemic plans until the middle of March 2020, when the NCTV took over, and the whole thing switched to a lockdown-until-vaccine paradigm.

This tracks exactly with the timeline followed by most (if not all) NATO and Five Eyes allies in the global Covid response:

....

148 *Bomen & Bos Substack*

149 Van den Bos, "Corona policy set by the European Commission."

January – February 2020: Public health agencies seem to be in charge of responding to the outbreak. It is mostly confined to China, so there is not widespread panic. The public health plan is the same as always: monitor for local clusters of serious disease requiring treatment, and be prepared to scale up hospital capacity if needed. Guidelines are to wash your hands a lot, and stay home if you're sick.

End of February – Mid-March 2020: The media switches from criticizing China's draconian, anti-democratic lockdowns to praising them. Massive increase in panic propaganda and in calling on the public to play an active role in "flattening the curve" by wearing masks and "social distancing."

Mid-March – Mid-May 2020: States of Emergency intended for times of war/terrorism are declared everywhere, even where there are no cases of Covid. **Without telling the public, pandemic response is officially moved from public health agencies to military/ intelligence-led bodies (US Task Force, UK Biosecurity Centre, among others) operating largely in secret. (Before mid-March these bodies were already in charge behind the scenes.) Public health agencies switch from traditional public health plans to nonstop lockdown-until-vaccine propaganda.**

End of 2020 – End of 2022: Populations grow weary of lockdown measures, but new waves of panic propaganda focused on "cases" and "variants" lead to repeated lockdowns and a desperate desire for vaccines, followed by cult-like embrace of mandates, refusal to examine any evidence contradicting the "safe and effective" claims, and brutal ostracism of skeptics. The public accepts the necessity for repeated, endless vaccine boosters – contrary to everything it was initially told.

End of 2022 – today: Government commissions spend many months and many millions of dollars examining their countries' pandemic responses. Every commission in nearly every country finds that the public health agencies were woefully inadequate, that the public health response in January-February was catastrophically misguided, and that the lockdown-until-vaccine plan should have been implemented as soon as the first cases were discovered in China. Covid vaccines are now recommended along with seasonal flu vaccines. The mRNA platform is viewed as an unmitigated success, and tested against dozens of diseases and pathogens. Reports of injuries and deaths are ignored, obfuscated, and censored by every single government in the world.

The Covid Coup in Germany

Recent revelations from the "RKI (Robert Koch Institute) Leak" demonstrate that the same pattern was followed in Germany, as well.

Highlights of these revelations are presented on Sasha Latypova's Substack by Dr. Stefan Hamburg.[150] Dr. Hamburg's testimony in the German Bundestag is here[151] (German with subtitles). A transcript in English is here.[152]

As Dr. Hamburg reports, the RKI Leak shows the same timeline, as detailed above, being followed in the German Covid response. The leaked documents also show that Germany followed the same patterns of propaganda and censorship, as detailed in The Catastrophic Covid Convergence,[153] **switching from a scientifically and ethically sound public health approach, to a biodefense lockdown-until-vaccine framework.**

Here's how Dr. Hamburg describes the utterly non-scientific, shockingly foreordained risk assessment leading to lockdowns in Germany:

I quote from 16 March, 2020: 'During the weekend a new risk assessment was prepared.' Before a court, RKI stated the assessment was prepared outside, so it was not based on a scientific evaluation. Further quote: **'Risk is scheduled to be scaled up this week.'** One

150 Latypova, "Dr. Stefan Homburg: Some Interesting Excerpts from the RKI-Leak."

151 Homburg, "Whistleblow Uncovers Covid Scam."

152 Greaterisrahell, "Transcription of Pro. Dr. Stefan Homburg, Leibnitz University in Hanover, Germany."

153 Lerman, "The Catastrophic Covid Convergence - revisited (part 2)."

day later the RKI report stated that there was a high risk, and we went into lockdown.

Here are additional excerpts from Dr. Hamburg/Sasha Latypova:

Regarding schools, the experts advised against comprehensive closures on 11 March 2020. Only five days later, policy makers closed all German schools for a long period of time:

ROBERT KOCH INSTITUT Protokoll 11.03.2020
(Exzerpt: @SHomburg)

Schulschließungen in Gebieten die nicht besonders betroffen sind, sind nicht empfohlen

• • •

School closures in areas that are not particularly affected are not recommended

While RKI's speakers emphasized the existence of a medical public emergency, they knew only too well that corona was comparable with influenza. They noted this in March 2021, during a strict lockdown, which was tightened by curfews shortly thereafter:

ROBERT KOCH INSTITUT Protokoll 19.03.2021
(Exzerpt: @SHomburg)

COVID-19 sollte nicht mit Influenza verglichen werden, bei normaler Influenzawelle versterben mehr Leute

Das Hauptrisiko, an COVID-19 zu sterben, ist das Alter

* * *

COVID-19 should not be compared to influenza, more people die in a normal influenza wave

The main risk of dying of COVID-19 is age

Here is some of Dr. Hamburg's testimony regarding what the RKI Leak says about the German government's Covid vaccine policy:

> We read the following in April of 2020: 'There is currently no experience with RNA and DNA vaccines, EMA [European Medicines Agency] and Phizer(sic) are considering whether to skip phase 3 trials.'
>
> Two weeks later: 'A number of vaccines will become available that have been tested in quick succession. Relevant data will be collected post-marketing.' Put differently: Let's first vaccinate the entire population, and then afterwards let's learn whether the stuff helps or harms. That was the plan, and that's how it was implemented.
>
> On 27 December, 2020 vaccination started in Germany. On 8 January, 2021, in the very early phase we read: 'Vaccine effectiveness is not yet known. The duration of protection is also unknown.' That just repeats what we could read in the EMA approval, namely, that only protection from a positive PCR test was really confirmed. Everything else like protection from severe illnesses, death and the like was not confirmed in the admission process.

Who was actually in charge of the German Covid response?
As in the Netherlands, it was not just the "politicians." It was leaders on a higher, global level. As Dr. Hamburg testified:

> In June of 2020, not only were the number of colds low, as is typical for the season, but even the PCR numbers approached the zero line. .... RKI members thought that now the official risk level could be reduced again, but then we read about **NATO General Holtherm, who was top boss of the RKI,** two hierarchy levels above Mr. Wieler [RKI President], the figure head or mouth piece. **Holtherm decided on Tuesday that the risk assessment in the next week must not be changed.** [boldface added]

What about military/intelligence agencies? I do not have definitive documentation to prove they were in charge of the German response, but here are some suggestive data points:

In a report in *Exemplars in Global Health*, the very Mr. Wieler – who was RKI President – mentioned by Dr. Hamburg above, writes that:

On February 27, with a total of 26 confirmed cases, the government set up **an inter-ministerial national crisis management group.**[154] [boldface added]

Wikipedia reports that the new crisis team was led jointly by the Federal Ministry of the Interior (BMI) and the Federal Ministry of Health. The BMI, according to Wikipedia,[155] "is comparable to the UK Home Office or a combination of the U.S. Department of Homeland Security and the U.S. Department of Justice...It maintains, among other agencies, the two biggest federal law enforcement agencies in Germany...**It is also responsible for the federal domestic intelligence agency, the Federal Office for the Protection of the Constitution.**"
[boldface added]

Interestingly, on the same day that the national crisis management group was set up, as Wikipedia notes:

On 27 February 2020, Lothar Wieler, President of the Robert Koch Institute (RKI), announced that there would be daily press briefings on the development of the spread of COVID-19 in the country.

As detailed in Chapter 4.2, February 27, 2020, was an important date in the Covid response narrative. That's when the messaging switched from mostly reasonable public health directives to military-style lockdown-until-vaccine propaganda.

Cees van den Bos notes that this was also an important date in the coordinated Covid response in the EU:

....

154 Exemplars in Global Health, *Emerging COVID-19 Success Story: The Challenge of Maintaining Progress.*

155 Wikidpedia, "Federal Ministry of the Interior (Germany)," accessed February 12, 2025.

This was the date of the activation of the Integrated Political Crisis Response (IPCR) on the EU level. All member states of the EU sit in the IPCR. It was activated in 'full mode.' All countries were represented by their intelligence agencies (including NCTV for Holland). [FOIA documents attesting to the IPCR activation can be found here.][156]

Additionally, in Holland, the first coronavirus patient was announced on this very same date, although the announcement had been prepared weeks in advance. The story of the announcement is on van den Bos' Substack[157] (right click for the translate-to-English function).

"Very powerful forces" ordered the U.S. and EU to time Covid vax approvals until after the U.S. elections.
Finally, the revelation from the RKI Leak that might be the most scandalous, and that Dr. Homburg rightly points out **"proves that the so-called pandemic was staged and steered by very powerful forces"** is this:

> ROBERT KOCH INSTITUT   28 September 2020
>
>
>
> „Zulassung bei FDA vor US Wahlen ist nicht ge-wünscht, auch nicht bei europäischer Behörde, d.h. es wird erste Ergebnisse nicht vor November geben"
>
> Translation, the passage concerns new vaccines:
> " Approval by the FDA before US elections is not desired, nor by European authorities, i.e. first results will not be available before November "

....

156 Van den Bos, "Corona policy set by the European Commission."

157 Van den Bos, "Bruins' note," translated to English from Dutch.

As Dr. Homburg summarizes: "Unknown political forces favored Biden and they ordered American as well as European authorities to obstruct emergency approval" of the mRNA Covid vaccines – products that the authorities claimed would save lives.

If NATO were in charge of the Covid response, enacted and enforced through the Biodefense Global Public-Private Partnership, which encompasses the military and intelligence industrial complexes in all of the participating countries, then we can surmise that it was more important for NATO, and the Biodefense GPPP, to prevent the re-election of President Trump than to rush what they said were life-saving measures to the world's population.

Whatever their motives, it is clear that the "very powerful forces" that ran the global Covid response did not have the best interests of the world's citizens in mind.

CENSORSHIP AND PROPAGANDA
DURING COVID AND BEYOND

*O*ne *of the scariest parts of the Covid response was the massive censorship and propaganda campaign, carried out by the global censorship/propaganda-industrial-complex, to disseminate the biodefense lockdown-until-vaccine agenda, and to silence any dissent.*

Each of the first five sections in this chapter contains a detailed analysis of one manifestation of the Covid propaganda industrial complex: a best-selling author's book, a date on which multiple propaganda pieces appeared simultaneously, and several New York Times articles. These give the sense of the depth and breadth of the narrative control exercised during the pandemic.

The last three sections expand the analysis to discuss how the censorship industrial complex is working in the post-Covid information landscape to regulate the flow of information over the internet and control the narrative everywhere.

4.1 BEST-SELLING AUTHOR MICHAEL LEWIS REVEALED AS COVID PROPAGANDIST

When I read *The Premonition*,[158] by Michael Lewis – renowned author of *The Big Short* and *Moneyball*, among other best-sellers – I had the same eerie Twilight Zone feeling as when I read Deborah Birx's *Silent Invasion* (discussed in detail in Chapter 3). The book brimmed with so many contradictions, obfuscations, and downright falsehoods that it was clearly intended as something other than an ordinary work of nonfiction.

The author, I sensed, was telling some very tall tales in order to obscure and draw attention away from uncomfortable truths.

In this section I present an imaginary conversation between myself and Michael Lewis, examining the elaborate fabrications in *The Premonition*, and attempting to expose the truths I think he's hiding.

The terrifying takeaways from this analysis are: First, that what Lewis is hiding – or trying to divert attention away from – is a massive CIA involvement in the Covid response. Second, that the intelligence and national security leaders who coordinated the Covid response did not just censor information that contradicted their narrative; they also recruited widely trusted voices – including internationally renowned authors – to disseminate their propaganda.

Why is exposing Covid propagandists so important?

In Chapter 3, I explained how the lockdown-until-vaccine response to the "novel coronavirus" in the U.S. and other countries was led by the military/intelligence – not the public health – arms of government.

In order to gain widespread acceptance of this entirely unprecedented draconian response, its directors had to run a massive global propaganda campaign, which is still ongoing.

What does this campaign entail? The biodefense global public-private partnership (GPPP) has to convince the world of what I believe are four major lies:

---

158 Tucker, "With Premonition, Michael Lewis Gets It Backwards."

1. SARS-CoV-2 was a naturally occurring virus that in no way could possibly have been engineered as a potential bioweapon.
2. Although it was most definitely caused by a naturally occurring respiratory virus (see #1 lie), Covid-19 was nothing like the flu or like any previous flu-like pandemic. It did not confer natural immunity, it was equally dangerous to everyone, and there were zero existing early treatments that might work against it.
3. The only way to respond to this particular novel pathogen was to lock everything down and wait for a vaccine.
4. This had always been the public health plan for pandemic management, not a totally unprecedented, untested, unscientific response copied from totalitarian China.

As Toby Green and Thomas Fazi meticulously document in their excellent book *The Covid Consensus*,[159] most of the world indeed came to believe this utterly false – and ultimately devastating – narrative.

The consensus was achieved through what Robert Malone has described[160] as "military-grade information warfare capability and technology that was designed for our opponents outside the U.S. and has been turned on American citizens." Basically, the intelligence and national security agencies in many countries, not just the U.S., turned their military propaganda playbooks, originally intended to counter terrorists and topple foreign regimes, on their own people.

We must expose as much of the propaganda network as possible, in order to dismantle the consensus narrative and arrive at the truth.

Propaganda succeeds when it both silences opposition and propagates lies

For the Covid propaganda to succeed, it has to apply equal pressure from two sides: suppression of dissenting views and propagation of the consensus narrative.

....

159 Lerman, "The Covid Consensus: To Understand the Global Pandemic Disaster, Read This Book."

160 Malone, "Lies My Government Told Me," *RFK Jr Podcast.*

Many investigations in the years following the initial Covid lockdowns have exposed the elaborate efforts to suppress alternative Covid narratives (and dissenting opinions on other topics), through direct government pressure, as well as indirect actions by "anti-disinformation" organizations. Examples include:

- Censorship of doctors and scientists[161]
- Fusing of national security infrastructure with social media platforms[162]
- Twitter Files on Covid[163]
- Discovery in *Missouri v Biden* Covid censorship lawsuit[164]
- Potential discovery in *Berenson v Biden* lawsuit[165]
- Censorship-Industrial Complex: Top 50 Organizations[166]

Less well-researched, and perhaps even more insidious, was the blanket dissemination of the consensus storyline through the publications of widely trusted media outlets, medical journals, and even famous writers.

This section takes a step toward exposing the very covert, alarmingly ubiquitous, propagation of the national security/biodefense false Covid storyline. These revelations are alarming particularly because they mean anyone – even a trusted, seemingly independent internationally celebrated author like Michael Lewis, with ostensibly no government, military, or intelligence ties – can be a purveyor of military/intelligence/biodefense propaganda.

....

161 Shir-Raz et al., "Censorship and Suppression of Covid-19 Heterodoxy: Tactics and Counter-Tactics."

162 Siegel, "A Guide to Understanding the Hoax of the Century."

163 Zweig (@davidzweig), "The Twitter Files: How Twitter Rigged The Covid Debate."

164 Kheriaty, "The Censors are Exposed: Major Update to Missouri v. Biden from Tracy Beanz."

165 Brownstone Institute, "Berenson v. Biden: The Potential and Significance."

166 Schmidt et al., "Report on the Censorship-Industrial Complex: The Top 50 Organizations to Know."

Covid Propaganda in Michael Lewis's *The Premonition*

The following is an imaginary conversation between me and Michael Lewis, with his answers quoted from *The Premonition* and from articles and interviews about the book.

Q: A New York Times review[167] says that in *The Premonition* you follow "medical renegades" who warned for years that something like the Covid-19 pandemic was bound to happen, while the federal government proved to be inordinately unhelpful. Similarly, a *Time Magazine* article[168] asks "Why this 'rogue group of patriots,' as you call them, had to find one another and do the work their bosses weren't doing?"

Who were these so-called rogue renegades, and how did you find them?

Lewis: In late March 2020 Richard Danzig introduced me to the Wolverines, (*TP* p. 303) a kind of secret group of doctors who were kind of trying to shadow manage the pandemic.[169]

Q: Did you know Richard Danzig chairs the board of the Center for New American Security,[170] a national security think tank? According to their website, Danzig's "primary activities in recent years have been as a consultant to U.S. Intelligence Agencies and the Department of Defense on national security issues."

You might also be interested to know (or already know?) that in 2009, Danzig wrote A Policymaker's Guide to Bioterrorism and What to Do About It,[171] in which he explained that understanding potential bioterror-

167 Szalai, "The Pandemic Gets the Michael Lewis Treatment, Heroic Technocrats and All."

168 Vick, "Michael Lewis Found the People Who Should Have Been in Charge During the Pandemic."

169 Ritholtz, "Transcript: Michael Lewis."

170 Center for a New American Security, Richard J. Danzig profile.

171 Danzig, *A Policymaker's Guide to Bioterrorism and What to Do About It.*

ism agents is a very specialized field, "obscure to the typical CIA agent." Thus, he argued, it was important to grant security clearances to "first rate experts and convene them regularly to discuss intelligence issues and hypotheses." (p. 37)

Do you think a group of first-rate bioterrorism experts with security clearances convening regularly to discuss intelligence issues might be another way to describe the Wolverines?

Lewis: They were a secret group of doctors who were influencing policy all over the US. Carter Mecher was sitting at the center of it. No one in the world, so far as I knew, knew who they were.[172]

Q: They were influencing policy all over the U.S. even though they were rogue renegades, who nobody in the world knew, doing what you call "redneck epidemiology" (*TP* p. 102)? Seems a bit far-fetched.

Who is this Carter Mecher [pronounced MESH-er] guy who's "sitting at the center of it?"

Lewis: He was not a policy person, not a Washington person, not a person who knew anything about pandemics, but a doctor from Atlanta. He had only ever wanted to be a doctor. (*TP* p. 59) From the moment he walked into an ICU, he sensed it was where he was meant to be. (*TP* p. 61)

In 2005 he was surprised by a call from the White House, and even more surprised by what they wanted him to do: help create a national pandemic response plan. He'd learned a lot about infectious disease by treating it in various intensive care units. He knew nothing about pandemics, and hadn't given any thought to how to plan for them. 'But it was the White House calling,' he said. 'I figured, Yeah, yeah, what the hell.' (*TP* p. 74)

....

172 *Politics and Prose*, "Michael Lewis, *The Premonition.*"

Q: So Carter Mecher, who described himself as "kind of the doofus from the VA" (TP p. 75), who knew nothing about pandemics, was invited to the White House in 2005, at which point you claim he basically "invented the idea of pandemic response?"[173]

Let me just add that, according to Rajeev Venkayya, another of your Wolverines, Mecher "was recruited because they needed someone who understood how a hospital actually worked."[174]

It's quite a story. A totally unknown doofus ICU doc from the VA, with no pandemic expertise, is called into the White House out of the blue to work on pandemic planning because he understands how a hospital works. I'm guessing maybe there were other reasons why he was on Bush's pandemic response team, but we'll get to that in a sec.

Let's fast forward to the Covid pandemic. What was Mecher doing when the pandemic hit?

Lewis: Carter had been back in Atlanta for nine years. He'd left the White House at the end of President Obama's first term and returned to the Veterans Health Administration. The people around him either never knew, or soon forgot, where he'd been for the previous six years, and what he'd done there. No one ever brought up the White House, or pandemics. (TP p. 160)

He's in the federal government but he's — he basically — he's working out of his house for the VA and the VA doesn't even know they employ him. His superpower is invisibility.[175]

Outside the VA, at least a few people from his White House days had not lost track of him. Tom Bossert, for example. Donald Trump had named

---

173 Ritholtz, "Transcript: Michael Lewis."

174 Lipton and Steinhauer, "The Untold Story of the Birth of Social Distancing."

175 *Politics and Prose*, "Michael Lewis, "The Premonition"."

Bossert his first homeland security adviser. Bossert built a team of people to deal with biological risks, and instantly called Richard Hatchett and Carter Mecher. (*TP* p. 162)

Q: To recap: Carter Mecher, an unassuming ICU doc, who "had no formal training in epidemiology or virology or any other relevant field" (*TP* p. 164) and had been sitting at home being invisible and doing nothing for the VA for nine years – was the first person Trump's homeland security advisor called (along with Richard Hatchett – his Wolverine partner) to deal with biological risks?

I have a theory to run by you: Perhaps Bossert called Mecher and Hatchett because they were deeply embedded in the intelligence community's counterterrorism/biological weapons program – and were known as experts in the field?

Before you answer that, let me provide some interesting information that may or may not surprise you: The only shred of evidence I could find online of any activity at all by super-invisible Carter Mecher between 2011 and 2020 was his participation in a 2015 conference[176] at the Hudson Institute entitled: Biological and Chemical Threat Preparedness, Emergency Response.

The Hudson Institute (a national security think tank) and Inter-University Center for Terrorism Studies published a report from that conference in October 2015 entitled: *A National Blueprint for Biodefense.*[177] It was mostly about how unprepared we were to face bioterrorist attacks. Here's the general gist: "The Nation failed to heed the advice of the 9/11 Commission, the WMD [Weapons of Mass Destruction] Commission, and many other experts who warned of the dangers of biological terrorism and warfare. We must now add the failure to

....

176 C-SPAN, "User Clip: Mecher April 2015 Hudson."

177 Bipartisan Commission on Biodefense, A National Blueprint for Biodefense: Leadership and Major Reform Needed to Optimize Efforts, October 2015.

appreciate the threat, generate political will, and take action in the face of looming danger."

At the conference, Mecher's talk addressed an "Anthrax Scenario." He said:

> Although we tend to focus on the public health and medical conse-
> quences of a large-scale biological attack, it would be much more
> than a public health emergency. It'd be a national security crisis. By
> definition this would not be a naturally occurring disease outbreak
> and would not behave as such.

Let's pause for a moment and apply these words to the Covid-19 pandemic, which the biodefenders describe not as a public health and medical problem, but as a national security crisis, even a war,[178] against a pathogen that behaves like no other naturally occurring disease outbreak ever known. Did you notice the uncanny parallels between how Mecher describes a large-scale biological attack, and how he and his fellow Wolverines approached the Covid pandemic?

Getting back to Mecher specifically: It sure seems like he is some kind of bioterrorism expert who works very, very, very covertly, doesn't it? By the way, who was his boss during his four-year stint in the Obama White House, of which you write: "He wasn't quite sure how it happened, but his name wound up on a list of experts asked to stick around for a few months to advise the new administration in case of emergency" (*TP* p. 111)?

Lewis: The official in charge of him, Heidi Avery, came from some deep place in the intelligence community and was now called deputy assistant to the president for homeland security. (*TP* p. 114)

Q: You mean the Heidi Avery who was described by former CIA Director John Brennan in his 2020 biography[179] as a CIA director "within the Office

----

178 Tucker, "Sorry, This is Not Going Away."

179 Brennan, *Undaunted*.

of Intelligence Programs at the National Security Council, which was responsible for supporting the president, vice president, and national security adviser on all matters dealing with intelligence, including covert action?"

Lewis: Avery told Carter Mecher that the Obama administration had decided to dissolve the Biodefense Directorate, which he was on, and fold it into something called the Resilience Directorate.

Q: Wait. That reminds me of something. You said the Wolverines were kind of, sort of secretly shadow running the pandemic response from outside the federal government. But according to the U.S. Government's COVID-19 Response Plan dated March 13, 2020, here's who was in charge of the government's Covid policy:

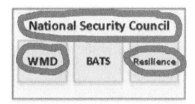

Are you seeing the overlap that I'm seeing?
As we've learned, our rogue doofus renegade Carter Mecher:

- was probably a deeply undercover WMD (weapons of mass destruction) expert
- was on the Biodefense Directorate that was folded into the Resilience Directorate
- had a CIA director boss who advised the National Security Council on covert action

Moving right along to Carter's bestie, Richard Hatchett: You start.

Lewis: In 2001 Richard entered the subculture of federal emergency response. A pair of recent events had pushed the threat of bioterrorism to the front of the minds of the people who worked in and around national security. One was the series of anthrax attacks on Capitol Hill in October 2001. (*TP* p. 56)

In 2005, the possibility that Saddam Hussein had preserved the smallpox virus preoccupied the Bush administration.

Richard had no obvious place in the national security conversation and was surprised that when the conversation turned to bioterrorism. His new colleagues assumed, because he was a doctor, he might have something to offer. 'I was going to stuff I didn't really belong at,' he said. 'I would be going to these meetings at the White House or the Homeland Security Council.' (*TP* p. 57)

Q: I'm noticing a pattern here: as with Mecher, you say Hatchett was just a regular ol' doc with no national security experience, yet somehow he found himself – who knows why or how – working at the White House with the Homeland Security Council.

In fact, Aaron Kheriaty in *The New Abnormal*[180] reports that "in 2001, Richard Hatchett, a member of the CIA who served also on George W. Bush's National Security Council was already recommending obligatory confinement of the entire population in response to biological threats." (p. 9)

Additional details of Hatchett's biography[181] include serving on Obama's National Security Staff, and as Deputy Director, and then Director, of the U.S. Biomedical Advanced Research and Development Authority (BARDA), a government body established in 2006, responsible for the procurement and development of medical countermeasures, principally

....

180 Kheriaty, *The New Abnormal.*

181 London School of Hygiene and Tropical Medicine, Richard Hatchett profile.

against bioterrorism, including chemical, biological, radiological and nuclear CBRN threats.[182]

In 2017, Hatchett was appointed CEO of the Coalition for Epidemic Preparedness Innovations (CEPI), which according to its website[183] "was one of the first organizations to respond to the Covid-19 pandemic, announcing its first three Covid-19 vaccine partnerships on 23 January 2020 – when there were just 581 confirmed cases worldwide."

In May 2020, he was appointed to the expert advisory group for the UK Government's Vaccine Task Force. In 2021, he was appointed to the UK Government's Pandemic Preparedness Partnership.[184]

Sounds like Hatchett was the opposite of a doctor with no national security experience running things from outside the federal government. In fact, he was a bioterrorism and medical countermeasures expert, directly involved in the UK government's pandemic response and in the global vaccine effort, starting all the way back in January 2020, when it wasn't even a pandemic and before Covid-19 had even been named.

Lewis: Richard was actually the jungle guide for the book. Richard is the one who held my hand through the whole book.[185]

Q: Richard, the CIA agent and BARDA Director, held your hand through the book in which you wrote that he "had no obvious place in the national security conversation?" And he didn't correct you? Or was he the one dictating the story to you?

Lewis: [no answer]

....

182 Kraft and Marks, *U.S. Government Counterterrorism*.

183 Coalition for Epidemic Preparedness Innovations, "Q+A: How CEPI-funded research is supporting the COVID-19 vaccine rollout."

184 Wikipedia, "Richard Hatchett," accessed February 12, 2025.

185 *Politics and Prose*, "Michael Lewis, "The Premonition"."

More *Premonition* Propaganda

In addition to the many inaccuracies and inconsistencies revealed in the above Q&A, there is so much more fiction in *The Premonition*, it would take an entire book to expose it all. Here are some highlights:

- All the Wolverines, so innocently described by Lewis as "seven men, all doctors," (*TP* p. 164) actually have impressive military/intelligence/biodefense pedigrees, like Mecher and Hatchett's. You'll find some of the salient elements in their biographies, along with several other noteworthy biodefense figures mentioned in *The Premonition*, at the end of this section.
- Lewis portrays the non-Wolverine characters who star in the book – most notably Charity Dean and Joe DeRisi – as playing elaborate roles in the pandemic response, when in fact they played almost no role at all. Their most important characteristic is that they supposedly had "premonitions" about how bad the Wuhan virus was, long before most people even knew about it.
- Lewis's main argument in the book is that the federal government, mostly represented in this story by the CDC, is risk-averse and dysfunctional, and only rogue patriot outsiders are creative and open-minded enough to come up with solutions to big problems like pandemics.

According to Lewis, the Wolverines were those renegade outsiders – just seven obscure doctors doing their doctoring things – who came up with the wonderful solution of extreme social distancing, otherwise known as lockdowns, to what they viewed as the problem of pandemics.

They did this way back in 2005, when the Bush administration was obsessing about bioterrorism and biowarfare, but they of course had nothing at all to do with national security or biodefense.

This ragtag group, as Lewis tells it, came up with the brilliant idea of lockdowns by analyzing how two cities responded to the 1918 flu pandemic, and combining this analysis with a computer simulation inspired[186] by a 14-year-old's science project. No joke. That's how Lewis says they did it. And, needless to say, they did so with no input from anyone at the CDC or any other public health agency, and without consulting any experts in epidemiology, virology or any related field.

This leads to some pretty absurd passages in *The Premonition*, like the following:

> Public-health people who did not actually know all that much about the subject, for instance, would insist that if you closed schools, all sorts of bad things would happen: crime would rise with kids on the streets; the thirty million kids in the school-lunch program would lack nutrition; parents wouldn't be able to go to work; and so on. (*TP* p. 105)

> Carter couldn't get over that an actual medical professor at Stanford named John Ioannidis became a sensation on U.S. cable news in the spring of 2020 by claiming the virus posed no real threat. He condemned social distancing policies as a hysterical overreaction. That was all that those who wished to deny the reality needed to be able to say, Look, we have experts, too. To say: See, all the experts are fake. Carter had received threats in the mail from such people, who had learned of his role in the strategy. (*TP* p. 295)

Allow me to ask Lewis a few rhetorical questions before returning to the main story:

Q: Carter received threats in the mail????? Who the heck sends threats in the mail? And how could anyone "learn of his role in the strategy" when he was so deeply deeply deeply undercover? You know who actually did

---

186 Tucker, "Lockdown Ideology Originated in 2006 Under George W. Bush."

receive threats? John Ioannidis.[187] As well as other[188] pandemic and epidemiology experts who tried to speak out against the lockdown policy.

But let's return to the propaganda narrative:

After the Wolverines came up with their brilliant but rogue lockdown plan, claims Lewis, the CDC miraculously adopted it, because disappearance master Carter Mecher managed to secretly insert it into their documents, without anybody noticing. Not only that, but the entire world adopted the secretly inserted lockdown plan. As Lewis claimed in an interview: "Whatever the CDC's relationship to the American people is, its relationship to the rest of the world is extremely powerful. And it goes out in itself, this plan, all over the world."[189]

The Premonition accomplishes all of the Covid propaganda goals

Thus Michael Lewis's *The Premonition* promotes exactly what the national security/biodefense pandemic managers need the consensus narrative to be:

The lockdown-until-vaccine plan was not a military response to a potential bioweapon, planned and executed by a group of covert CIA and military biowarfare experts, and modeled after the draconian response of China's totalitarian regime.

Rather, it was invented by a group of rogue doctors way back in 2005, and when in 2020 the CDC for some reason refused to follow that plan that had been internationally accepted as the standard pandemic response (although it had never been implemented or even considered for any prior pandemic), those same heroic renegades came back and somehow, from outside the federal government, worked hard to make sure it was implemented this time.

....

187 Jamison, "A top scientist questioned virus lockdowns on Fox News. The backlash was fierce."

188 Colton, "Stanford professor who challenged lockdowns and 'scientific clerisy' declares academic freedom 'dead'."

189 Ritholtz, "Transcript: Michael Lewis."

Pulling Premonition threads to unravel the giant Covid propaganda juggernaut

Not only is *The Premonition* an excellent exemplar of Covid consensus propaganda, but we can also follow threads from Lewis's book to numerous other influential publications whose sole purpose, I would contend, is to promulgate the four lies listed in my introduction: that SARS-CoV-2 was not a potential bioweapon; that Covid-19 was, nonetheless, unlike any respiratory viral illness ever known; that lockdowns and vaccines were the only appropriate response; and that the unprecedented lockdown-until-vaccine paradigm was – and had always been – an integral part of public health pandemic planning.

Here are some of what I believe to be Covid propaganda publications emanating from, and working in tandem with, *The Premonition*:

- Lewis's baseless and reprehensible takedown of acclaimed Stanford epidemiologist and biomedical data expert John Ioannidis in Lewis's podcast (Season 3, 5/24/2022)[190]
- The takedowns of Prof. John Ioannidis, Prof. Jay Bhattacharya and Prof. Bhattacharya's wife by BuzzFeed reporter Stephanie Lee – interviewed by Lewis in his aforementioned podcast
- The "Red Dawn" emails[191] – "leaked" to *The New York Times*[192] and quoted in an astonishing number of Covid propaganda pieces. In these emails, doofus-cum-undercover-CIA-biowarfare-expert Carter Mecher provides lengthy dissertations on how dangerous the virus is and how important it is to begin locking down immediately. Dozens of high-level government officials are cc'd on these emails, yet almost none except a Wolverine here and there, and a biodefense expert named Eva Lee, ever participate in the conversation.

....

190 Lewis, "The Person Who Knows," *Against the Rules Podcast*.

191 The 'Red Dawn' emails, hosted at https://int.nyt.com/data/documenthelper/6879-2020-covid-19-red-dawn-rising/66f590d5cd41e11bea0f/optimized/full.pdf#page=1

192 Lipton, "The 'Red Dawn' Emails: 8 Key Exchanges on the Faltering Response to the Coronavirus."

- *Lessons from the Covid War*[193] – an "investigative report" by the self-appointed "Covid Crisis Group," whose members include four Wolverines (Mecher, Hatchett, Lawler and Venkayya), one honorary Wolverine (Michael Callahan) and several additional Premonition characters (Charity Dean, Marc Lipsitch, John Barry). For an idea on how reliable it is as a factual document, note that Deborah Birx's propaganda tome is referenced seven times. Although it is a masterpiece of misinformation, this is an extremely valuable document, because so many of the sources it quotes are almost certainly prominent Covid propagandists, including Michael Lewis.
- Lewis's forward[194] to *We Want Them Infected*, one of the most ridiculous and egregious pandemic propaganda books, written by a prolific Covid propagandist, Dr. Jonathan Howard.[195]
- *The Vaccine*,[196] by Joe Miller. In this book about the development of the BioNTech/Pfizer mRNA vaccine, which I believe to be mostly fictional, the author thanks none other than Richard Hatchett for "helping me map my thoughts" (p. 251). If that sounds eerily similar to how Lewis called Hatchett a "jungle guide," get this: one of the main characters in *The Vaccine* is gripped by what can only be described as a supernatural premonition about lockdowns. In January 2020, before anyone even heard about the virus, this character – with no background, publications or experience in viruses or pandemics – suddenly had an "extreme revelation" that very soon "all human contact would be considered perilous, ripping apart families, societies, and the global economy." (p. 8)

You can't make this stuff up. Or maybe you can.

....

193 Tucker, "Sorry, This Is Not Going Away."

194 Howard, ""We Want Them Infected" - My Book Is Done!"

195 *Science-Based Medicine*, Jonathan Howard author archive.

196 O'Connor-May, "Book review: The Vaccine."

APPENDIX
Biographies of the Wolverines and closely affiliated characters

James Lawler[197]

- One of the few uniformed physicians ever to become qualified in biosafety level-4 (BSL-4) laboratory operations, directing animal model research for highly dangerous pathogens (like at the Wuhan Institute of Virology).
- Assisted in initiating some of the first collaborative clinical research programs for DoD Cooperative Threat Reduction efforts in the Caucasus (international bioterrorism work).
- Served on the White House staff in the Homeland Security Council Biodefense Office during the George W. Bush administration and the National Security Council (NSC) Resilience Directorate under the Obama administration (with Mecher and Hatchett).

Duane Caneva

- Chief Medical Officer for the Department of Homeland Security (2018-2021), serving as advisor to the Assistant Secretary for Countering WMD, the Secretary, and the Administrator to FEMA.
- Former Director of Medical and Public Health Preparedness Policy at the National Security Council (2017-2018); overseeing policy development and implantation on national biodefense, health sector preparedness, and chemical defense.
- Former Director of Medical Preparedness Policy at the Homeland Security Council (2007-2009),
- Served as the CBRN (Chemical, Biological, Radiological and Nuclear) consultant to the Office of the Attending Physician at the U.S. Capitol, as Adjunct Professor and as co-director of the postgraduate level Weapons of Mass Destruction Course at the

197 The Asia Group, James Lawler profile.

Uniformed Services University of the Health Sciences.[198]

Matt Hepburn[199]

- Clinical Research Director at the U.S. Army Medical Research Institute for Infectious Diseases (2007-2009), leading domestic and international clinical research efforts on biodefense products. This role entailed extensive service with the Cooperative Threat Reduction program in the republics of the former Soviet Union.
- Joint Project Lead of Enabling Biotechnologies for the Joint Program Executive Office for CBRN Defense.
- Program Manager at DARPA (2013-2019).
- Director of Medical Preparedness on the White House National Security Staff (2010-2013).
- Vaccine Development Lead for Operation Warp Speed.

Dave Marcozzi[200]

- Completed a Congressional fellowship in 2006, serving on the Bioterrorism and Public Health Preparedness Subcommittee.
- Director of the National Healthcare Preparedness Programs within the Office of the Assistant Secretary for Preparedness and Response (ASPR).
- Completed a 3-year detail at the White House National Security Council as Director of All-Hazards Medical Preparedness Policy.

....

198 U.S. Senate Committee on Homeland Security & Governmental Affairs, *Historically Unprepared: Examination of the Federal Government's Pandemic Preparedness and Initial COVID-19 Response,* December 2022.

199 The International Society for Pharmaceutical Engineering, Matthew Hepburn profile.

200 Nationwide Response Issues After an Improvised Nuclear Device Attack: Medical and Public Health Considerations for Neighboring Jurisdictions: Workshop Summary, "Biographical Sketches of Speakers and Panelists."

Rajiv Venkayya[201, 202]

- Director for Biodefense and Health at the White House Homeland Security Council (2003-2005).
- Special Assistant to President Bush for Biodefense at the White House Homeland Security Council, directing the development of policies to prevent, protect, and respond to bioterrorism and naturally occurring biological threats such as avian influenza and SARS, as well as the medical consequences of weapons of mass destruction.
- President of the Vaccine Business Unit at Takeda starting in 2012.

Michael Callahan, noted by Lewis as an "honorary Wolverine" is a known CIA agent involved in bioweapons research who called Robert Malone from China in early January 2020 to tell him about the emerging virus.[203,204]

Robert Kadlec, described by Lewis as "the head of an abstruse but possibly powerful division inside the HHS called the Office of the Assistant Secretary for Preparedness and Response, or ASPR" and as the person who supposedly "way back at the end of the Bush administration, had dubbed Carter and the others 'Wolverines'"(*TP* p. 183), has had a lengthy career in bioweapons, biowarfare, and medical countermeasures as meticulously documented by researcher Paula Jardine.[205, 206, 207, 208]

....

201 NRIdoctors.com, Rajeev Venkayya profile.

202 Takeda Pharmaceutical Company, Rajeev Venkaya profile.

203 Diego, "DARPA's Man in Wuhan."

204 Malone, "A Minority Report on Pandemic Origins."

205 Jardine, "A Manhattan Project for the Biomedical Security State."

206 Jardine, "The Early Career of Covid Czar Robert Kadlec."

207 Jardine, "Robert Kadlec's 20-Year Plot."

208 Jardine, "The Bio-Security Cabal: A 20-Year Entrenchment."

Ken Cuccinelli, who was acting Deputy Secretary of Homeland Security and is mentioned by Lewis as having participated in a phone call with some Wolverines, has a noteworthy accomplishment, mentioned in his Wikipedia bio:

> "Under his tenure, Cuccinelli reduced oversight of the DHS's intelligence arm, making it unnecessary for it to get approval from the DHS's civil liberties office in producing intelligence products."[209]

I find this particularly chilling, given the disdain for civil liberties that seems to permeate the biodefense network's Covid response.

209 Wikipedia, "Ken Cuccinelli," accessed February 12, 2025.

4.2 FEBRUARY 27, 2020: THE PROPAGANDA MACHINE SWITCHES TO LOCKDOWNS

February 27th, 2020, was a very strange day.

I did not know it at the time. I was preparing for a trip to Utah with my husband. I was vaguely aware that there was a virus of concern in China, but I wasn't too worried about it. I was not even aware that the WHO had reported[210] a total of 59 confirmed cases and zero deaths in the U.S. from the virus on that day.

My husband wasn't worried either. He was actually reassured by the official reaction to the virus, which was exactly what he had learned in medical school. Public health officials, politicians, and major media outlets were telling the public not to panic. The advice was: wash your hands a lot and stay home if you're sick. That's what the CDC, the WHO, Anthony Fauci, President Trump, and everyone in between was saying.

Everyone knew masks did not provide protection from airborne respiratory viruses. It was generally agreed that the draconian lockdowns in China were the product of totalitarian overreaction.

However, a radically different approach was about to be implemented. It was an approach concocted in the shadowy realm of biowarfare and bioterrorism, and it entailed fomenting panic in order to gain compliance with lockdowns until countermeasures became available.

The 27th of February is such a noteworthy date, because it's when a jarring narrative flip occurred: reassurance and established protocols became suspect. Panic and doomsday predictions became the new norm. At the time, the shift was not immediately apparent. In retrospect, it is astonishing.

The following is a detailed analysis of some of the private communications, international events, and public propaganda narratives from February 27, 2020. All had the goal of priming the public for the heretofore unthinkable response to a novel pathogen: lock everything down and wait for vaccines.

....

210 World Health Organization, *Coronavirus disease 2019 (COVID-19) Situation Report - 38.*

Private Messaging by Top Officials: Expect Lockdowns

Dr. Anthony Fauci

On February 27th, 2020, Anthony Fauci, the public health face of the not-yet-pandemic response, did a 180 in his private communications (which became available many months later through Freedom of Information Requests).

As reported by Jeffrey Tucker:

> On February 26, Fauci was writing: 'Do not let the fear of the unknown...distort your evaluation of the risk of the pandemic to you relative to the risks that you face every day...do not yield to unreasonable fear.'
>
> The next day, February 27, Fauci wrote actress Morgan Fairchild: 'Be prepared to mitigate an outbreak in this country by measures that include social distancing, teleworking, temporary closure of schools, etc.'[211]

What changed between the 26th and the 27th to make Fauci change his messaging so drastically? Nothing about the virus was different. But the switch from a measured public health to a brutal bioterrorism response had been thrown. The new paradigm, which Fauci began to explain in private and the media began to blast to the public (see below) was: start panicking and prepare for lockdowns.

Senator Richard Burr

Senator Burr, who was serving as Chair of the Senate Intelligence Committee at the time, was caught in a secret recording from February 27th, 2020, making prescient lockdown predictions.

As reported by NPR:

> On Feb. 27, when the United States had 15 confirmed cases of COVID-19 [NPR had even lower numbers than the WHO], President

....

211 Tucker, "What Might Have Been: Calm, Protection, and Care."

Trump was tamping down fears and suggesting that the virus could be seasonal.

On that same day, Burr attended a luncheon held at a social club called the Capitol Hill Club. And he delivered a much more alarming message.

'There's one thing that I can tell you about this: it is much more aggressive in its transmission than anything that we have seen in recent history,' he said, according to a secret recording of the remarks obtained by NPR. 'It is probably more akin to the 1918 pandemic.'

Sixteen days before North Carolina closed its schools over the threat of the coronavirus, Burr warned it could happen.

And Burr invoked the possibility that the military might be mobilized to combat the coronavirus.[212]

What did Burr know that even President Trump did not?

Burr was a member of the "Gang of Eight" – the top lawmakers on the Senate and House intelligence committees. And, as reported by Just Security:

The U.S. intelligence community is able to share the nation's most sensitive secrets with this small group without anyone else outside the administration knowing.[213]

In addition, Senator Burr was closely allied with biowarfare operative Robert Kadlec,[214] with whom he had created ASPR[215] – the biodefense sub-agency within HHS – and BARDA,[216] the Biomedical Advanced

212 Mak, "Weeks Before Virus Panic, Intelligence Chairman Privately Raised Alarm, Sold Stocks."

213 Goodman, "Who is Richard Burr, Really? Why the public can't trust his voice in the Russia probe."

214 Jardine, "The Bio-Security Cabal: A 20-Year Entrenchment."

215 U.S. Administration for Strategic Preparedness and Response, "Pandemic and All Hazards Preparedness Act (PAHPA)."

216 U.S. Administration for Strategic Preparedness and Response, "About BARDA."

Research and Development Authority, which was responsible for developing countermeasures to bioterrorism.[217]

International Lockdown Warnings and Shifts Toward Panic Policy

On February 27th, 2020, a surprising number of countries made major changes, or announced abrupt policy reversals, in their response to the novel coronavirus:

In England, which had been following the same established public health guidelines as the United States, the *Guardian* reported, in an article entitled, "UK schools and offices could close for up to two months":[218] "Prof Chris Whitty [the government's Chief Scientific Advisor] said the country should prepare to face disruption to many normal activities 'for quite a long period' and to pay a heavy 'social cost' for efforts to thwart the virus."

In Australia, as reported by the *Guardian:*[219] "PM initiates emergency response plan as Australia prepares for global pandemic." The plan, according to the article, included "mass vaccinations and stadium quarantines."

In Japan, "Prime Minister Shinzo Abe took the drastic step of asking all the country's schools to close for about a month." The move, as reported by France 24,[220] "which would make Japan one of a few countries, including China, to suspend classes nationwide, "appeared to be an abrupt reversal of the more cautious stance the administration had taken on the virus."

....

217 Borrell, *The First Shots.*

218 Campbell and Siddique, "Coronavirus: UK schools and offices could close for up to two months."

219 Doherty and Murphy, "Australia declares coronavirus will become a pandemic as it extends China travel ban."

220 France 24, "France faces coronavirus 'epidemic,' Macron warns, as confirmed cases double."

In France, President Emmanuel Macron said[221] the country was "preparing for a jump in the number of coronavirus cases."

In Germany, as reported by German broadcaster DW:[222] "The government has announced a new crisis team to handle its response to the spread of the disease."

In Holland, as reported by Dutch researcher Cees van den Bos,[223] the first coronavirus patient was announced, although the announcement had been prepared weeks in advance.

In the European Union, as van den Bos also reported,[224] the Integrated Political Crisis Response (IPCR) – in which all countries were represented by their intelligence agencies – was activated in "full mode."

As the case and death counts[225] demonstrate, there was nothing particularly scary about what the virus was doing in each country on that day. Yet all these governments, on the same day, started preparing for "jumps" in cases, long lockdowns, quarantines, and vaccines.

U.S. Covid Task Force – Change in Leadership

In the United States, February 27th, 2020, was the day on which leadership of the pandemic Task Force, the group in charge of the entire U.S. government's pandemic response, got transferred from HHS Secretary Alex Azar, to the new "Coronavirus Response Coordinator" and National Security Council representative, Deborah Birx. (See Chapter 3 for more details)

Here's how this was reported by the White House:

....

221 Ibid

222 Thurau, "How Germany is preparing for COVID-19."

223 Van den Bos, "Bruins' note," translated to English from Dutch.

224 Van den Bos, "Corona policy set by the European Commission."

225 World Health Organization, *Coronavirus disease 2019 (COVID-19) Situation Report - 38.*

Today, Vice President Mike Pence announced the following individual to a key position on his team to combat the spread of the Coronavirus:

Ambassador Deborah Birx, to serve as the White House Coronavirus Response Coordinator.

Ambassador Birx is a world-renowned global health official and physician. She will be detailed to the Office of the Vice President and will report to Vice President Mike Pence. She will also join the Task Force led by Health and Human Services Secretary Alex Azar. She will be supported by the National Security Council staff.[226]

It's important to note that on the Covid response org chart, the Task Force is placed above all the other agencies, including HHS. Birx is not just "joining the Task Force" – she is replacing Azar as the de facto leader of the response. And she is "supported" not by the staff of the Vice President or the HHS, but by the National Security Council, which is in charge of the response policy.

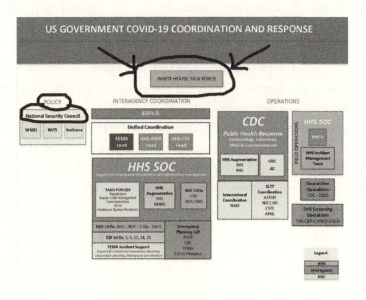

226 The White House, Press Release, "Vice President Pence Announces Ambassador Debbie Birx to Serve as the White House Coronavirus Response Coordinator," February 27, 2020.

The fact that this happened on February 27th is particularly relevant because, on the same day, responsibility for all government communications about the not-yet-pandemic were diverted from the public health agencies to the Task Force, now controlled by the National Security Council.

Covid Communications Must Go Through VP/Task Force

As reported by *The New York Times*,

> The White House moved on Thursday [February 27, 2020] to tighten control of coronavirus messaging by government health officials and scientists, directing them to coordinate all statements and public appearances with the office of Vice President Mike Pence, according to several officials familiar with the new approach.[227]

This means that starting on February 27th, the public health agencies could no longer communicate about the virus, or the response, directly with the public. It all had to go through the National Security Council-led Task Force.

Propaganda-Industrial Complex

It is fascinating to note that on the same day when the key change in Covid response leadership and communications happened, several central themes and figures in the Covid propaganda campaign also emerged:

NYT Op-Ed by EcoHealth Alliance's Peter Daszak

In a February 27, 2020, op-ed that is now findable only if you already know the URL (it is not listed anywhere on *The New York Times* site), Peter Daszak,[228] the person most closely identified with the probable creation of SARS-CoV-2 in a Wuhan bioweapons lab, wrote this:

....

227 Shear and Haberman, "Pence Will Control All Coronavirus Messaging From Health Officials."

228 Senger, "Fauci has Awarded Peter Daszak of EcoHealth Another $650,000 to Study Bat Coronaviruses."

We Knew Disease X Was Coming. It's Here Now.

In early 2018, during a meeting at the World Health Organization in Geneva, a group of experts I belong to (the R&D Blueprint) coined the term 'Disease X': We were referring to the next pandemic, which would be caused by an unknown, novel pathogen that hadn't yet entered the human population.

In a nutshell, Covid-19 is Disease X.

The looming pandemic will challenge us in new ways, as people try to evade quarantines, and misinformation campaigns and conspiracy theorists ply their trade in open democracies.

Pandemics are like terrorist attacks: We know roughly where they originate and what's responsible for them, but we don't know exactly when the next one will happen. They need to be handled the same way — by identifying all possible sources and dismantling those before the next pandemic strikes.[229]

NYT Podcast by Pandemic Panic-Meister Donald McNeil Jr.

In his February 27, 2020, podcast Donald McNeil Jr., a science and health reporter for _The New York Times_ specializing in pandemics, said:

I'm trying to bring a sense that if things don't change, a lot of us might die. If you have 300 relatively close friends and acquaintances, six of them would die in a 2.5 percent mortality situation.

We can do it, but we're not used to being controlled from the top down the way people have been in China. So I don't know what's going to happen in the United States. We're not mentally prepared to fight a sort of people's war against an epidemic, which is what happened in China.[230]

229 Daszak, "We Knew Disease X Was Coming. It's Here Now."

230 McNeil, "The Coronavirus Goes Global," _The Daily Podcast._

This is an incredibly scary prediction from someone whose *New York Times* bio[231] says he specializes in "plagues and pestilences" and who "covers diseases of the world's poor and wider epidemics, including Covid-19, AIDS, Ebola, malaria, swine and bird flus and Zika."

It is also at best ignorant and, at worst, intentionally fear-mongering. There was no credible reason to believe that 2.5% of the entire population would die of Covid-19. That would mean 9 million deaths in the United States alone.

Obviously, this is neither realistic nor is "mortality situation" the correct scientific way to refer to fatality rates, as McNeil surely knows, given his many years of writing about plagues.

In fact, when McNeil aired the podcast, it was already known that the fatality rate was as low as the flu for most age groups. Anthony Fauci himself co-wrote an article in *The New England Journal of Medicine*, which appeared online on February 28th (presumably having been written a few days prior):

> If one assumes that the number of asymptomatic or minimally symptomatic cases is several times as high as the number of reported cases, the case fatality rate may be considerably less than 1%. This suggests that the overall clinical consequences of Covid-19 may ultimately be more akin to those of a severe seasonal influenza (which has a case fatality rate of approximately 0.1%) or a pandemic influenza (similar to those in 1957 and 1968)...[232]

In all of his writing on the pandemic[233] after February 27th, McNeil consistently hyped fear of the virus, of "misinformation" about it, and of other pathogens.

....

231 *The New York Times*, Donald G. McNeil Jr. profile.

232 Fauci et al., "Covid-19 - Navigating the Uncharted."

233 *The New York Times*, Donald G. McNeil Jr. profile.

Scientific American Article by Pandemic Propagandist
Zeynep Tufekci

On February 27th, 2020, an obscure sociologist named Zeynep Tufekci, who rocketed to international fame as a highly celebrated Covid[234] "expert," appeared on the scene with her *Scientific American* article "Preparing for Coronavirus to Strike the U.S. – Getting ready for the possibility of major disruptions is not only smart; it's also our public duty."[235]

Here is a particularly noteworthy paragraph:

> All of this means that the only path to flattening the curve for COVID-19 is community-wide isolation: the more people stay home, the fewer people will catch the disease. The fewer people who catch the disease, the better hospitals can help those who do. Crowding at hospitals doesn't just threaten those with COVID-19; if emergency rooms are overwhelmed, more flu patients, too, will die because of lack of treatment, for example.

Note the mention of "flattening the curve" – a term that only appeared as a meme via Twitter (see below) on the same day this article came out, and only circulated widely several days/weeks after. How would readers know what "flattening the curve for COVID-19" meant here? Was it mere happenstance that Tufekci used this as-yet-unfamiliar phrase on the same day the Twitter meme appeared?

I don't know for sure, but I'm guessing it was not a coincidence.

Other statements and actions by Tufekci suggesting that she did not spontaneously come up with her Covid pronouncements include:

- In a podcast interview with Sam Harris,[236] dated February 1, 2021, she claimed she wrote the *Scientific American* article because everyone who had any credentials – epidemiologists, infectious disease experts, even the mainstream media – was telling the

234 Smith, "How Zeynep Tufekci Keeps Getting the Big Things Right."

235 Tufekci, "Preparing for Coronavirus to Strike the U.S."

236 Tufekci, "Persuasion and Control," *Making Sense Podcast.*

public to remain calm and not to panic. But with her background in computers and sociology, she was certain people had to prepare to "stay home for a few weeks."

- After this initial article, Tufekci went on to supposedly single-handedly convince the CDC and the WHO to change their masking policies,[237] by publishing an op-ed in *The New York Times*[238] that went against all established science and all previous studies on masking.

Then, in the weeks and months after February 27th, 2020, following Tufekci – who wrote articles directly contradicting all the experts and established epidemiological knowledge, with no training in any related field herself – became "following the science."

I would argue that such an unlikely and even absurd turn of events did not happen by accident, but rather because Tufekci was intentionally promoted and celebrated by the Covid propaganda machine.

The Economist/ Flatten the Curve

A little after midnight between February 27th and 28th, 2020, a formerly unknown podiatrist-turned-public-health expert, who had found his way to a leadership position in the biodefense-industrial complex in New Jersey in the years following 9/11, tweeted out a graph that was perhaps the single most important propaganda prop for the lockdown panic:

....

237 Wikipedia, "Zeynep Tufekci," accessed February 12, 2025.

238 Tufekci, "Why Telling People They Don't Need Masks Backfired."

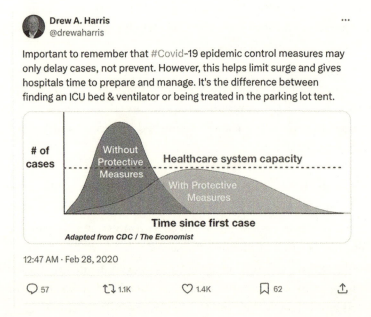

Drew A. Harris
@drewaharris

Important to remember that #Covid-19 epidemic control measures may only delay cases, not prevent. However, this helps limit surge and gives hospitals time to prepare and manage. It's the difference between finding an ICU bed & ventilator or being treated in the parking lot tent.

12:47 AM · Feb 28, 2020

57   1.1K   1.4K   62

There are many strange things about this tweet and how it "went viral," suggesting that Dr. Harris was probably just a conduit for the propaganda-industrial-complex, which sent it out on that night, and then blasted it around the globe a few weeks later.

Here are some clues that support this hypothesis:

1. Dr. Harris's CV[239] shows an abrupt and heavily funded switch from podiatry to biodefense right after 9/11.
Training:

- 1983 Doctor of Podiatric Medicine (i.e., podiatrist — a doctor who treats feet)
- 1999 Master of Public Health

....

239 Drew A. Harris, D.P.M., M.P.H. Curriculum Vitae, hosted at https://www. jefferson.edu/content/dam/academic/cabe/faculty/faculty-documents/Harris-CV-11-20.pdf

Experience:

- 1984-2001 Podiatric Medicine, private practice
- 2001-2004 University of Medicine & Dentistry of New Jersey, Executive Director for Special Projects for Sr VP for Academic Affairs. Coordinator, UMDNJ's Bioterrorism response efforts
- 2004-2008 Director, Public Health Leadership Initiative for Emergency Response
- 2004-2008 Assistant Director, NJ Center for Public Health Preparedness at UMDNJ

According to Wikipedia:

The Centers for Public Health Preparedness (CPHP) program was established in 2000 by the Centers for Disease Control and Prevention (CDC) to strengthen bioterrorism and emergency preparedness by linking academic expertise to state and local health agency needs.

These centers were awarded through a competitive submission process...[2] to build a response to the events on September 11, 2001.

From 2004 to 2010, the CDC gave $134 million in funding to the Centers for Public Health Preparedness (CPHP) Cooperative Agreement program; 27 CPHPs within accredited schools of public health received the funds.[240]

- 2008-2010 President, NJ Association for Biomedical Research

This last item is very strange. What qualifies a podiatrist with a Masters in Public Health to head up a Biomedical Research Association? I'm reminded of BARDA – the Biomedical Advanced Research and Development Authority mentioned in the section on Senator Burr above, which was created in 2005 to develop countermeasures to bioterrorism.

Dr. Drew's funding also highlights the importance of bioterrorism

---

240 Wikipedia, "Center for Public Health Preparedness," accessed February 12, 2025.

response efforts in his career: Of the 15 items listed under 'SUPPORT,' eleven are between $5,000 and $50,000. Then there are three items related to the Center for Public Health Preparedness (see above), with a total value of over $2.3 million.

2. Dr. Drew claims a graph he saw in The Economist as one of his sources, but the graph appeared in an article dated February 29th – and can at most be backdated to the 27th.

The print edition of *The Economist,* dated February 27, 2020, featured an authorless article entitled "Going Global" — online title: "The virus Is coming."[241]

This article does not include any "flatten the curve" imagery. It uses the awkward term "flatten the spike" in discussing how China managed the pandemic.

It does, however, link to a second article: "Covid-19 is now in 50 countries, and things will get worse,"[242] dated February 29th, which contains this graphic:

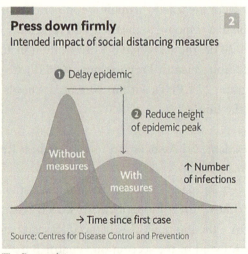

The Economist

....

241 *The Economist*, "The virus is coming."

242 *The Economist*, "Covid-19 is now in 50 countries, and things will get worse."

A March 27th *New York Times* article suggests that Dr. Harris managed to see the second article on February 27th (even though it's dated February 29th), fly from Portland, Oregon, to Philadelphia, redesign the graph, and tweet it out, all by a little after midnight:

> At the end of February, Drew Harris, a population health analyst at Thomas Jefferson University in Philadelphia, had just flown across the country to visit his daughter in Eugene, Ore., when he saw an article on his Google news feed. It was from *The Economist*, and was about limiting the damage of the coronavirus.
>
> Dr. Harris was waiting for his return flight in Portland when the first Oregon coronavirus case was announced; he had dinner at a busy airport bar and thought about how quiet the place would be in a week or two when the reality of the outbreak set in. Once home, he recreated his graphic and posted it on Twitter and LinkedIn, and was pleased to see the enthusiastic interest in flattening the curve.
>
> 'Now I know what going viral means,' Dr. Harris said.[243]

3. The famous tweet had minimal engagement on Dr. Harris's generally very low-engagement Twitter feed.

Here's what his Twitter profile looked like when I accessed it in December 2024:

Drew A. Harris
@drewaharris

#PopHealth, #HealthPolicy, thought leader, consultant, advocate, analyst, Mission: Be good, Do good. AKA @DrewAHarris on places that dare not speak their names.

◎ Philadelphia, PA   ⊘ Drewaharris.com   🗓 Joined February 2009

46 Following   **2,157** Followers

Not followed by anyone you're following

....

243 Roberts, "Flattening the Coronavirus Curve."

Most of his posts have little to no engagement, even now after he supposedly became a Covid hero. The "flatten the curve" post has 57 comments, none of which (as far as I can tell) were posted before March 6th. None of the comments has any engagement.

On March 13th there are multiple comments, stating that the post will appear in articles that day in: Fast Company, *Forbes*, the *Washington Post*, *People*, and NPR.

On LinkedIn[244] the same post has 4 comments and 13 reposts.

Somehow, this initially little-noticed tweet from February 27th became a global sensation.

Of particular note is that it was republished simultaneously in at least 5 different nationally prominent media outlets on March 13th, the date of President Trump's National Emergency Declaration, and the date of the *Pan-CAP-A* (discussed in detail in chapter 3).

I believe it is very difficult to dismiss all those simultaneous publications of a hitherto unnoticed tweet, magically created by a completely unknown individual with no social media presence, as coincidence.

CONCLUSION

As the "novel coronavirus" spread throughout the world in the early months of 2020, two diametrically opposed responses to such a virus were in play:

The public health response, which was initially followed everywhere except China, involved telling the public not to panic, wash hands, and stay home when sick. This was standard protocol for a novel flu-like virus. Chapter 2 provides a detailed discussion of what a public health response to Covid would have looked like.

Behind the scenes, the biodefense-industrial-complex was gearing up for its bioterrorism-inspired response: lockdown-until-vaccine.

On February 27th, the biodefense response went public. A few weeks later, much of the world went into lockdown, convinced by a global propaganda campaign that this was the only appropriate response.

....

244 Harris, LinkedIn post, https://www.linkedin.com/posts/drewaharris_covid-activity-6639033165660901376-JML4/

4.3 NYT PROPAGANDA: ACADEMIC LOSSES CAUSED BY LOCKDOWN POLICY, NOT PANDEMIC

My family used to get The New York Times *print edition delivered to our house every day. This continued through the first two years of Covid, during which I spent nearly every morning ranting about how much propaganda the newspaper was disseminating. It was particularly upsetting because alternative outlets were receiving negative truth ratings from "fact checkers" while* The New York Times *spouted distortions and lies with abandon. I wrote several pieces analyzing various insidious ways in which the propagandizing was accomplished. Shortly thereafter, my husband and I canceled our NYT delivery.*

• • •

On September 1, 2022, *The New York Times* ran a front page story[245] entitled: "The Pandemic Erased Two Decades of Progress in Math and Reading."

The Pandemic Erased Two Decades of Progress in Math and Reading

The results of a national test showed just how devastating the last two years have been for 9-year-old schoolchildren, especially the most vulnerable.

The first paragraph states that "National test results released on Thursday showed in stark terms the pandemic's devastating effects on American schoolchildren, with the performance of 9-year-olds in math and reading dropping to the levels from two decades ago."

Further down, the article says: "Then came the pandemic, which shuttered schools across the country almost overnight" and "experts say

....

245 Mervosh, "The Pandemic Erased Two Decades of Progress in Math and Reading."

it will take more than the typical school day to make up gaps created by the pandemic."

The definition of a pandemic, according to the Bulletin of the World Health Organization[246] (ref: Last JM, editor. A dictionary of epidemiology, 4th edition. New York: Oxford University Press; 2001) is "an epidemic occurring worldwide, or over a very wide area, crossing international boundaries and usually affecting a large number of people."

According to the Association for Professionals in Infection Control and Epidemiology, "an epidemic occurs when an infectious disease spreads rapidly to many people."

Thus, a pandemic is a disease that spreads rapidly to many people all over the world.

Based on this pretty much universally accepted definition, a pandemic can do exactly one thing: it can spread disease to many people around the world.

What can a pandemic NOT do?
- A pandemic cannot impose mandates or lockdowns.
- A pandemic cannot block borders or force people to stop traveling.
- A pandemic cannot shutter schools – overnight or otherwise.
- A pandemic cannot impact math and reading.
- A pandemic cannot cause learning gaps.

What can our response to a pandemic do?
If we decide to shut down schools for months and years on end in response to a pandemic, then it is our response that has caused whatever educational deficits and devastation to children ensue. It is not the pandemic.

In case there's any doubt that the effects of a pandemic are separate and distinct from society's response to the pandemic, we can take a look at Sweden, where schools were never shut down, and where there was no learning loss[247] and much less devastation to schoolchildren than in

---

246 Kelly, "The classical definition of a pandemic is not elusive."

247 Hallin et al., "No learning loss in Sweden during the pandemic: Evidence from primary school reading assessments."

countries that closed schools[248] during the Covid pandemic.

Blaming the pandemic for anything other than disease and/or death is misinformation.

The New York Times headline and article contain clear and uncontestable instances of misinformation.

Here is the information from the article, stated in a factually correct way:

US public health leaders and politicians mandated prolonged school shutdowns in response to the Covid pandemic, and these school shutdowns had devastating effects on schoolchildren, creating learning gaps and erasing decades of progress in math and reading.

....

248 Vira and Skoog, "Swedish middle school students' psychosocial well-being during the COVID-19 pandemic: A longitudinal study."

4.4 *NYT* PROPAGANDA: ZERO COVID ENDS BUT ZERO SENSE CONTINUES

China decided to finally drop its disastrous draconian zero-Covid policies. In response, major Western news outlets have revealed how completely and absolutely nonsensical their coverage of the pandemic in China has been from the very beginning.

A front-page article[249] in *The New York Times* from December 30, 2022, is a perfect example. The title: "How Bad is China's Covid Outbreak? It's a Scientific Guessing Game" seemingly makes sense. As the subhead explains, there is an "absence of credible information from the Chinese government," so it's difficult to figure out what's actually going on.

The rest of the article belies the notion that anything resembling sense has informed the reporters and editors at this once venerable newspaper of record.

Let's look at the claims in the article, starting with the first paragraph:

As Covid barrels through China, scientists around the world are searching for clues about an outbreak with sprawling consequences – for the health of hundreds of millions of Chinese people, the global economy and the future of the pandemic.

Here are the unproven – and, according to the headline and subhead of this article unprovable, – assumptions underlying these claims:

1) Covid is barreling through China. Says who? If there is no reliable data coming out of the country, how do we know there's any barreling going on? The word "barrels" is linked to a *New York Times* article about the confusion and chaos following the end of zero Covid policies. No proof of barreling.

....

249 Stevenson and Mueller, "How Bad is China's Covid Outbreak? It's a Scientific Guessing Game."

2) The unproven outbreak has sprawling consequences – why? The rest of the world has gone back more or less to normal, post-pandemic functioning, and China is attempting to do the same. Even if there are hundreds of millions of Covid cases in China, we know that the overall Covid mortality rate is extremely low[250] in all except the elderly and infirm, and as Western media (including the *NYT*) reported[251] ad nauseam in 2020, China built lots of extra capacity, so no reason to imagine its hospitals will be overrun.

Next paragraph:

> But in the absence of credible information from the Chinese government, it is a big scientific guessing game to determine the size and severity of the surge in the world's most populous country.

The overarching assumption in this paragraph, and in the entire article, is that there is a fundamental "absence of credible information from the Chinese government." Again, this assumption makes sense, given what we know about the Chinese government's manipulation of information[252] to serve its various agendas. It means that whatever China's leaders say about the pandemic in their country is not credible.

Yet just a few paragraphs down, the article makes these astonishing claims:

> Until this month, the world seemed to have a reasonably clear understanding of what was happening with the virus in China. The ruling Communist Party proudly published low daily case numbers and deaths as a testament to its stringent 'zero Covid' policy. A countrywide system of lockdowns, quarantines and mass testing

....

250 Pezzullo et al., "Age-stratified infection fatality rate of COVID-19 in the non-elderly population."

251 Qin, "China Pledged to Build a New Hospital in 10 Days. It's Close."

252 Senger, "Why Did Intellectuals and Officials Celebrate and Copy China's Lockdown Model?"

largely kept the virus at bay.

But in early December, the government abruptly abandoned 'zero Covid,' leaving the scientific community largely in the dark.

Wait, what?

When they were pursuing the clearly unattainable, unscientific and incredibly destructive zero Covid policies, the Chinese Communist Party (CCP) was completely credible, and all the data they published was 100 percent reliable? For example, this data, as presented in Michael Senger's excellent article[253] on this subject:

Total Coronavirus Deaths in China

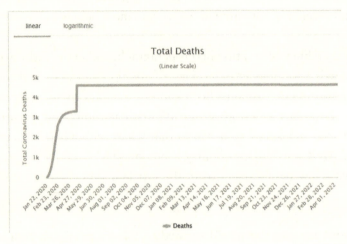

In case there's any doubt: This graph, based on the data reported by the CCP, shows no Covid deaths in China for two years, starting in March 2020. It means that, while the entire world was reportedly affected by an extremely contagious respiratory virus that caused millions of deaths, one country of 1.4 billion people managed to avoid it completely. That is the data that *The New York Times* and the scientific community deemed credible.

....

253 Senger, "China's Covid Numbers are Manifestly Absurd."

Then, suddenly, when the CCP decided to stop with the terrible, misguided, and destructive policies, their reported data is not credible and scientists are "in the dark" about what's happening in China?

The absurdity of these claims is so glaring, it should discredit anything anyone has to say about the data from China now, if they do not acknowledge that it was equally incredible from the very beginning. One cannot help but wonder: where are the fact-checkers when such levels of misinformation and blatant fear-mongering are published on the front page of *The New York Times*?

4.5 *NYT* PROPAGANDA: CIA AGENT CLOAKS LOCKDOWN PROPAGANDA IN CONCERN FOR CHINA

On January 24, 2023, Dr. Michael V. Callahan published an opinion piece in *The New York Times* entitled "The Indirect Ways the U.S. Can Help China Avoid Covid Catastrophe."[254]

If we assume this was written by a prominent doctor at a Harvard-affiliated hospital – an academic professional who bases his opinions on sound medical principles and scientific knowledge – it makes no sense at all. In fact, it is an embarrassment to the writer and the institution he represents.

If, however, we realize that this is just the latest in the lockdown-until-vaccine propaganda campaign of a CIA agent[255] and top biosecurity[256] intelligence operator, everything suddenly makes perfect sense.

The following are the medical and scientific fictions (or, if you prefer, lies) supposedly advocated by infectious-disease-physician Callahan, followed by an explanation of why CIA-agent/biosecurity-propagandist Callahan would want to promulgate them:

Fiction #1: Zero Covid works

Callahan opens his article with a bold statement: "China rolled back its longstanding pandemic strategy 'zero Covid,' which had protected the country for nearly three years." As many, including myself, have noted, there is no evidence – except the repeated statements of people like Callahan and the lockdown-narrative-promoting mainstream press[257] – for the fact that the "zero Covid" strategy protected anyone from anything.[258]

....

254 Callahan, "The Indirect Ways the U.S. Can Help China Avoid Covid Catastrophe."

255 Malone, "A Minority Report on Pandemic Origins."

256 Diego, "DARPA's Man in Wuhan."

257 British Broadcasting Corporation, "Trusted News Initiative."

258 Alexander, "More Than 400 Studies on the Failure of Compulsory Covid Interventions (Lockdowns, Restrictions, Closures)."

Callahan, who has worked for the intelligence community in Asia, knows (as we all should) that information from the Chinese Communist Party (CCP) is not reliable, to say the least. Therefore, there is no reason to think he believes the CCP's absurd claims that there were no Covid deaths in China for three years thanks to lockdowns.

So why is this his lede? Because the biosecurity propaganda machine has to maintain the illusion that lockdowns, at least to some degree, are effective, and that ending them is somehow undesirable.

Fiction #2: China's Lunar New Year is a very scary time

Callahan returns to a favorite trope of the lockdown-until-vaccine narrative from early 2020: the Lunar New Year in China. Due to "enormous" travel, "densely packed transit systems, winter conditions and multigenerational gatherings," Callahan tells us "the Lunar New Year is a common tabletop simulation for training public health officials." What about the real world? Do we have any proof that it was disastrous in 2020, as mainstream media warned,[259] or will be disastrous in 2023?

Furthermore, if Lunar New Year travel in 2020 already exported Covid far and wide (we know that by the time lockdowns were initiated in China on January 23, 2020, the virus had already spread to nearly every Chinese province,[260] and many other countries) – what use were lockdowns in one or two specific areas for containing its worldwide spread? And if it spread everywhere, including in China, despite lockdowns, how can we believe the "Zero deaths for three years" narrative?

Fiction #3: the most dangerous subvariant

Ever since Delta, variants and subvariants have provided a never-ending source of fear-mongering[261] for the lockdown-until-vaccine propagandists. In his op-ed, Callahan makes an unsubstantiated claim that the "subvariant XBB1.5" is "the most infectious to date." There is no reference, so I'm

....

259 Pasley, "People in China are making 3 billion trips to celebrate the Lunar New Year, and it's not going to help the Wuhan coronavirus outbreak."

260 WawumuStats, "Timeline of the Coronavirus by Map (Since January 2020)."

261 Lerman, "Why this Nonstop Fear Mongering?"

not sure where the information is from. I found one doctor[262] in North Carolina saying it "seems to be the most infectious" with no meaningful data to support the claim. A WHO official says[263] it's the "most transmissible" (again, no numbers or data) but adds "there's no indication it makes people more sick than previous subvariants."

As has been true for SARS-CoV-2 and every one of its mutations, and as is true for every infectious disease humanity has ever encountered: If it's not very lethal to most people, it can infect the entire world's population while causing very little serious disease or death.

Dr. Callahan knows this. Propagandist Callahan is using the tried and true biodefense network's tactic of constantly citing high case numbers (regardless of illness or death) to send the media and public into paroxysms of panic.

Fiction #4: vaccines work

Next, Callahan says the United States has a high vaccination rate using "highly protective vaccines." If he means against the original SARS-CoV-2 virus, Callahan might be able to dig up some evidence (though it is highly contestable). But if he means against this subvariant, he has zero evidence, and he knows it.

Fiction #5: some vaccines (ours) are better than others (theirs)

"Domestically made Chinese vaccines," according to Callahan, "may provide less lasting protection against the virus and its variants."

Since he says "may," this is clearly just a hypothesis. Since we know our vaccines provide at most a few months of protection from the original strain (again, a contestable statement) and none from any variant or subvariant thereafter, the meaning of "less lasting protection" basically is "less than zero," which again makes no sense.

However, as a member of the lockdown-until-vaccine biosecurity

....

262 Rivera, "XBB1.5: 'Of all the COVID variants, this one is the most infectious of them all' says NC health experts."

263 Kimball, "XBB.1.5 omicron subvariant is the most transmissible version of Covid yet, WHO says."

network, Callahan is using this piece of propaganda to bolster the case that lockdowns and vaccines work.

How anyone can believe such preposterous fiction is a mystery.

Postscript: a very scary non-fiction

The vast expansion of surveillance in general, and biosurveillance[264] in particular, is one of the biosecurity GPPP's biggest achievements during Covid, and Callahan manages to include a plug for more:

> In December, at least one online pharmacy in China began selling the Covid drug Paxlovid, made by the American pharmaceutical company Pfizer, directly to patients. The pharmacy shipped Paxlovid to any Chinese person with a positive coronavirus test. If the Beijing government were to tie the government's home test result reporting system to the commercial Paxlovid home delivery providers, many lives could be saved.

If anyone is wondering why it's important to debunk and expose all of the fictions and propaganda of the Covid biosecurity agenda, this tiny window into the terrifying vision they have for our future is the answer.

---

264 Kheriaty, "Why It Is Ethical To Resist the Biosecurity Surveillance State."

<u>4.6</u> INTERNET CENSORSHIP, EVERYWHERE ALL AT ONCE

After analyzing some pieces of glaring Covid propaganda in mainstream publications, I turned to the broader phenomenon of what is now known as the "censorship industrial complex." In this section, written at the beginning of 2024, I reported on the frightening simultaneous actions taken in multiple countries to censor content on the Internet, in the name of "preserving democracy."

• • •

It used to be a truth universally acknowledged by citizens of democratic nations, that freedom of speech was the basis not just of democracy, but of all human rights.

When a person or group can censor the speech of others, there is – by definition – an imbalance of power. Those exercising the power can decide what information and which opinions are allowed, and which should be suppressed. In order to maintain their power, they will naturally suppress information and views that challenge their position.

Free speech is the only peaceful way to hold those in power accountable, challenge potentially harmful policies, and expose corruption. Those of us privileged to live in democracies instinctively understand this nearly sacred value of free speech in maintaining our free and open societies.

Or do we?

Alarmingly, it seems like many people in what we call democratic nations are losing that understanding. And they seem willing to cede their freedom of speech to governments, organizations, and Big Tech companies who, supposedly, need to control the flow of information to keep everyone "safe."

The locus for the disturbing shift away from free speech is the 21st century's global public square: the Internet. And the proclaimed reasons for allowing those in power to diminish our free speech on the Internet are: "disinformation" and "hate speech."

In this section, I will review the three-step process by which anti-disinformation laws are introduced. Then, I will review some of the laws rolled out in multiple countries almost simultaneously, and what such laws entail in terms of vastly increasing the potential for censorship of the global flow of information.

How to Pass Censorship Laws

Step 1: Declare an existential threat to democracy and human rights
Step 2: Assert that the solution will protect democracy and human rights
Step 3: Enact anti-democratic, anti-human rights censorship fast and in unison

Lies, propaganda, "deep fakes," and all manner of misleading information have always been present on the Internet. The vast global information hub that is the World Wide Web inevitably provides opportunities for criminals and other nefarious actors, including child sex traffickers and evil dictators.

At the same time, the Internet has become the central locus of open discourse for the world's population, democratizing access to information and the ability to publish one's views to a global audience.

The good and bad on the Internet reflect the good and bad in the real world. And when we regulate the flow of information on the Internet, the same careful balance between blocking truly dangerous actors, while retaining maximum freedom and democracy, must apply.

Distressingly, a recent slew of laws governing Internet information are significantly skewed in the direction of limiting free speech and increasing censorship. The reason, the regulators claim, is that fake news, disinformation, and hate speech are existential threats to democracy and human rights.

Here are examples of dire warnings, issued by leading international organizations, about catastrophic threats to our very existence purportedly posed by disinformation:

> Propaganda, misinformation and fake news have the potential to polarise public opinion, to promote violent extremism and hate speech and, ultimately, to undermine democracies and reduce trust in the democratic processes. –Council of Europe[265]

....

265 Council of Europe, "Dealing with propaganda, misinformation and fake news."

The world must address the grave global harm caused by the proliferation of hate and lies in the digital space. –United Nations[266]

Online hate speech and disinformation have long incited violence, and sometimes mass atrocities. –World Economic Forum (WEF)/ The New Humanitarian[267]

Considering the purported existential peril of disinformation and hate speech, these same groups assert that any solution will obviously promote the opposite:

Given such a global threat, we clearly need a global solution. And, of course, such a solution will increase democracy, protect the rights of vulnerable populations, and respect human rights. –WEF[268]

Moreover, beyond a mere assertion that increasing democracy and respecting human rights are built into combating disinformation, international law must be invoked.

In its Common Agenda Policy Brief from June 2023, "Information Integrity on Digital Platforms,"[269] the UN details the international legal framework for efforts to counter hate speech and disinformation.

First, it reminds us that freedom of expression and information are fundamental human rights:

Article 19 of the Universal Declaration of Human Rights and article 19 (2) of the Covenant protect the right to freedom of expression,

....

266 United Nations, "Guardrails Urgently Needed to Contain 'Clear and Present Global Threat' of Online Mis- and Disinformation and Hate Speech, says UN Secretary-General."

267 Stremlau and De Gregorio, "Why we need an international body to rein in hate speech during conflict."

268 World Economic Forum, "The Clear and Present Danger of Disinformation."

269 United Nations, *Our Common Agenda Policy Brief 8: Information Integrity on Digital Platforms*, June 2023.

including the freedom to seek, receive and impart information and ideas of all kinds, regardless of frontiers, and through any media.

Linked to freedom of expression, freedom of information is itself a right. The General Assembly has stated: "Freedom of information is a fundamental human right and is the touchstone of all the freedoms to which the United Nations is consecrated." (p. 9)

Then, the UN brief explains that disinformation and hate speech are such colossal, all-encompassing evils that their very existence is antithetical to the enjoyment of any human rights:

Hate speech has been a precursor to atrocity crimes, including genocide. The 1948 Convention on the Prevention and Punishment of the Crime of Genocide prohibits 'direct and public incitement to commit genocide.'

In its resolution 76/227, adopted in 2021, the General Assembly emphasized that all forms of disinformation can negatively impact the enjoyment of human rights and fundamental freedoms, as well as the attainment of the Sustainable Development Goals. Similarly, in its resolution 49/21, adopted in 2022, the Human Rights Council affirmed that disinformation can negatively affect the enjoyment and realization of all human rights.

This convoluted maze of legalese leads to an absurd, self-contradictory sequence of illogic:

- Everything the UN is supposed to protect is founded on the freedom of information, which along with free speech is a fundamental human right.
- The UN believes hate speech and disinformation destroy all human rights.
- THEREFORE, anything we do to combat hate speech and disinformation protects all human rights, even if it abrogates the fundamental human rights of free speech and information, on which all other rights depend.
- Because: genocide!

In practice, what this means is that, although the UN at one point in its history considered the freedom of speech and information fundamental to all other rights, it now believes the dangers of hate speech and disinformation eclipse the importance of protecting those rights.

The same warping of democratic values, as delineated by our international governing body, is now occurring in democracies the world over.

Censorship Laws and Actions All Happening at Once

If hate speech and disinformation are the precursors of inevitable genocidal horrors, the only way to protect the world is through a coordinated international effort. Who should lead this campaign?

According to the WEF,[270] "Governments can provide some of the most significant solutions to the crisis by enacting far-reaching regulations."

Which is exactly what they're doing.

United States

In the US, freedom of speech is enshrined in the Constitution, so it's hard to pass laws that might violate it.

Instead, the government can work with academic and nongovernmental organizations to strong-arm social media companies into censoring disfavored content. The result is the Censorship-Industrial Complex,[271] a vast network of government-adjacent academic and nonprofit "anti-disinformation" outfits, all ostensibly mobilized to control online speech in order to protect us from whatever they consider to be the next civilization-annihilating calamity.

The Twitter Files and several court cases reveal how the U.S. government uses these groups to pressure online platforms to censor content it doesn't like.

---

270 Romeo, "Disinformation is a growing crisis. Governments, business and individuals can help stem the tide."

271 Schmidt et al., "Report on the Censorship-Industrial Complex: The Top 50 Organizations to Know."

[Twitter Files on Covid[272]
Discovery in Missouri v Biden Covid censorship lawsuit[273]
Potential discovery in Berenson v. Biden lawsuit[274]]

Google

In some cases, companies may even take it upon themselves to control the narrative according to their own politics and professed values, with no need for government intervention. For example: Google, the most powerful information company in the world, has been reported to fix its algorithms to promote, demote, and disappear content according to undisclosed internal "fairness" guidelines.

This was revealed by a whistleblower named Zach Vorhies[275] in his almost completely ignored book, *Google Leaks*,[276] and by Project Veritas, in a sting operation against Jen Gennai,[277] Google's Head of Responsible Innovation.

In their benevolent desire to protect us from hate speech and disinformation, Google/YouTube immediately removed[278] the original Project Veritas video from the Internet.

European Union

The Digital Services Act[279] came into force November 16, 2022. The European Commission[280] rejoiced that "The responsibilities of users,

....

272 Zweig (@davidzweig), "The Twitter Files: How Twitter Rigged The Covid Debate."

273 Kheriaty, "The Censors are Exposed: Major Update to Missouri v. Biden from Tracy Beanz."

274 Brownstone Institute, "Berenson v. Biden: The Potential and Significance."

275 Vorhies, "Google Leaks: Censorship Exposed."

276 Vorhies and Heckenlively, *Google Leaks*.

277 Project Veritas, "Jen Gennai - Google."

278 AllSides, "YouTube Removes Project Veritas Video on Google Bias."

279 European Commission, "The Digital Services Act package."

280 European Commission, "The Digital Services Act."

platforms, and public authorities are rebalanced according to European values." Who decides what the responsibilities and what the "European values" are?

- very large platforms and very large online search engines [are obligated] to prevent the misuse of their systems by taking risk-based action and by independent audits of their risk management systems
- EU countries will have the primary [oversight] role, supported by a new European Board for Digital Services

Brownstone Institute contributor David Thunder explains how the act provides an essentially unlimited potential for censorship:

This piece of legislation holds freedom of speech hostage to the ideological proclivities of unelected European officials and their armies of "trusted flaggers."

The European Commission is also giving itself the power to declare a Europe-wide emergency that would allow it to demand extra interventions by digital platforms to counter a public threat.[281]

UK

The Online Safety Bill[282] was passed September 19, 2023. The UK government says "It will make social media companies more responsible for their users' safety on their platforms."

According to Internet watchdog *Reclaim the Net*, this bill constitutes one of the widest sweeping attacks on privacy and free speech in a Western democracy:

The bill imbues the government with tremendous power; the capability to demand that online services employ government-approved software to scan through user content, including photos, files, and

---

281 Thunder, "You Should Be Very Worried About the Digital Services Act."
282 U.K. Government, "A guide to the Online Safety Bill."

messages, to identify illegal content.[283]

The Electronic Frontier Foundation,[284] a nonprofit dedicated to defending civil liberties in the digital world, warns: "the law would create a blueprint for repression around the world."

Australia

The Communications Legislation Amendment (Combatting Misinformation and Disinformation) Bill 2023 was released in draft form June 25, 2023 and was expected to pass by the end of 2023. It was ultimately defeated a year later.

It is instructive to note how the Australian government tried to justify the bill:

> The new powers will enable the ACMA [Australian Communications and Media Authority] to monitor efforts and require digital platforms to do more, placing Australia at the forefront in tackling harmful online misinformation and disinformation, while balancing freedom of speech.[285]

Reclaim the Net explains:

> This legislation hands over a wide range of new powers to ACMA, which includes the enforcement of an industry-wide "standard" that will obligate digital platforms to remove what they determine

---

283 Frieth, "The UK Passes Sweeping New Surveillance and Censorship Measures in The Online Safety Bill."

284 Electronic Frontier Foundation, "The UK Online Safety Bill: A Massive Threat to Online Privacy, Security, and Speech."

285 Australian Department of Infrastructure, Transport, Regional Development, Communications and the Arts, "New ACMA powers to combat misinformation and disinformation."

as misinformation or disinformation.[286]

Australian journalist Rebekah Barnett elaborates:

> Controversially, the government will be exempt from the proposed
> laws, as will professional news outlets, meaning that ACMA will
> not compel platforms to police misinformation and disinformation
> disseminated by official government or news sources.
>
> The legislation will enable the proliferation of official narratives,
> whether true, false or misleading, while quashing the opportunity
> for dissenting narratives to compete.[287]

Canada

The Online Streaming Act (Bill C-10) became law April 27, 2023. Here's
how the Canadian government describes it, as it relates to the Canadian
Radio-television and Telecommunications Commission (CRTC):

> The legislation clarifies that online streaming services fall under the
> Broadcasting Act and ensures that the CRTC has the proper tools
> to put in place a modern and flexible regulatory framework for
> broadcasting. These tools include the ability to make rules, gather
> information, and assign penalties for non-compliance.[288]

According to Open Media, a community-driven digital rights organization,

> Bill C-11 gives the CRTC unprecedented regulatory authority to
> monitor all online audiovisual content. This power extends to
> penalizing content creators and platforms and through them, content
> creators that fail to comply.[289]

....

286 Maas, "TV Networks Join The Pushback Against Australia's Proposed Anti-
"Misinformation" Law."

287 Barnett, "Australia's Misinfo Bill Paves Way for Soviet-Style Censorship."

288 Government of Canada, "Online Streaming Act."

289 Bhuller, "What's wrong with Bill C-11."

World Health Organization

In its proposed new Pandemic Treaty and in the amendments to its International Health Regulations, all of which it hopes to pass in 2024, the WHO seeks to enlist member governments to:

> Counter and address the negative impacts of health-related misinformation, disinformation, hate speech and stigmatization, especially on social media platforms, on people's physical and mental health, in order to strengthen pandemic prevention, preparedness and response, and foster trust in public health systems and authorities.[290]

David Bell, Senior Scholar at Brownstone Institute, is a public health physician and biotech consultant in global health. He is also a former medical officer and scientist at the World Health Organization (WHO), and he writes that essentially this will give the WHO, an unelected international body,

> power to designate opinions or information as 'mis-information or disinformation, and require country governments to intervene and stop such expression and dissemination. This…is, of course, incompatible with the Universal Declaration of Human Rights, but these seem no longer to be guiding principles for the WHO.[291]

CONCLUSION

We are at a pivotal moment in the history of Western democracies. Governments, organizations, and companies have more power than ever to decide what information and views are expressed on the Internet, the global public square of information and ideas.

It is natural that those in power should want to limit expression of ideas and dissemination of information that might challenge their position.

....

290 World Health Organization, "WHO welcomes historic commitment by world leaders for greater collaboration, governance and investment to prevent, prepare for and respond to future pandemics."

291 Bell, "Amendments to WHO's International Health Regulations: An Annotated Guide."

They may believe they are using censorship to protect us from grave harms of disinformation and hate speech, or they may be using those reasons cynically to consolidate their control over the flow of information.

Either way, censorship inevitably entails the suppression of free speech and information, without which democracy cannot exist.

Why are the citizens of democratic nations acquiescing to the usurpation of their fundamental human rights? One reason may be the relatively abstract nature of rights and freedoms in the digital realm.

In the past, when censors burned books or jailed dissidents, citizens could easily recognize these harms and imagine how awful it would be if such negative actions were turned against them. They could also weigh the very personal and imminent negative impact of widespread censorship against much less prevalent dangers, such as child sex trafficking or genocide. Not that those dangers would be ignored or downplayed, but it would be clear that measures to combat such dangers should not include widespread book burning or jailing of regime opponents.

In the virtual world, if it's not your post that is removed, or your video that is banned, it can be difficult to fathom the wide-ranging harm of massive online information control and censorship. It is also much easier online than in the real world to exaggerate the dangers of relatively rare threats, like pandemics or foreign interference in democratic processes. The same powerful people, governments, and companies that can censor online information can also flood the online space with propaganda,[292] terrifying citizens in the virtual space into giving up their real-world rights.

The conundrum for free and open societies has always been the same: How to protect human rights and democracy from hate speech and disinformation without destroying human rights and democracy in the process.

The answer embodied in the recent coordinated enactment of global censorship laws is not encouraging for the future of free and open societies.

....

292 Malone, "Propaganda and the U.S. Government."

4.7 GOVERNMENT FUNDS AI TOOLS FOR WHOLE-OF-INTERNET SURVEILLANCE AND CENSORSHIP

I feel scared. Very scared.

Internet-wide surveillance and censorship, enabled by the unimaginably vast computational power of artificial intelligence (AI), is here.

This is not a futuristic dystopia. It's happening now.

Government agencies are working with universities and nonprofits to use AI tools to surveil and censor content on the Internet.

This is not political or partisan. This is not about any particular opinion or idea.

What's happening is that a tool powerful enough to surveil everything that's said and done on the Internet (or large portions of it) is becoming available to the government to monitor all of us, all the time. And, based on that monitoring, the government – and any organization or company the government partners with – can then use the same tool to suppress, silence, and shut down whatever speech it doesn't like.

But that's not all. Using the same tool, the government and its public-private, "non-governmental" partners (think, for example: the World Health Organization, or Monsanto) can also shut down any activity that is linked to the Internet. Banking, buying, selling, teaching, learning, entertaining, connecting to each other – if the government-controlled AI does not like what you (or your kids!) say in a tweet or an email, it can shut down all of that for you.

Yes, we've seen this on a very local and politicized scale with, for example, the Canadian truckers.[293]

But if we thought this type of activity could not, or would not, happen on a national (or even scarier – global) scale, we need to wake up right now and realize it's happening, and it might not be stoppable.

....

293 Tucker, "And Now, It's Economic Warfare."

February 2024 Documents Show Government-Funded AI Intended for Online Censorship

The U.S. House Select Subcommittee on the Weaponization of the Federal Government[294] was formed in January 2023 "to investigate matters related to the collection, analysis, dissemination, and use of information on U.S. citizens by executive branch agencies, including whether such efforts are illegal, unconstitutional, or otherwise unethical."

Unfortunately, the work of the committee is viewed, even by its own members, as largely political: Conservative lawmakers are investigating what they perceive to be the silencing of conservative voices by liberal-leaning government agencies.

Nevertheless, in its investigations, this committee has uncovered some astonishing documents related to government attempts to censor the speech of American citizens.

These documents have crucial and terrifying all-of-society implications.

In the Subcommittee's interim report, dated February 5, 2024,[295] documents show that academic and nonprofit groups are pitching a government agency on a plan to use AI "misinformation services" to censor content on internet platforms.

Specifically, the University of Michigan is explaining to the National Science Foundation (NSF) that the AI-powered tools funded by the NSF can be used to help social media platforms perform censorship activities without having to actually make the decisions on what should be censored.

Here's how the relationship is visualized in the Subcommittee's report:

....

294 Establishment of the Select Subcommittee on the Weaponization of the Federal Government, H.R.12, 118th Cong. (2023-2024)

295 Committee on the Judiciary and the Select Subcommittee on the Weaponization of the Federal Government, *The Weaponization of the National Science Foundation: How NSF is Funding the Development of Automated Tools to Censor Online Speech "At Scale" and Trying to Cover Up its Actions*, February 5, 2024.

Here's a specific quote presented in the Subcommittee's report. It comes from "Speaker's notes from the University of Michigan's first pitch to the National Science Foundation (NSF) about its NSF-funded, AI-powered WiseDex tool." The notes are on file with the committee.

> Our misinformation service helps policy makers at platforms who want to...push responsibility for difficult judgments to someone outside the company...by externalizing the difficult responsibility of censorship.

This is an extraordinary statement on so many levels:

1. It explicitly equates "misinformation service" with censorship.
This is a crucial equation, because governments worldwide are pretending to combat harmful misinformation when in fact they are passing massive censorship bills (as discussed in the previous section). In 2024, the WEF declared "misinformation and disinformation" the biggest short-term risk" in the next two years[296], which presumably means their biggest efforts will go toward censorship.

When a government contractor explicitly states that it is selling a "misinformation service" that helps online platforms "externalize censorship" – the two terms are acknowledged as being interchangeable.

....

296 Heading, "These are the biggest global risks we face in 2024 and beyond."

2. It refers to censorship as a "responsibility."

In other words, it assumes that part of what the platforms should be doing is censorship. Not protecting children from sex predators or innocent citizens from misinformation – just plain and simple, unadulterated censorship.

3. It states that the role of AI is to "externalize" the responsibility for censorship.

The Tech platforms do not want to make censorship decisions. The government wants to make those decisions but does not want to be seen as censoring. The AI tools allow the platforms to "externalize" the censorship decisions and the government to hide its censorship activities.

All of this should end the illusion that what governments around the world are calling "countering misinformation and hate speech" is not straight-up censorship.

What Happens When AI Censorship Is Fully Implemented?

Knowing that the government is already paying for AI censorship tools, we have to wrap our minds around what this entails.

No manpower limits: As the Subcommittee report points out, the limits to government online censorship have, up to now, involved the large numbers of humans required to go through endless files and make censorship decisions. With AI, barely any humans need to be involved, and the amount of data that can be surveilled can be as vast as everything anyone says on a particular platform. That amount of data is incomprehensible to an individual human brain.

No one is responsible: One of the most frightening aspects of AI censorship is that when AI does it, there is no human being or organization – be it the government, the platforms, or the university/nonprofits – who is actually responsible for the censorship. Initially, humans feed the AI tool instructions for what categories or types of language to censor, but then the machine goes ahead and makes the case-by-case decisions all by itself.

No recourse for grievances: Once AI is unleashed with a set of censorship instructions, it will sweep up gazillions of online data points and apply censorship actions. If you want to contest an AI censorship action, you will have to talk to the machine. Maybe the platforms will employ humans to respond to appeals. But why would they do that, when they have AI that can automate those responses?

No protection for young people: One of the claims made by government censors is that we need to protect our children from harmful online information, like content that makes them anorexic, encourages them to commit suicide, turns them into ISIS terrorists, and so on. Also from sexual exploitation. These are all serious issues that deserve attention. But they are not nearly as dangerous to vast numbers of young people as AI censorship is.

The danger posed by AI censorship applies to all young people who spend a lot of time online, because it means their online activities and language can be monitored and used against them – maybe not now, but whenever the government decides to go after a particular type of language or behavior. This is a much greater danger to a much greater number of children than the danger posed by any specific content, because it encompasses all the activity they conduct online, touching on nearly every aspect of their lives.

Here's an example to illustrate this danger: Let's say your teenager plays lots of interactive video games online. Let's say he happens to favor games designed by Chinese companies. Maybe he also watches others play those games, and participates in chats and discussion groups about those games, in which a lot of Chinese nationals also participate.

The government may decide next month, or next year, that anyone heavily engaged in Chinese-designed video games is a danger to democracy. This might result in shutting down your son's social media accounts or denying him access to financial tools, like college loans. It might also involve flagging him on employment or dating websites as dangerous or undesirable. It might mean he is denied a passport or put on a watchlist.

Your teenager's life just got a lot more difficult. Much more difficult than if he was exposed to an ISIS recruitment video or suicide-glorifying TikTok post. And this would happen on a much larger scale than the sexual exploitation the censors are using[297] as a Trojan Horse for normalizing the idea of online government censorship.

Monetize-able censorship services: An AI tool owned by the government can theoretically be used by a non-governmental entity with the government's permission, and with the blessing of the platforms that want to "externalize" the "responsibility" for censorship. So while the government might be using AI to monitor and suppress, let's say as an example, anti-war sentiment – a company could use it to monitor and suppress, let's say as an example, anti-fast food sentiment. The government could make a lot of money selling the services of the AI tools to third parties. The platforms could also conceivably ask for a cut. Thus, AI censorship tools can potentially benefit the government, tech platforms, and private corporations. The incentives are so powerful, it's almost impossible to imagine that they will not be exploited.

Can We Reverse Course?

I do not know how many government agencies and how many platforms are using AI censorship tools. I do not know how quickly they can scale up.

I do not know what tools we have at our disposal – other than raising awareness and trying to lobby politicians and file lawsuits to prevent government censorship and regulate the use of AI tools on the internet.

If anyone has any other ideas, now would be the time to implement them.

....

297 Shepardson and Brice, "Tech CEOs told 'you have blood on your hands' at U.S. Senate child safety hearing."

4.8 THE CLOSING OF THE INTERNET MIND

This section was co-authored by members of the Brownstone Working Group on Censorship and Propaganda: Jeffrey Tucker, Aaron Kheriaty, Andrew Lowenthal, and Debbie Lerman. It was first published in The American Mind.[298]

• • •

The definition of online freedom has been depressingly constricted over the last thirty years.

You have surely heard that your search results[299] on Google (with 92 percent share of the search market) reflect not your curiosities and needs but someone or something else's views on what you need to know. That's hardly a secret.

And on Facebook, you are likely inundated by links to official sources to correct any errors you might carry in your head, as well as links to corrections to posts as made by any number of fact-checking organizations.

You have likely also heard of YouTube videos being taken down, apps deleted from stores, and accounts being canceled across a variety of platforms.

You might have even adjusted your behavior in light of all of this. It is part of the new culture of Internet engagement. The line you cannot cross is invisible. You are like a dog with an electric shock collar. You have to figure it out on your own, which means exercising caution when you post, pulling back on hard claims that might shock, paying attention to media culture to discern what is sayable and what is not, and generally trying to avoid controversy as best you can in order to earn the privilege of not being canceled.

Despite all the revelations[300] regarding the Censorship Industrial Complex, and the wide involvement of government in these efforts, plus

....

298 Kheriaty et al., "The Closing of the Internet Mind."

299 White, "Google.gov(.)"

300 Kheriaty, "Slaying the Censorship Leviathan."

the resulting lawsuits[301] that claim that this is all censorship, the walls are clearly closing in further by the day.

Users are growing accustomed to it, for fear of losing their accounts. For example, YouTube (which feeds 55 percent of all video content online) allows three strikes before your account is deleted permanently. One strike is devastating and two existential. You are frozen in place and forced to relinquish everything–including your ability to earn a living if your content is monetized – if you make one or two wrong moves.

No one needs to censor you at that point. You censor yourself.

It was not always this way. It was not even supposed to be this way.

It's possible to trace the dramatic change from the past to the present by following the trajectory of various Declarations that have been issued over the years. The tone was set at the dawn of the World Wide Web in 1996 by digital guru, Grateful Dead lyricist, and Harvard University fellow John Perry Barlow, who died in 2018.

Barlow's Declaration of the Independence of Cyberspace, somewhat ironically written in Davos, Switzerland, is still hosted[302] by the Electronic Frontier Foundation that he founded. The manifesto waxes lyrical about the liberatory, open future of internet freedom:

> *Governments of the Industrial World, you weary giants of flesh and steel, I come from Cyberspace, the new home of Mind. On behalf of the future, I ask you of the past to leave us alone. You are not welcome among us. You have no sovereignty where we gather.*
>
> *We have no elected government, nor are we likely to have one, so I address you with no greater authority than that with which liberty itself always speaks. I declare the global social space we are building to be naturally independent of the tyrannies you seek to impose on us. You have no moral right to rule us nor do you possess any methods of enforcement we have true reason to fear.*
>
> *Governments derive their just powers from the consent of the*

....

301 Kheriaty, "The White House's 'Misinformation' Pressure Campaign Was Unconstitutional."

302 Barlow, "A Declaration of the Independence of Cyberspace."

governed. You have neither solicited nor received ours. We did not invite you. You do not know us, nor do you know our world. Cyberspace does not lie within your borders. Do not think that you can build it, as though it were a public construction project. You cannot. It is an act of nature and it grows itself through our collective actions.

And so on it went with a heady, expansive vision – tinged perhaps with a dash of sixties utopian anarchism – that shaped the ethos which drove the building of the Internet in the early days. It appeared to a whole generation of coders and content providers that a new world of freedom had been born that would shepherd in a new era of freedom more generally, with growing knowledge, human rights, creative freedom, and borderless connection of everyone to literature, facts, and truth emerging organically from a crowd-sourced process of engagement.

Nearly a decade and a half later, by 2012, that idea was fully embraced by the main architects of the emergent app economy and the explosion of smartphone use across the world. The result was the Declaration of Internet Freedom which went live in July 2012[303] and garnered a great deal of press attention at the time. Signed by the EFF, Amnesty International, Reporters Without Borders, and other liberty-focused organizations, it read:

---

303 Declaration of Internet Freedom, archived July 2, 2012.

DECLARATION

W̲e stand for a free and open Internet.

We support transparent and participatory processes for making Internet policy and the establishment of five basic principles:

Expression: Don't censor the Internet.

Access: Promote universal access to fast and affordable networks.

Openness: Keep the Internet an open network where everyone is free to connect, communicate, write, read, watch, speak, listen, learn, create and innovate.

Innovation: Protect the freedom to innovate and create without permission. Don't block new technologies and don't punish innovators for their users' actions.

Privacy: Protect privacy and defend everyone's ability to control how their data and devices are used

To be sure, it was not quite as sweeping and visionary as the Barlow original but maintained the essence, putting free expression as the first principle with the lapidary phrase: "Don't censor the Internet." It might have stopped there, but given the existing threats coming from growing industrial cartels and the stored-data marketplace, it also pushed openness, innovation, and privacy as first principles.

Again, this outlook defined an era and elicited broad agreement. "Information freedom supports the peace and security that provides a foundation for global progress," said[304] Hillary Clinton in an endorsement of the freedom principle in 2010. The 2012 Declaration was neither right-wing nor left-wing. It encapsulated the core of what it meant to favor freedom on the Internet, exactly as the title suggests.

If you go to the site internetdeclaration.org now, your browser will not reveal any of its contents. The secure certificate is dead. If you bypass

----

304 Clinton, "Remarks on Internet Freedom," The Newseum, Washington DC. January 21, 2010.

the warning, you will find yourself forbidden from accessing any of the contents. The tour through Archive.org shows that the last living presentation of the site was in February 2018.[305]

This occurred three years after Donald Trump publicly advocated[306] that "in some places" we have to talk about "closing up the Internet." He got his wish, but it came after him personally following his election in 2016. The very free speech about which he made fun turned out to be rather important to him and his cause.

Two years into the Trump presidency, precisely as the censorship industry started coalescing into full operation, the site of the Declaration site broke down and eventually disappeared.

Fast forward a decade from the writing of the Internet Declaration of Freedom. The year is 2022 and we had been through a rough two years of account takedowns, particularly against those who doubted the wisdom of lockdowns or vaccine mandates. The White House revealed on April 22, 2022 a Declaration for the Future of the Internet.[307] It comes complete with a parchment-style presentation and a large capital letter in old-fashioned script. The word "freedom" is removed from the title and added only as a part of the word salad that follows in the text.

A DECLARATION *for the* FUTURE *of the* INTERNET

*W*e are united by a belief in the potential of digital technologies to promote connectivity, democracy, peace, the rule of law, sustainable development, and the enjoyment of human rights and fundamental freedoms. As we increasingly work, communicate, connect, engage, learn, and enjoy leisure time using digital technologies, our reliance on an open, free, global, interoperable, reliable, and secure Internet will continue to grow. Yet we are also aware of the risks inherent in that reliance and the challenges we face.

We call for a new Declaration for the Future of the Internet that includes all partners who actively support a future for the Internet that is an open, free, global, interoperable, reliable, and secure. We further affirm our commitment to protecting and respecting human rights online and across the digital ecosystem. Partners in this Declaration intend to work toward an environment that reinforces our democratic systems and promotes active participation of every citizen in democratic processes, secures and protects individuals' privacy, maintains secure and reliable connectivity, resists efforts to splinter the global Internet, and promotes a free and competitive global economy. Partners in this Declaration invite other partners who share this vision to join us in working together, with civil society and other stakeholders, to affirm guiding principles for our role in the future of the global Internet.

---

305 Declaration of Internet Freedom, archived February 11, 2018.

306 Statt, "Donald Trump thinks he can call Bill Gates to 'close up' the internet."

307 The White House, "A Declaration for the Future of the Internet," archived April 28, 2022.

Signed by 60 nations, the new Declaration was released to great fanfare, including a White House press release.[308] The signatory nations, in addition to the United States, were all NATO-aligned while excluding others. The signatories are: Albania, Andorra, Argentina, Australia, Austria, Belgium, Bulgaria, Cabo Verde, Canada, Colombia, Costa Rica, Croatia, Cyprus, Czech Republic, Denmark, Dominican Republic, Estonia, the European Commission, Finland, France, Georgia, Germany, Greece, Hungary, Iceland, Ireland, Israel, Italy, Jamaica, Japan, Kenya, Kosovo, Latvia, Lithuania, Luxembourg, Maldives, Malta, Marshall Islands, Micronesia, Moldova, Montenegro, Netherlands, New Zealand, Niger, North Macedonia, Palau, Peru, Poland, Portugal, Romania, Serbia, Slovakia, Slovenia, Spain, Sweden, Taiwan, Trinidad and Tobago, the United Kingdom, Ukraine, and Uruguay.

The core of the new declaration is very clear and represents a good encapsulation of the essence of the structures that govern content today: "The Internet should operate as a single, decentralized network of networks – with global reach and governed through the multi-stakeholder approach, whereby governments and relevant authorities partner with academics, civil society, the private sector, technical community and others."

The term "stakeholder" (as in "stakeholder capitalism") became popular in the nineties as distinct from "shareholder" meaning a partial owner. A stakeholder is not an owner or even a consumer but a party or institution with a strong interest in the outcome of the decision-making by the owners, whose rights might need to be overridden in the broader interests of everyone. In this way, the term came to describe an amorphous group of influential third parties that deserve a say in the management of institutions and systems. A "multi-stakeholder" approach is how civil society is brought inside the tent, with financing and seeming influence, and told that they matter as an incentive to woke-wash their outlooks and operations.

Using that linguistic fulcrum, part of the goal of the new Declaration is explicitly political: "Refrain from using the Internet to undermine the

....

308 The White House, Press Release, "Fact Sheet: United States and 60 Global Partners Launch Declaration for the Future of the Internet," April 28, 2022.

electoral infrastructure, elections and political processes, including through covert information manipulation campaigns." From this admonition we can conclude that the new Internet is structured to discourage "manipulation campaigns" and even goes so far as to "foster greater social and digital inclusion within society, bolster resilience to disinformation and misinformation, and increase participation in democratic processes."

Following the latest in censorship language, every form of top-down blockage and suppression is now justified in the name of fostering inclusion (that is, "DEI," as in Diversity [3 mentions], Equity [2 mentions], and Inclusion [5 mentions]) and stopping dis- and mis-information, language identical to that invoked by the Cybersecurity Infrastructure Security Agency (CISA) and the rest of the industrial complex that operates to stop information spread.

This agency was created in the waning days of the Obama administration and approved by Congress in 2018, supposedly to protect our digital infrastructure against cyberattacks from computer viruses and nefarious foreign actors. But less than one year into its existence, CISA decided that our election infrastructure was part of our critical infrastructure (thereby asserting Federal control over elections, which are typically handled by the states). Furthermore, part of protecting our election infrastructure included protecting what CISA director Jen Easterly called our "cognitive infrastructure."

Easterly, who formerly worked at Tailored Access Operations, a top-secret cyber warfare unit at the National Security Agency, coined the queen of all Orwellian euphemisms: "cognitive infrastructure," which refers to the thoughts inside your head. This is precisely what the government's counter-disinformation apparatus, headed by people like Easterly, is attempting to control. True to this stated aim, CISA pivoted by 2020 to become the nerve center of the government's censorship apparatus – the agency through which all government and "stakeholder" censorship demands are funneled to social media companies.

Now consider what we've learned about Wikipedia, which is owned by Wikimedia, the former CEO of which was Katherine Maher, now the President and CEO of National Public Radio. She has been a consistent and public defender of censorship, even suggesting[309] that the First Amendment is "the number one challenge."

The co-founder of Wikipedia, Larry Sanger, has said[310] he suspects that she turned Wikipedia into an intelligence-operated platform. "We know that there is a lot of backchannel communication," he said in an interview. "I think it has to be the case that the Wikimedia Foundation now, probably governments, probably the CIA, have accounts that they control, in which they actually exert their influence. And it's fantastic, in a bad way, that she actually comes out against the system for being 'free and open.' When she says that she's worked with government to shut down what they consider 'misinformation,' that, in itself, means that it's no longer free and open."

What happened to Wikipedia, which all search engines privilege among all results, has befallen nearly every prominent venue on the Internet. The Elon Musk takeover of Twitter has proven to be aberrant and highly costly in terms of advertising dollars, and hence elicits vast opposition from the venues that are on the other side. That his renamed platform X even exists at all seems to run contrary to every wish of the controlled and controlling establishment today.

We have traveled a very long way from the vision of John Perry Barlow in 1996, who imagined a cyberworld in which governments were not involved to one in which governments and their "multi-stakeholder partners" are in charge of "a rules-based global digital economy." In the course of this complete reversal, the Declaration of Internet Freedom became the Declaration for the Future of the Internet, with the word freedom consigned to little more than a passing reference.

The transition from one to the other was – like bankruptcy – gradual at first and then all at once. We've traveled rather quickly from "you [governments and corporate interests] are not welcome among us" to a "single, decentralized network of networks" managed by "governments and relevant authorities" including "academics, civil society, the private

309 End Wokeness (@endwokeness), "The number one challenge that we see is the First Amendment in the United States."

310 Rufo, "Larry Sanger Speaks Out."

sector, technical community and others" to create a "rules-based digital economy."

And that is the core of the Great Reset affecting the main tool by which today's information channels have been colonized by the corporatist complex.

mRNA VACCINES

The second most scary outcome of the global pandemic response, after the worldwide censorship and propaganda campaigns, was the normalization of mRNA products as "safe and effective." This goal of the biodefense global public-private partnership was achieved through legal loopholes and maneuverings over decades. These enabled billions of injectables to be manufactured and administered with no legal or regulatory oversight. In this chapter I explain the legal paths used, and expose the fact that they were intended for situations involving weapons of mass destruction, not naturally occurring viruses.

5.1 COVID mRNA VACCINES REQUIRED NO SAFETY OVERSIGHT

When everyone from the President to your primary care doctor declared loudly and wholeheartedly in December 2020 that the newly FDA-authorized Covid mRNA vaccines were "safe and effective" – what were those claims based on?

There are two aspects of drug production that are regulated to protect our safety:

1. Manufacturing standards: regulations are supposed to ensure that a medical product contains what the label says it contains. This means testing for consistency across manufactured batches of the product, consistency within each batch, testing for impurities, ensuring that manufacturing facilities adhere to certain standards, etc.

Here's how the FDA explains Current Good Manufacturing Practice (CGMP) Regulations:

> CGMP provides for systems that assure proper design, monitoring, and control of manufacturing processes and facilities. Adherence to the CGMP regulations assures the identity, strength, quality, and purity of drug products by requiring that manufacturers of medications adequately control manufacturing operations. This includes establishing strong quality management systems, obtaining appropriate quality raw materials, establishing robust operating procedures, detecting and investigating product quality deviations, and maintaining reliable testing laboratories.[311]

2. Safety and efficacy: Before they are manufactured on a large scale, medical products are supposed to be tested in clinical trials to ensure that they do not cause serious side effects or death, and to verify that they actually are effective at doing whatever the manufacturer says they can do.

....

311 U.S. Food and Drug Administration, "Facts About the Current Good Manufacturing Practice (CGMP)."

Here's how the FDA explains how it approves new drugs:

The FDA makes careful, informed decisions about which new drugs to approve based on evaluation of whether treatments are safe and effective. It follows a comprehensive, multistep process that can take several years to complete. The process is governed by laws and regulations to protect the rights, safety, and welfare of volunteers.[312]

In this chapter, I will show that both manufacturing oversight and safety oversight were bypassed in bringing the Covid mRNA shots to market. I will use the BioNTech/Pfizer agreements to illustrate the process. The analysis will show that:

- The Covid mRNA vaccines were acquired and authorized through mechanisms designed to rush medical countermeasures to the military during emergencies involving weapons of mass destruction.
- These mechanisms did not require the application of, or adherence to, any laws or regulations related to vaccine development or manufacturing.
- The FDA's Emergency Use Authorization for the vaccines was based on clinical trials and manufacturing processes conducted with no binding legal standards, no legally proscribed safety oversight or regulation, and no legal redress from the manufacturer for potential harms. (This last point is being challenged in multiple court cases, so far to no avail.)

What all of this means is that none of the laws or regulations that we count on to protect us from potentially harmful, or deadly, medical products was applied to the Covid mRNA vaccines. The assertion of "safe and effective" was based entirely on aspirations, opinions, beliefs,

....

312 U.S. Food and Drug Administration, "How the FDA Regulates and Approves Drugs."

and presumptions of government employees.

In Part 1 of this section, I will examine the contracts between the U.S. government, represented by the Department of Defense, and Pfizer/BioNTech, represented by Pfizer. In Part 2, I will dissect the laws that were applied to the authorization of the mRNA Covid vaccines.

The regulations covered in this chapter are complicated and convoluted. Nevertheless, it is crucial to understand them, in order to document that there has never been (as of the printing of this book) a properly conducted prospective controlled clinical trial of any mRNA product. Thus, no reliable data exists to support any "safe and effective" claims regarding these products.

PART 1: COVID mRNA VACCINE MANUFACTURING CONTRACTS – A FRAMEWORK INTENDED FOR MILITARY COUNTERMEASURES

When the U.S. government entered into its Covid vaccine agreement with Pfizer, which was acting on behalf of the BioNTech/Pfizer partnership, in July 2020, the agreement encompassed a minimum of 100 million doses of a "vaccine to prevent COVID-19" and a payment of at least $1.95 billion. The agreement also allowed for future procurement of hundreds of millions of additional doses.

That's a lot of money for a lot of items, especially since the vaccines had not yet been tested, approved, or manufactured to scale and, as the agreement stated, were purely "aspirational."

Obviously, this is not normal procedure. But, then, those were not normal times. The government declared that we were "at war" with a catastrophically dangerous virus that would kill millions and millions of people of all ages unless we could develop "medical countermeasures" (a military term) and get everyone to take them as quickly as possible.

In keeping with the declaration of war, it was a military framework that was used for acquiring the aspirational products that became known as Covid mRNA vaccines.

Military Acquisition

The government side to the agreement with Pfizer was the Department of Defense (DoD), represented by a convoluted chain of parties, each operating as a subcontractor, or co-contractor, for the next.

The important point to recognize is that all of these bodies are charged exclusively with military objectives: "ensuring military readiness," "enhancing the mission effectiveness of military personnel," and "supporting the Army and Unified Land Operations, anytime, anywhere."

This is crucial, because the laws and procedures governing military procurement have a very different set of assumptions and cost-benefit considerations than those used in civil society.

In fact, agencies governing civilian and public health, like the HHS, NIH, and NIAID, do not have the authority to grant certain types of special acquisition contracts, which is why the Covid vaccine contracts had to be overseen by the Department of Defense.

Thus, as stated in a July 2021 document entitled, *Report to Congressional Committees: COVID-19 CONTRACTING*, **the Department of Health and Human Services (HHS) "partnered" with the Department of Defense (DoD) to "leverage DoD's OTA authorities … which HHS lacked."**[313]

Translation: HHS did not have the authority to enter into a type of agreement called OTA with Pfizer. Therefore, the agreement had to be signed by the Department of Defense.

This is a cryptic statement, and a crucial one. It suggests that there was something about the agreements between the U.S. government and mRNA vaccine manufacturers that was not covered by civilian laws. The key to this is the "OTA authorities."

What Is Other Transaction Authority/Agreement (OTA)?

(NOTE: OTA is used interchangeably to refer to Other Transaction Agreement and Other Transaction Authority.)

A thorough review of the use of OTA by the Department of Defense, including its statutory history, can be found in the *February 22, 2019*

---

313 U.S. Government Accountability Office, Report to Congressional Committees, *COVID-19 Contracting: Actions Needed to Enhance Transparency and Oversight of Selected Awards,* July 2021.

Congressional Research Service report.[314] This report, along with every other discussion of OTA, specifies that it is an alternative acquisition path for defense and military purposes. It is not intended, nor has it ever been used before Covid, for anything intended primarily for civilian use.

If you look for OTA laws in the U.S. Code,[315] this is the path you will go down:

Armed Forces -> General Military Law -> Acquisition -> Research and Engineering -> Agreements -> Authority of the DoD to carry out certain prototype projects

This legal pathway very clearly shows that OTA laws are intended for acquisition of research and engineering prototypes for the armed forces.

According to the Defense Advanced Research Projects Agency (DARPA) website,

The Department of Defense has authority for three different types of OTs: (1) research OTs, (2) prototype OTs, and (3) production OTs.

These three types of OTs represent three stages of initial research, development of a prototype, and eventual production.[316]

Within those three types, there are specific categories of projects to which OTA can apply:

- Originally, according to the OTA Overview[317] provided by the DoD, the Other Transaction Authority was "limited to apply to

----

314 U.S. Congressional Research Service, *Department of Defense Use of Other Transaction Authority: Background, Analysis, and Issues for Congress*, February 22, 2019.

315 10 U.S. Code § 4022 - Authority of the Department of Defense to carry out certain prototype projects

316 Defense Advanced Research Projects Agency, "What are OTs?"

317 Other Transaction Authority (OTA) Overview, hosted at https://acqnotes.com/wp-content/uploads/2014/09/Other-Transaction-Authority-Overview.pdf

weapons or weapon systems proposed to be acquired or developed by the DoD."

- OTA was later expanded to include "any prototype project directly related to enhancing the mission effectiveness of military personnel and the supporting platforms, systems, components, or materials proposed to be acquired or developed by the DoD, or to improvement of platforms, systems, components, or materials in use by the Armed Forces."

So far, none of that sounds like an acquisition pathway for millions of novel medical products intended primarily for civilian use.

Is There any Exception for Civilian Use of OTA That Might Apply to Covid mRNA Vaccines?

The FY2004 National Defense Authorization Act (P.L. 108-136)[318] contained a section that gave Other Transaction Authority to "the head of an executive agency who engages in basic research, applied research, advanced research, and development projects" that "have the potential to facilitate defense against or recovery from terrorism or nuclear, biological, chemical or radiological attack."

This provision was extended until 2018, but does not appear to have been extended beyond that year. Also, note that even in this exceptional case of non-DoD use of OTA, the situation must involve terrorism or an attack with weapons of mass destruction (CBRN).

What Other OTA Laws Might Apply?

The 2019 CRS report cited above provides this chart, showing that a few non-DoD agencies have some OTA or related authorities:

....

318 National Defense Authorization Act for Fiscal Year 2004, Pub. L. 108-136, 117 Stat. 1392.

Table B-1. Selected Non-DOD Federal Agencies with OT or Related Authorities

Agency	R&D Authority	Prototype Authority	Permanent Authority	Temporary Authority	OT Authority as Currently Enacted
Advanced Research Project Agency – Energy (ARPA-E)	√(	X	√(		42 U.S.C. §16538
Department of Energy (DOE)	√(	X		√(Sunset Sept. 30, 2020)	42 U.S.C. §7256
Department of Health and Human Services (HHS)	√(	X	√(		42 U.S.C. §247d-7e
Department of Homeland Security (DHS)	√(	√(		√((Sunset Sept. 30, 2018)	6 U.S.C. §391 and §538, Division F, P.L. 115-141
Department of Transportation (DOT)	√(	X	√(		49 U.S.C. §5312
Domestic Nuclear Detection Office (DNDO)	√(	√(	√(		6 U.S.C. §596
Federal Aviation Administration (FAA)	√(	X	√(		49 U.S.C. §106(l)
National Aeronautics and Space Administration (NASA)	√(	√(	√(		51 U.S.C. §20113(e)
Transportation Security Administration (TSA)	√(	X	√(		49 U.S.C. §114(m)

Source: CRS review of the *United States Code* and Congress.gov.

Notes: The authorities listed may be restricted to specific agency or department programs.

According to this table, The Department of Health and Human Services (HHS) has some research and development (R&D) Other Transaction Authorities. The law pertaining to the OT Authority of HHS is 42 U.S.C. §247d-7e.[319]

Where is this law housed and what does it say?

The Public Health and Welfare -> Public Health Service -> General Powers and Duties -> Federal-State Cooperation -> Biomedical Advanced Research and Development Authority (BARDA) -> Transaction Authorities

So there is a place in the law related to civilian health and welfare where OTA might be applicable, although it is valid only for research and development, not prototypes or manufacturing.

....

319 42 U.S. Code § 247d–7e - Biomedical Advanced Research and Development Authority.

The law states that the BARDA secretary has OT Authority

> with respect to a product that is or may become a qualified coun-
> termeasure or a qualified pandemic or epidemic product, activities
> that predominantly—
> (i) are conducted after basic research and preclinical development
> of the product; and
> (ii) are related to manufacturing the product on a commercial
> scale and **in a form that satisfies the regulatory requirements under
> the Federal Food, Drug, and Cosmetic Act [21 U.S.C. 301 et seq.]
> or under section 262 of this title.**
> [boldface added]

The "regulatory requirements," enumerated in the laws mentioned above, mean that it would be impossible for BARDA/HHS to enter into agreements – even just R&D – for any medical products (like the mRNA vaccines) that did not undergo rigorous safety testing and strict manufacturing oversight.

HHS "Partnership" with DoD Circumvented Civilian Protection Laws

To summarize the predicament of Other Transaction Authority/Agreements with respect to civilian authorities, in general, and Covid mRNA vaccines, in particular:

1. OTA was written and codified as a way for the military to acquire weapons and other necessary systems and equipment without a lot of bureaucratic red tape. It covers research and development, prototypes, and subsequent manufacturing.
2. The only OTA for a public health agency is the HHS and it only covers Research & Development, not prototypes or manufacturing.
3. Even the R&D OTA given to the HHS still requires products to be manufactured "in a form that satisfies the regulatory requirements" for drug and vaccine safety.

In other words: There is no way HHS could have used its very limited OTA to sign contracts for hundreds of millions of novel medical products. So what did HHS do?

As mentioned at the beginning of this chapter, and as the Government Accountability Office (GAO) noted in its July 2021 report on "Covid-19 Contracting:"[320] HHS "partnered" with DoD to "leverage DoD's OTA authorities...which HHS lacked." (p. 24)

What are DoD's OT Authorities for Medical Products?

As discussed above, OTA is intended to help the military get equipment and technology without a lot of bureaucratic hassle. None of the original laws pertaining to OTA mentioned anything other than "platforms, systems, components, or materials" intended to "enhance the mission effectiveness of military personnel."

But five years before Covid, an exceptional use of OTA was introduced:

In 2015, DoD announced[321] the establishment of the CBRN Medical Countermeasure Consortium, whose purpose was to use the OTA acquisition pathway to "work with DoD to develop FDA licensed chemical, biological, radiological, and nuclear medical countermeasures." [FDA = Food & Drug Administration]

As described in the 2015 announcement, this included "prototype technologies for therapeutic medical countermeasures targeting viral, bacterial, and biological toxin targets of interest to the DoD." The list of agents included the top biowarfare pathogens, such as anthrax, ebola, and marburg.

The announcement went on to specify that "enabling technologies can include animal models of viral, bacterial or biological toxin disease and pathogenesis (multiple routes of exposure), assays, diagnostic technologies or other platform technologies that can be applied to development of approved or licensed MCMs [medical countermeasures]."

Although this still does not sound anything like the production of 100 million novel vaccines for civilian use, it does provide more leeway for OTA than the very limited Other Transaction Authority given to HHS.

....

320 U.S. Government Accountability Office, Report to Congressional Committees, *COVID-19 Contracting: Actions Needed to Enhance Transparency and Oversight of Selected Awards*, July 2021.

321 Global Biodefense, "DoD CBRN Medical Countermeasure Consortium."

Pfizer's Other Transaction Agreement (OTA)

The Department of Defense (DoD) can make three types of agreements under OTA: research, prototypes, and manufacturing. Importantly, according to *National Defense Magazine*,[322] the agreements (which are "other than contracts") are supposed to start with prototypes and then move "from prototypes to production contracts." In other words, you start with an OTA for a prototype and then get an actual production contract.

In contrast, the agreement between Pfizer and the U.S. government, routed through the Department of Defense and the CBRN Medical Countermeasure Consortium, classified what Pfizer agreed to deliver as a "prototype project" and "manufacturing demonstration." As stated in the agreement:

> The intent of this prototype project is to demonstrate that Pfizer has the business and logistics capability to manufacture 100M doses of its currently unapproved mRNA-based COVID-19 vaccine for the Government [(b)(4) redaction][323]

So the military acquisition branch of the government is paying Pfizer to show that it can manufacture 100 million doses of a never-before produced or tested product, while also acquiring those 100 million doses, and potentially hundreds of millions more. The "prototype" somehow includes not just the manufacturing process, but also the 100 million doses created through that process.

Nowhere in the history of Other Transaction Agreements is there anything remotely resembling this conflation of a prototype ("a preliminary model of something," according to the *Oxford English Dictionary*) and the manufacturing of millions of exemplars of that prototype. Actually, it is unclear from the wording of the OTA whether the "prototype" applies to the mRNA Covid vaccine, the mRNA platform for manufacturing the

....

322 *National Defense Magazine*, "Special Report: Other Transaction Authority."

323 U.S. Department of the Army, Statement of Work for Covid-19 Pandemic - Large Scale Vaccine Manufacturing Demonstration, RPP #: 20-11, Project Identifier: 2011-003.

vaccine, the actual manufacturing of 100 million vaccines, or all of the above.

Why OTA is so important

Why should we care about the Other Transaction Authorities of our public health agency (HHS) as compared to the OTA of our military (DoD), and how the latter were applied to the Covid mRNA vaccine purchasing agreements?

While the public health (HHS) OTA requires adherence to extensive development and manufacturing regulations, the OTA pathway for the military (DoD) to develop medical countermeasures requires only "FDA licensure."

Thus, using DoD Other Transaction Authorities, it would theoretically be possible to bypass any safety regulations – depending on the requirements for FDA licensing of an OTA-generated product.

And, as we will see in Part 2 of this chapter, for the Covid mRNA vaccines, Emergency Use Authorization was granted, requiring no legal safety oversight at all.

PART 2: REGULATORY FRAMEWORK FOR COVID mRNA VACCINES

In part 1 of this chapter, we revealed that the Covid mRNA vaccine agreements (defined as "other than contracts") between the military and Pfizer/bioNTech were based on Other Transaction Authorities, defined by law as pertaining to military acquisition of equipment and countermeasures.

How is development and manufacturing of "medical countermeasures" regulated under military OTA? Are the regulations the same as the CGMP and clinical trial standards that apply to FDA-regulated medical products, as discussed in Part 1 of this chapter?

The answer, as we will learn, is: not at all.

First, we need to understand who is responsible for quality and safety oversight in the context of Pfizer's OTA (the agreement between Pfizer/BioNTech and the U.S. military). Here's what the agreement says:

Pfizer will meet the necessary FDA requirements for conducting ongoing and planned clinical trials, and with its collaboration partner, BioNTech, will seek FDA approval or authorization for the vaccine, assuming the clinical data supports such application for approval or authorization.[324]

Sounds like the FDA is in charge of safety regulations here. But what are the FDA requirements "for approval or authorization" in the context of Other Transaction Authority (OTA)?

According to the Pfizer OTA, those requirements are whatever it takes to "grant an Emergency Use Authorization ("EUA") under Section 564 of the Federal Food, Drug, and Cosmetic Act."

What is Emergency Use Authorization (EUA)?

Even before explaining what EUA is, and by way of understanding where EUA stands in relation to other pathways for authorizing or approving medical products, it is helpful to look at what EUA is not:

EUA is not a designation for an experimental product undergoing a clinical trial

If we only understand one thing about EUA it should be this: EUA does not apply to a product undergoing a clinical trial governed by FDA regulations or other legal requirements.

EUA is also not the same as Expanded Access Use (EAU), often called "compassionate use" access, which applies to granting patients with severe, incurable diseases access to experimental products before they are fully approved.

This table from an FDA-CDC 2020 presentation[325] summarizes the differences between products undergoing clinical trials, products given

----

324 U.S. Department of the Army, Statement of Work for Covid-19 Pandemic - Large Scale Vaccine Manufacturing Demonstration, RPP #: 20-11, Project Identifier: 2011-003.

325 U.S. Food and Drug Administration, "FDA-CDC Joint Learning Session: Regulatory Updates on Use of Medical Countermeasures," Preparedness Summit, August 25-27, 2020.

to patients through expanded "compassionate" access, and products authorized through EUA:

Comparison of Access Mechanisms

Consideration	Clinical Trial	Expanded Access (IND/IDE)	EUA
Ability to inform effectiveness	Yes – designed to provide evidence of safety and effectiveness	Not likely; possibly anecdotal information with larger population size	Not likely
Ability to inform safety	Yes – designed to provide evidence of safety and effectiveness	Safety signals might be identified	Safety signals might be identified
Ability to obtain useful information to benefit future patients	Yes - designed and intended to benefit future patients – randomized/blinded	Not likely; with larger sized populations, possibly some safety data in patient subgroups that could inform broader labeling	Not likely
Availability of findings	Eventually published in medical journals. If part of a regulatory approval, FDA makes reviews public.	Individual medical records are not released to the general public. Case reports might be published in medical journals.	Generally there is no systematic data collection. Retrospectives studies may be conducted and published.
Informed consent required?	Yes	Yes	No, but requires informing the volunteer of 1) right to refuse and 2) that product is unapproved/available under an EUA
Institutional review board (IRB) required?	Yes	Yes, but no prior approval needed for individual patient access	No
Level of access to investigational product	Depends on trial design P1 typically 20 – 100 P2 typically several 100 P3 typically 300 – 3,000	Depends on type of expanded access, which ranges from individual patient (e-IND/IDE) to large (e.g., 100-1,000) populations	Can enable access to a large number of patients

Here's what this table tells us about EUA:

1. The process of granting EUA is not likely to generate any information about a product's effectiveness.
2. The process of granting EUA is not designed to provide evidence of safety or effectiveness, but safety signals might be identified.
3. It is unlikely, once a product is granted EUA and administered to some patients, that any useful information will be obtained to benefit any future patients.
4. There is no systematic data collection on effectiveness or safety with EUA, and no data is published in medical journals as part of the regulatory approval process.
5. No informed consent is required, but patients who "volunteer" to take the product must be told they can refuse and that the product is unapproved/available under EUA.

6. No institutional review board (IRB) is required. [IRB[326] is a board that is supposed to protect the well-being of human subjects in clinical trials]

To clarify even further how separate EUA is from any normal approval process, in a 2009 Institute of Medicine of the National Academies publication,[327] we find this statement:

> **It is important to recognize that an EUA is not part of the development pathway; it is an entirely separate entity that is used only during emergency situations and is not part of the drug approval process. (p. 28)**

To summarize:

The process of granting a product EUA is unlikely to generate any evidence of safety or effectiveness. Once a product is granted EUA and administered to patients, it is unlikely that any useful information will be obtained to benefit future patients, because there is no systematic data collection on effectiveness or safety.

Based on all this very clear information from the CDC/FDA and the IMNA, it would be fair to conclude that Emergency Use Authorization is a process that should be applied very judiciously and only in cases of dire emergencies.

Now let's look at what types of emergency situations EUA is legally designed to address.

EAU is meant for WMD emergencies

The laws permitting the EUA "Access Mechanism" described above were drawn up for cases of extreme, immediate emergencies involving weapons of mass destruction (WMD), also referred to as CBRN (chemical, biological, radiological, nuclear) agents.

....

326 Grady, "Institutional Review Boards."

327 Institute of Medicine of the National Academies, *Medical Countermeasures Dispensing: Emergency Use Authorization and the Postal Model.*

Here's how the Food & Drug Administration (FDA) describes its EUA powers:

> Section 564 of the FD&C Act (21 U.S.C. 360bbb–3) allows FDA to strengthen public health protections against biological, chemical, nuclear, and radiological agents.
>
> With this EUA authority, FDA can help ensure that medical countermeasures may be used in emergencies to diagnose, treat, or prevent serious or life-threatening diseases or conditions caused by biological, chemical, nuclear, or radiological agents when there are no adequate, approved, and available alternatives (among other criteria).[328]

It's extremely important to understand that these EUA powers were granted in 2004 under very specific circumstances related to preparedness for attacks by weapons of mass destruction, otherwise known as CBRN (chemical, biological, radiological, nuclear) agents.

As explained in Harvard Law's *Bill of Health*,

> Ultimately, it was the War on Terror that would give rise to emergency use authorization. After the events of September 11, 2001 and subsequent anthrax mail attacks, Congress enacted the Project Bioshield Act of 2004. The act called for billions of dollars in appropriations for purchasing vaccines in preparation for a bioterror attack, and for stockpiling of emergency countermeasures. To be able to act rapidly in an emergency, Congress allowed FDA to authorize formally unapproved products for emergency use against a threat to public health and safety (subject to a declaration of emergency by HHS). **The record indicates that Congress was focused on the threat of bioterror specifically, not on preparing for**

---

328 U.S. Food and Drug Administration, Federal Register Notice, "Authorization of Emergency Use of an In Vitro Diagnostic Device in Response to an Outbreak of Mpox; Availability," February 7, 2020.

a naturally-occurring pandemic.[329]

[boldface added]

Given such a narrow type of truly extreme emergency situation involving a WMD attack, it is understandable why the EUA "access mechanism" does not require a lot of regulatory oversight or adherence to any manufacturing or clinical trial standards.

So what does the EUA access mechanism actually require?

The 3 Steps for Emergency Use Authorization (EUA)

Three things have to happen in order for EUA to be granted to a medical product:

1. The Secretary of Homeland Security, the Secretary of Defense, or the Secretary of Health and Human Services needs to determine that there is an emergency involving an attack or a threat of an attack with a CBRN agent or a disease caused by such an agent.
2. The FDA needs to make sure that it meets four "statutory criteria" when it issues the EUA.
3. The FDA has to "impose certain required conditions" in the EUA.

EUA Step 1: Declaring a CBRN emergency

The emergency declaration for EUA is separate and unrelated to any other emergency declarations that may be issued by the President, the HHS Secretary, or anyone else. It must be issued specifically for the purpose of activating EUA and can be ended or extended independently of any other emergency declaration.

Here's what the EUA law states[330] are the four possible scenarios for activating the EUA "access mechanism:"

....

329 Iwry, "From 9/11 to COVID-19: A Brief History of FDA Emergency Use Authorization."

330 21 U.S. Code § 360bbb–3 - Authorization for medical products for use in emergencies.

1. a determination by the Secretary of Homeland Security that there is a domestic emergency, or a significant potential for a domestic emergency, involving a heightened risk of attack with a biological, chemical, radiological, or nuclear agent or agents;

2. a determination by the Secretary of Defense that there is a military emergency, or a significant potential for a military emergency, involving a heightened risk to United States military forces, including personnel operating under the authority of Title 10 or Title 50, of attack with—
   a. a biological, chemical, radiological, or nuclear agent or agents; or
   b. an agent or agents that may cause, or are otherwise associated with, an imminently life-threatening and specific risk to United States military forces;

3. a determination by the Secretary [of Health and Human Services] that there is a public health emergency, or a significant potential for a public health emergency, that affects, or has a significant potential to affect, national security or the health and security of United States citizens living abroad, and that involves a biological, chemical, radiological, or nuclear agent or agents, or a disease or condition that may be attributable to such agent or agents; or

4. the identification of a material threat pursuant to section 319F–2 of the Public Health Service Act [42 U.S.C. 247d–6b][331] sufficient to affect national security or the health and security of United States citizens living abroad.

Nowhere in these four situations is there any mention of a naturally occurring epidemic, pandemic, or any other kind of public health situation that is not caused by "biological, chemical, radiological or nuclear agent/s."

....

331 42 U.S. Code § 247d–6b - Strategic National Stockpile and security countermeasure procurements.

Could SARS-CoV-2 qualify as such an agent?

If you look for the definition of "**biological agents**" in the U.S. Legal Code, you will go down the following pathway:

Crimes and Criminal Procedure -> Crimes -> Biological Weapons -> Definitions

So in the context of United States law, the term "biological agents" means biological weapons, and the use of such agents/weapons is regarded as a crime. Wikipedia provides this definition:

A biological agent (also called bio-agent, biological threat agent, biological warfare agent, biological weapon, or bioweapon) is a bacterium, virus, protozoan, parasite, fungus, or toxin that can be used purposefully as a weapon in bioterrorism or biological warfare (BW).[332]

On What Legal Basis was EUA Issued for Covid mRNA Vaccines?

It would seem, based on the laws regarding EUA, that none of the four possible situations described in the law could be applied to a product intended to prevent or treat a disease caused by a naturally occurring pathogen.

Nevertheless, this law was used to authorize the mRNA Covid vaccines.

Given the four choices listed in the EUA law, the one that was used for Covid "countermeasures" was

C) a determination by the Secretary [of HHS] that there is a public health emergency, or a significant potential for a public health emergency, that affects, or has a significant potential to affect, national security or the health and security of United States citizens living abroad, and that involves a biological, chemical, radiological, or nuclear agent or agents, or a disease or condition that may be attributable to such agent or agents.

....

332 Wikipedia, "Biological agent," accessed February 12, 2025.

When applied specifically to Covid, this is how it was worded:

> the Secretary of the Department of Health and Human Services (HHS) determined that there is a public health emergency that has a significant potential to affect national security or the health and security of United States citizens living abroad, and that involves the virus that causes Coronavirus Disease 2019 (COVID-19)...[333]

There is no doubt here that "the virus that causes COVID-19" is deemed to be the equivalent of "a biological, chemical, radiological, or nuclear agent or agents." In other words, it is considered a weapon of mass destruction – not a naturally occurring disease.

It is also important to remember that the EUA "determination of a public health emergency" is completely separate from, and not in any way reliant on, any other public health emergency declarations, like the ones that were made by the WHO, the U.S. government, and the President at the beginning of the Covid-19 pandemic.

So even when the WHO, the U.S. government, and the President declare that the pandemic is over, there can still be Emergency Use Authorization if the HHS Secretary continues to claim that the situation described in section C) exists.

Looking at all of the EUAs for hundreds of Covid-related medical products,[334] it is very difficult to see how the HHS secretary could justify the claim that "there is a public health emergency that has a significant potential to affect national security or the health and security of U.S. citizens living abroad" in most, if not all, of these cases.

....

333 U.S. Food and Drug Administration, Letter to Pfizer Inc., May 10, 2021.

334 U.S Food and Drug Administration, "Emergency Use Authorization."

EUA Step 2: Meeting the statutory criteria

Once one of the secretaries has declared that there is an emergency that warrants EUA, there are four more "statutory criteria" that have to be met in order for the FDA to issue the EUA.

Here's how the FDA explains these requirements:[335]

1. Serious or Life-Threatening Disease or Condition

For FDA to issue an EUA, the CBRN agent(s) referred to in the HHS Secretary's EUA declaration must be capable of causing a serious or life-threatening disease or condition.

NOTE: This criterion repeats the specification of a CBRN agent, which is legally defined as a weapon whose use is a crime.

2. Evidence of Effectiveness

Medical products that may be considered for an EUA are those that "may be effective" to prevent, diagnose, or treat serious or life-threatening diseases or conditions that can be caused by a CBRN agent(s) identified in the HHS Secretary's declaration of emergency or threat of emergency under section 564(b).

The "may be effective" standard for EUAs provides for a lower level of evidence than the "effectiveness" standard that FDA uses for product approvals. FDA intends to assess the potential effectiveness of a possible EUA product on a case-by-case basis using a risk-benefit analysis, as explained below.

LEGAL QUESTION: How can anyone legally claim that a product authorized under EUA is "safe and effective" if the legal standard for EUA is "may be effective" and the FDA declares that this is a "lower level of evidence" than the standard used for regular product approvals?

....

335 U.S Food and Drug Administration, Guidance for Industry and Other Stakeholders, *Emergency Use Authorization of Medical Products and Related Authorities*, January 2017.

3. Risk-Benefit Analysis

A product may be considered for an EUA if the Commissioner determines that the known and potential benefits of the product, when used to diagnose, prevent, or treat the identified disease or condition, outweigh the known and potential risks of the product.

In determining whether the known and potential benefits of the product outweigh the known and potential risks, FDA intends to look at the totality of the scientific evidence to make an overall risk-benefit determination. Such evidence, which could arise from a variety of sources, may include (but is not limited to): results of domestic and foreign clinical trials, in vivo efficacy data from animal models, and in vitro data, available for FDA consideration. FDA will also assess the quality and quantity of the available evidence, given the current state of scientific knowledge.

NOTE: There is no legal standard and there are no legal definitions for what it means for "known and potential benefits" to outweigh "known and potential risks." There is also no qualitative or quantitative legal definition for what constitutes acceptable "available evidence" upon which the risk-benefit analysis "may be" based. There could be zero actual evidence, but a belief that a product has a lot of potential benefit and not a lot of potential risk, and that would satisfy this "statutory requirement."

4. No Alternatives

For FDA to issue an EUA, there must be no adequate, approved, and available alternative to the candidate product for diagnosing, preventing, or treating the disease or condition. A potential alternative product may be considered "unavailable" if there are insufficient supplies of the approved alternative to fully meet the emergency need.

Here's how all of these "statutory criteria" were satisfied in the actual Emergency Use Authorization for the BioNTEch/Pfizer Covid mRNA vaccines (signed by the FDA Chief Scientist):

I have concluded that the emergency use of Pfizer-BioNTech COVID-19 Vaccine for the prevention of COVID-19 when administered as described in the Scope of Authorization (Section II) meets the criteria for issuance of an authorization under Section 564(c) of the Act, because:

1. SARS-CoV-2 can cause a serious or life-threatening disease or condition, including severe respiratory illness, to humans infected by this virus;

2. Based on the totality of scientific evidence available to FDA, it is reasonable to believe that Pfizer-BioNTech COVID-19 Vaccine may be effective in preventing COVID-19, and that, when used under the conditions described in this authorization, the known and potential benefits of Pfizer-BioNTech COVID-19 Vaccine when used to prevent COVID-19 outweigh its known and potential risks; and

3. There is no adequate, approved, and available alternative to the emergency use of Pfizer-BioNTech COVID-19 Vaccine to prevent COVID-19.[336]

NOTE: The only context in which the FDA weighed the potential benefits and risks of the vaccine, and in which the FDA determined it "may be effective," was in preventing Covid-19.

There is no consideration, no evidence of actual or potential benefit, and no determination that there is any potential effectiveness for the vaccine to do anything else, including: lowering the risk of severe disease, lowering the risk of hospitalization, lowering the risk of death, lowering the risk of any conditions actually or potentially related to Covid-19.

THEREFORE, one might reasonably question the legality of any claims that the vaccine is "safe and effective" in the context of anything other than "when used to prevent COVID-19" – which the vaccines were known NOT TO DO very soon after they were introduced.

If people were told the BioNTech/Pfizer mRNA vaccines were "safe and effective" at anything other than preventing Covid-19, and if they

---

336 U.S. Food and Drug Administration, Letter to Pfizer Inc., May 10, 2021.

were threatened with any consequences for failure to take the vaccine for anything other than preventing Covid-19, might they have a legitimate argument that they were illegally coerced into taking an unapproved product under fraudulent claims?

EUA Step 3: Imposing the required conditions

Once we have the EUA-specific emergency declaration, and once the FDA determines that the product may be effective and that whatever evidence is available shows that its benefits outweigh its risks, there is one more layer of related regulation.

Here's how a 2018 Congressional Research Service report on EUA explains this:

> *FFDCA §564 directs FDA to impose certain required conditions in an EUA and allows for additional discretionary conditions where appropriate. The required conditions vary depending upon whether the EUA is for an unapproved product or for an unapproved use of an approved product. For an unapproved product, the conditions of use must:*
>
> *(1) ensure that health care professionals administering the product receive required information;*
>
> *(2) ensure that individuals to whom the product is administered receive required information;*
>
> *(3) provide for the monitoring and reporting of adverse events associated with the product; and*
>
> *(4) provide for recordkeeping and reporting by the manufacturer.[337]*

LEGAL QUESTION: What exactly is the "required information?" We know that people were informed that the vaccines were given Emergency Use Authorization. But were they told that this means "a lower level of evidence" than is required for "safe and effective" claims on other medical products? Were they informed that there are different levels of "safe and

---

337 U.S. Congressional Research Service, *Emergency Use Authorization and FDAs Related Authorities*, August 13, 2018.

effective" depending on whether a product has EUA or another type of authorization?

NOTE: The law requires that there be a way to monitor and report adverse events. However, it does not state who monitors, what the standards are for reporting, and what the threshold is for taking action based on the reports.

No Legal or Regulatory Standards Apply to the FDA's Decision to Grant EUA

The EUA law does not impose any legal or regulatory standards that might determine whether a product is safe or effective. The only standards are whether the FDA believes the product may be effective and that its known benefits outweigh its known harms. If there are no known harms or known benefits, because the product has never been through the drug approval process, the FDA can use whatever information or standards it chooses to make that determination.

It follows from all of this that a company whose product is a candidate for EUA may attempt to demonstrate the product's safety and/or effectiveness through whatever means it chooses. The existence of such an attempt (whether a clinical trial or other data-collecting mechanism), and how that attempt is conducted, are all up to the company. Nothing in the EUA law applies to how the company designs, conducts or analyzes any studies or other data-collecting mechanisms it chooses to pursue.

Applied to Covid products this means:

- No safety or efficacy data from clinical trials were required in order for Covid products to receive EUA.
- Any clinical trials referred to in the EUA process were conducted with no legally applicable regulatory standards.
- When we find out that these products lack efficacy or safety, that is not a surprise. It is a highly likely result of the process.
- There is no data from the EUA process on which to base non-EUA decisions about safety or efficacy of the product. So any non-EUA use of the product would require going through the legal approval process for regular medical products from the beginning.

PREP Act

If you agree to develop, manufacture, and sell hundreds of millions of aspirational products to the government under the contract-like Other Transaction Agreement and bioterror-contingent Emergency Use Authorization, you need very good liability protection.

This is provided by the PREP (Public Readiness and Emergency Preparedness) Act that was designed to go hand-in-hand with EUA. Again, it is possible to envision a bioterrorism scenario, like an anthrax attack, in which the government needs to get lots of countermeasures very quickly. Many people will inevitably die in the attack, but if there's a chance that the countermeasure will work, it needs to get made and distributed as quickly as possible. If it has some bad side effects, or even if it kills some people, one could argue that the manufacturer should not be held liable.

Clearly, this was never intended to apply to a new, untested vaccine used to counter a naturally occurring virus in hundreds of millions of people.

What, then, are the standards for determining the necessity of a PREP Act declaration?

Here's how the Health and Human Services (HHS) website describes the factors considered by the HHS Secretary:

> In deciding whether to issue a PREP Act Declaration, HHS must consider the desirability of encouraging the design, development, clinical testing or investigation, manufacture, labeling, distribution, formulation, packaging, marketing, promotion, sale, purchase, donation, dispensing, prescribing, administering, licensing, and use of the countermeasure recommended in the Declaration. HHS may also consider other relevant factors.[338]

As with the EUA determination, there are no legally binding standards or directives for issuing a PREP Act. If the products made under EUA cause harm or death, no one involved in making or administering those products can be held accountable, as long as there is accompanying PREP Act protection.

....

338 U.S. Department of Health and Human Services, "PREP Act Q&As."

CONCLUSION

It is eminently apparent, given all the information in this chapter, that the BioNTach/Pfizer Covid mRNA vaccines were developed, manufactured, and authorized under military laws reserved for emergency situations involving biological warfare/terrorism, not naturally occurring diseases affecting the entire civilian population.

Therefore, the adherence to regulations and oversight that we expect to find when a product is deemed "safe and effective" for the entire civilian population was not legally required.

The BioNTech/Pfizer Covid mRNA vaccines were authorized for use in the entire population of the United States based on the application of the following sequence of agreements and determinations:

1. Department of Defense uses "contract-like" Other Transaction Authority (OTA) to buy aspirational products. DoD is not responsible for overseeing clinical trials or manufacturing. Pfizer is responsible for getting authorization from the FDA.

2. The FDA is permitted to issue Emergency Use Authorization (EUA) to Pfizer for mRNA vaccines because the HHS Secretary declares that there is an emergency that warrants EUA.

3. FDA makes its EUA determination based on whatever evidence and considerations it feels are appropriate, given the emergency situation. There are no legal standards that apply to the FDA's considerations, except that it believes the product may be effective, the benefits outweigh the risks based on available information, and there is no alternative product.

4. The Health and Human Services Secretary grants total legal immunity through the PREP Act to anyone involved in developing, making, shipping, or administering the vaccines, based on his determination that there is an emergency that justifies this action.

That's what the "safe and effective" claim for the BioNTech/Pfizer Covid mRNA vaccines was based on in December 2020, when millions of people – including children and pregnant women – were mandated to take the injections. Objectors were ridiculed, silenced, ostracized, and fired. Harms and deaths were, and continue to be in early 2025 (as this book goes to the publisher) covered up, uninvestigated, and uncounted.

Questions About the Legality of the EUA for Covid mRNA Vaccines

It sounds like something in this whole process must be illegal, right?

So far, trying to charge pharmaceutical companies with wrongdoing related to Covid vaccines has failed, because the EUA + PREP combo means they were not required to apply any legal/regulatory standards to their clinical studies or manufacturing processes.

But what about the government?

Since the OTA, EUA, and PREP regulations are intended for use during a catastrophic CBRN emergency, we might ask ourselves: did the U.S. government believe – or claim to believe – that SARS-CoV-2 was an engineered potential bioweapon? Did the government use what we might consider an extra-legal (in civilian terms) acquisition and authorization process based on the assumption that the entire population was threatened by the equivalent of a bioterrorism or biowarfare attack? It sure seems like they did. And if so, did they have a legal obligation to inform the public of this situation in order to resort to the OTA and EUA procurement and authorization pathway?

Moreover, even if the government considered, or claimed to consider, Covid-19 to be a disease caused by a potential bioterror agent, how could the HHS Secretary justify an Emergency Use Authorization that required him to determine that "there is a public health emergency that has a significant potential to affect national security" when it was known that Covid-19 was deadly almost exclusively in old and infirm populations?

In December 2020 the following facts were known about Covid-19 without a reasonable doubt:[339, 340, 341, 342, 343, 344]

- The infection fatality rate (IFR) for the entire population was less than 1%.
- The IFR for anyone under 55 was 0.01% or lower.
- The IFR for children was near zero.

A disease that has significant potential to affect national security has to be very severe, especially in its effect on the military. Yet in December 2020 military-aged people were known to be at nearly no risk from Covid-19. And still the HHS Secretary determined that there was an emergency that warranted EUA for the mRNA vaccines. And all military personnel were mandated to get the injections.

The government has not been held accountable for the subsequent injuries and deaths caused by these unregulated products.

ACKNOWLEDGEMENTS
Sasha Latypova[345] and Katherine Watt[346] have been trying to draw attention to this shocking legal and regulatory framework for a long time. I am deeply grateful for, and indebted to, their in-depth research and tireless work to disseminate this information.

....

339 Levin et al., "Assessing the age specificity of infection fatality rates for COVID-19: systematic review, meta-analysis, and public policy implications."

340 Meyerowitz-Katz and Merone, "A systematic review and meta-analysis of published research data on COVID-19 infection fatality rates."

341 Pei et al., "Burden and characteristics of COVID-19 in the United States during 2020."

342 Ioannidis, "Global perspective of COVID-19 epidemiology for a full-cycle pandemic."

343 Ioannidis, "Population-level COVID-19 mortality risk for non-elderly individuals overall and for non-elderly individuals without underlying diseases in pandemic epicenters."

344 Fairman, "COVID-19 Infection Fatality Rates."

345 Latypova, "Do C-19 Vax Manufacturers Violate cGxP?"

346 Watt, "Sasha Latypova and Katherine Watt discussing non-regulation of non-medicines known as 'vaccines,' and other U.S. military biochemical weapons."

5.2 WHY WAS THE BIONTECH/PFIZER mRNA VACCINE NOT RECALLED IN FEBRUARY 2021?

We learned in Part 1 of this chapter that the Covid mRNA vaccines were authorized without any meaningful legal oversight of manufacturing or safety standards. Once they were injected into millions of people, what was the followup mechanism to monitor for potential adverse events?

According to EUA regulations,[347] the FDA must "impose certain required conditions," including:

provide for the monitoring and reporting of adverse events associated with the product; and
provide for recordkeeping and reporting by the manufacturer.

In other words, there is supposed to be monitoring and reporting of adverse events, after a product is given Emergency Use Authorization. And, in fact, there was such monitoring and reporting of Covid mRNA vaccines, including "recordkeeping and reporting by the manufacturer."

The shocking fact is that, despite hundreds and thousands of reported adverse events in just the first few months after rollout, the products remained on the market.

This is just one example:

According to Stat News,[348] on May 5, 2022, The J&J adenovirus Covid vaccine "was limited to people 18 and older who cannot take one of the other available vaccines for medical reasons, or who simply will not agree to be vaccinated with one of the messenger RNA vaccines made by Moderna and by Pfizer and its partner BioNTech."

The reason?

Peter Marks, the FDA's vaccines lead, told STAT the agency reached its decision after a recent review of the data on the vaccine revealed another

....

347 U.S. Congressional Research Service, *Emergency Use Authorization and FDA's Related Authorities*, August 13, 2018.

348 Branswell, "FDA limits use of Johnson & Johnson's Covid-19 vaccine, citing clotting risk."

person in this country had died after receiving it — the ninth such death — in the first quarter of the year.

"If we see deaths and there is an alternative vaccine that is not associated with deaths but is associated with similar efficacy...we felt it was time at this point to make a statement on the [product's] fact sheet that this was not a first-line vaccine," said Marks.

With one death for every 2 million doses given in this country, the FDA decided that is a risk most people don't need to take, Marks said.

Nine deaths.

Compared to "an alternative vaccine that is not associated with deaths" – a statement made on May 5, 2022.

Let's look at one such "alternative vaccine:"

A document dated February 28, 2021[349] (almost a whole year BEFORE the Peter Marks statements), presents an analysis of "post-authorization adverse event reports" on the BioNTech/Pfizer Covid vaccine, as requested by the FDA for Pfizer/BioNTech's Biologics License Application (BLA).

This report, marked "CONFIDENTIAL" but publicly available on phmpt.org, is dated just 3 months after "the first temporary authorisation for emergency supply on 01 December 2020," which is when the UK gave Emergency Use Authorization to the product.

In the report, we see that there were 1,223 deaths among the 42,086 total cases analyzed in the report. NOTE: the total case number is not the number of people who received the vaccine. It is also not the number of people in a clinical trial. It is the number of adverse event "cases" that were analyzed by Pfizer "on behalf of BioNTech" (aside: the Pfizer-BioNTech relationship is worthy of a lot more analysis than it has received) after the product had been administered internationally for three months.

....

349 Pfizer, 5.3.6 *Cumulative Analysis of Post-Authorization Adverse Event Reports of PF-07302048 (BNT162B2) Received Through 28-Feb-2021.*

BNT162b2
5.3.6 Cumulative Analysis of Post-authorization Adverse Event Reports

Table 1 below presents the main characteristics of the overall cases.

Table 1. General Overview: Selected Characteristics of All Cases Received During the Reporting Interval

Characteristics		Relevant cases (N=42086)
Gender:	Female	29914
	Male	9182
	No Data	2990
Age range (years): 0.01 -107 years Mean = 50.9 years n = 34952	≤ 17	175[a]
	18-30	4953
	31-50	13886
	51-64	7884
	65-74	3098
	≥ 75	5214
	Unknown	6876
Case outcome:	Recovered/Recovering	19582
	Recovered with sequelae	520
	Not recovered at the time of report	11361
	Fatal	1223
	Unknown	9400

a. in 46 cases reported age was <16-year-old and in 34 cases <12-year-old.

Over 1,000 deaths in the first three months of administration. The actual number of doses that had been shipped when the report was published is redacted. The number that had been administered up to that date is not reported.

Pfizer's "DISCUSSION"

The data do not reveal any novel safety concerns or risks requiring label changes and support a favorable benefit risk profile of the BNT162b2 vaccine.

NOTE: I'm guessing that the key word here, for legal purposes, is "novel." They must have already known about all the adverse events in this report, including death, before the product was authorized and distributed, so technically this report does not include anything "novel," or new.

Pfizer's "SUMMARY AND CONCLUSION"

Review of the available data for this cumulative PM experience confirms a favorable benefit: risk balance for BNT162b2.

NOTE: There is no discussion of any benefits in the report.

My Conclusion

Distribution of the J&J shot was limited and the label was changed after NINE associated deaths. The "alternatives" were supposedly "not associated with deaths." But a report after just 3 months of the initial authorization of one of the two main alternatives shows OVER ONE THOUSAND deaths.

It sure seems like the BioNTech/Pfizer vaccine, for an undisclosed reason, was privileged over the J&J product by regulators, such that even more than 1,000 deaths in three months were not considered a "novel safety concern or risk requiring label changes." Not to mention withdrawing the product from the market.

My Hypothesis

I believe the BioNTech and Moderna Covid mRNA vaccines were predetermined as the only Covid vaccine products that would be not just aggressively marketed by the public health and regulatory bodies themselves, but also the only products that would remain on the market regardless of any reported adverse events, including thousands of deaths.

The reason for this, I surmise (not enough concrete proof yet to make this a definite claim), is that those two products were designed in tandem by the international biowarfare/biodefense network that ran the entire Covid pandemic and response. The biowarfare network was so hellbent on demonstrating the "safety and efficacy" of its precious mRNA platform that nothing could stand in the way of these products – especially not reports of their total lack of efficacy and jaw-droppingly horrendous safety profile.

5.3 DOD TOLD PHARMA EXEC THE VIRUS "POSED A NATIONAL SECURITY THREAT" ON FEB. 4, 2020

This chapter is based on an article I wrote in support of the claim that the SARS-CoV-2 virus, and the entire Covid-19 pandemic, were treated by the U.S. government/military and – by extension – by the global biodefense public-private partnership, as a bioterror event rather than a public health challenge.

• • •

A leaked recording obtained by investigator and writer Sasha Latypova features an executive at the pharmaceutical company AstraZeneca stating the following:

> It wasn't a surprise to me when I got a call on February 4th from the Defense Department here in the U.S. saying that the newly discovered Sars-2 virus posed a national security threat.[350]

This is an astonishing, major-newspaper headline-worthy revelation. Here's what was happening on February 4, 2020:

Virus Activity in the US

- According to CNN,[351] on February 4th there were 11 "confirmed cases of the novel coronavirus" in the United States.
- There were zero reported deaths from the virus in the US.
- As documented in my Covid Timeline Wiki Project,[352] *The New York Times* had two headlines about the virus focused on China and travelers from Wuhan. There were no op-eds on the virus.

....

350 Latypova, "Audio recording leaked from AstraZeneca: Covid was classified a national security threat by the U.S. Government/DOD on February 4, 2020."

351 Yeung et al., "February 4 coronavirus news."

352 Lerman, "Covid Timeline Wiki Project: February 4, 2020."

Virus Activity Internationally

- Approximately 490 reported deaths.
- The disease caused by the virus had not even been named "Covid-19" yet.
- The WHO said the outbreak "was not yet a pandemic."

Behind-the-Scenes Virus-Related Activity

EUA & PREP Act

Crucially, the FDA and HHS declared the first emergency basis for issuance of Emergency Use Authorization (EUA) for Covid on February 4th.[353]

As discussed extensively in part 1 of this chapter, EUA is an authority that was granted to the FDA "to strengthen public health protections against biological, chemical, nuclear, and radiological agents."

EUA powers were granted to the FDA to be used in situations of grave, immediate emergencies involving weapons of mass destruction. They were intended to allow the use of countermeasures against biological, chemical, nuclear, or radiological (CBRN) agents without going through all the usual steps of ensuring safety and efficacy, because the immediate threat of the CBRN attack would be so much greater than any potential risks caused by the countermeasure.

In conjunction with EUA, PREP Act protection was also granted retroactively to February 4th (announced March 17).[354] The Public Readiness and Emergency Preparedness (PREP) Act legally indemnifies from all liability anyone who does anything related to a product that receives Emergency Use Authorization. Again, this was intended for very extreme emergency situations involving CBRN agents, so that if a countermeasure caused harm while being used during the attack, no one would get sued.

....

353 U.S. Department of Health and Human Services, Federal Register Notice, "Determination of a Public Health Emergency," February 7, 2020.

354 U.S. Department of Health and Human Services, Federal Register Notice, "Declaration Under the Public Readiness and Emergency Preparedness Act for Medical Countermeasures Against COVID-19," March 17, 2020.

Origins Cover-Up

Anthony Fauci, Jeremy Farrar, Francis Collins, Eddie Holmes, and others in the international group of gain-of-function funders and researchers were conspiring to publish multiple documents denying the possibility that the virus could have emerged from the bioweapons lab they were funding/working with in Wuhan, China.

Emily Kopp at U.S. Right to Know compiled a detailed timeline[355] of these activities, many of which occurred on the days just before and just after February 4, 2020.

CONCLUSION

If the Department of Defense was telling pharmaceutical executives that the "novel coronavirus" was "a national security threat" on February 4, 2020 – when it had killed no one and infected 11 people in the country – there must have been a reason other than public health.

If EUA and PREP Act emergency declarations – reserved for dire situations involving attacks with CBRN agents – were issued on that same day, there must have been a reason other than public health.

If the heads of the U.S. public health agencies, including Anthony Fauci (NIAID) and Francis Collins (NIH), were spending a large portion of their time on that day frantically trying to come up with ways to claim the virus was not manufactured in a bioweapons lab – there must have been a reason other than public health.

The reason is becoming increasingly undeniable: The Covid crisis was a military/national security operation, not a public health event.

----

355 Kopp, "Timeline: the proximal origin of SARS-CoV-2."

<u>5.4</u> HOW mRNA COUNTERMEASURES ARE RELATED TO GAIN-OF-FUNCTION RESEARCH

In this chapter I explore the inextricable link between the type of research that attempts to produce biological weapons and the research intended to create countermeasures to such weapons.

Both are relevant to Covid, because SARS-CoV-2 was probably concocted in a lab in Wuhan (or maybe in a lab in the U.S. and then transported to Wuhan) where scientists from many different countries were working on potential bioweapons. And the same scientists were involved in "countermeasure research," resulting in the mRNA vaccine platform.

Even if it was not made as a bioweapon, I contend that the virus was treated as such, in order to scare world leaders into adopting the lockdown-until-vaccine scheme and to gain Emergency Use Authorization for the vaccines. And research on bioweapons using gain-of-function is real, whether or not it produces any viable results.

Taken together, the work on bioweapons, the lockdown-until-vaccine plan, and the design and manufacture of the mRNA products, were carried out by the organizations, academic institutions and government agencies that constitute the national and global biodefense public-private partnerships, as discussed in Chapter 1.

* * *

In the years immediately following the acute stage of the global Covid catastrophe, much finger-wagging and self-righteous condemnation took place in the halls of the U.S. government, regarding revelations that HHS, our umbrella public health agency, funded poorly supervised gain-of-function (GoF) research in Wuhan, China. The implication, though not the thrust of the condemnation, was that this research might have led to the creation of SARS-CoV-2 and thus to what became known as the Covid pandemic.

Peter Daszak and EcoHealth Alliance — the recipients of HHS grants for GoF research in Wuhan — have been the butt of all kinds of denunciations and performative threats of "funding suspension" and "future debarment." All total theater.[356]

Nobody, however, discussed the real nature of GoF research, the actual funders of it, and its underlying purpose[357] — which are critical for understanding the Covid pandemic response.

Bottom line: If we do not investigate the military/biodefense underpinnings of both gain-of-function research and countermeasure development, we will never understand the true corruption behind the Covid pandemic response. And we will be doomed to repeat it.

GoF Research and Medical Countermeasures Are Two Aspects of the Same Biodefense/Biowarfare Scheme

The point of GoF research is to engineer viruses that could be potential bioweapons and then develop countermeasures (medicines, vaccines) to protect your military and civilian populations from attacks with those bioweapons. (NOTE: "Pandemic preparedness" is the civilian cover/excuse for these efforts.)

This means that the beginning of the Covid saga – a real or potential lab leak, and its end – a global medical countermeasure (MCM) campaign, are not just related but mutually dependent.

Peter Daszak — a central figure in GoF-research-defunding theater, is a perfect case study, illustrating the entire Covid pandemic arc: from the possible escape of a bioengineered potential bioweapon, to the ongoing attempted coverup, to the non-public health lockdown-until-vaccine response and the culminating windfall for those engaged in all aspects of MCM deployment.

Case study: Peter Daszak

Before February 27, 2020[358] nobody had ever heard of him.

He was, and still is as of early 2025, the President of EcoHealth

---

356 Lerman, "Peter Daszak Gets DOD and CIA Funding. Why Don't They Ask About That?"

357 Lerman, "RFK, Jr.'s New Book: The Wuhan Cover-Up."

358 Lerman, "February 27, 2020: The Lockdown Plan Goes Public."

Alliance,[359] which according to its website is "a US-based organization that conducts research and outreach programs on global health, conservation and international development."

How is this related to Covid? "Dr. Daszak's research has been instrumental in identifying and predicting the origins and impact of emerging diseases across the globe. This includes identifying the bat origin of SARS…"

Daszak and GoF Research

So Daszak did research on emerging viruses, like SARS. Was he directly involved in engineering SARS-CoV-2 and possibly covering up a lab leak? It seems increasingly likely. EcoHealth Alliance whistleblower Dr. Andrew Huff[360] provided much proof of this way back in 2022. But even if you do not believe Dr. Huff's compelling testimony, and other mountains of evidence,[361] there's much more to consider:

On February 27, 2020, CNN's Zachary B. Wolf reported[362] about the novel coronavirus outbreak that "Health officials aren't even calling this outbreak a pandemic yet."

The *Washington Post* reported[363] that, according to experts, "in other parts of the world at least, most cases of the virus are mild…The United States has seen 60 cases, none fatal."

In other words, experts were following the outbreak as they would any other: by counting how many people got sick and how many died. And it seemed like most people had mild disease.

On that very same day,[364] however, *The New York Times* published a terrifying opinion piece by none other than Peter Daszak, entitled: We

359 EcoHealth Alliance, Peter Daszak profile.

360 Andrew Huff, X profile @AGHuff(.)

361 Kopp and Corin, "Emails show Wuhan lab collaborator played central role in public messaging about COVID-19 origins."

362 Wolf, "What U.S. officials today can learn from a 1918 flu."

363 Fowler et al., "California undertakes extensive effort to trace contacts of woman with coronavirus."

364 Lerman, "February 27, 2020: The Lockdown Plan Goes Public."

Knew that Disease X Was Coming. It's Here Now.[365]

[Interestingly, you can only find this opinion piece now if you directly search for it using the exact URL. If you look at the archived February 27, 2020 edition,[366] Daszak's piece is nowhere to be found. You have to know it was there to dig it up! Could the *NYT* be involved in a coverup?]

In the op-ed, the completely unknown author, presumably in his capacity as a student of emerging viruses, assumes the authority to tell us that the outbreak of SARS-CoV-2, which has yet to be called a pandemic and which has killed zero people in the United States, is the terrifying "Disease X."

But what exactly does that term mean, and where does it come from? Daszak tells us that: "In early 2018, during a meeting at the World Health Organization[367] in Geneva, a group of experts I belong to (the R&D Blueprint)[368] coined the term "Disease X."[369] [Links provided by Daszak]

Indeed, The WHO R&D Blueprint: 2018 review of emerging infectious diseases requiring urgent research and development efforts reports that:

> Disease X represents the awareness that a serious international epidemic could be caused by a pathogen currently not recognized to cause human disease. Disease X may also be a known pathogen that has changed its epidemiological characteristics, for example by increasing its transmissibility or severity.[370]

So, according to the 2018 report, Disease X was a kind of placeholder for a pandemic-causing pathogen we did not know about yet. The scariness

....

365 Daszak, "We Knew Disease X Was Coming. It's Here Now."

366 *The New York Times*, February 27, 2020 edition.

367 WHO Research and Development Blueprint, *2018 Annual review of diseases prioritized under the Research and Development Blueprint.*

368 The World Health Organization, R&D Blueprint, "About us."

369 Scutti, "World Health Organization gets ready for 'Disease X'."

370 Mehand et al., "The WHO R&D Blueprint: 2018 review of emerging infectious diseases requiring urgent research and development efforts."

of Disease X, according to this report, is that it is unknown. There is no way of knowing what the characteristics of such a virus would be. It could be a pathogen that has never infected humans before. Or it could be a known pathogen that becomes more transmissible or that causes more severe disease.

Yet in his February 27, 2020, opinion piece, Daszak claims he and his colleagues knew Disease X would be exactly like SARS-CoV-2:

> Disease X, we said back then, would likely result from a virus origi-nating in animals and would emerge somewhere on the planet where economic development drives people and wildlife together. Disease X would probably be confused with other diseases early in the outbreak and would spread quickly and silently; exploiting networks of human travel and trade, it would reach multiple countries and thwart containment. Disease X would have a mortality rate higher than a seasonal flu but would spread as easily as the flu.

I could not find any article or information from the WHO R&D Blueprint with this type of detail about Disease X.

What Daszak seems to be saying is that, somehow, he knew in 2018 that a virus would jump from animals to humans with exactly the char-acteristics that were the identifiers of the "novel coronavirus" and that were trumpeted by the biodefense planners and implementers of the Covid response as making it particularly scary:

– it would spread quickly and silently

Remember Deborah Birx's *Silent Invasion* (discussed extensively in Chapter 3)? This was the number one reason she, and all the Covid fear-mongers, used to claim we had to test everyone all the time and measure the severity of the virus by counting positive test results instead of cases of severe illness and death – all contrary to any previous management of a respiratory viral outbreak.

Also, no other zoonotic virus in recent memory (SARS-CoV-1, MERS, Ebola, Zika) behaved this way, so there was no reason to suspect Disease X would do so. Unless you knew that it was not zoonotic and had engineered characteristics that made it especially transmissible among humans.

– it would be deadlier than the flu but spread just as easily

Again, why would Daszak describe an unknown virus this way? All the other recent zoonotic viruses may have been deadlier than the flu but they spread much more slowly and were more easily containable. Unless he thought he knew something about the particular Disease X he was describing – because it had been engineered to easily spread among humans.

Disease X links right to...genetic vaccine platforms

It gets better. In the link Daszak provides from "Disease X" we find a 2018 CNN[371] article quoting a prominent expert who is mostly interested not in defining Disease X, but rather in explaining why we need to develop countermeasures to combat it. The expert? Dr. Anthony Fauci. The countermeasures he's advocating? Flexible platforms using customizable genetic information:

> When confronted with the unknown, the WHO recognizes that it must 'nimbly move' and that this involves creating platform technologies, explained Fauci.
>
> Essentially, scientists develop customizable recipes for creating vaccines. Then, when an outbreak happens, they can sequence the unique genetics of the virus causing the disease and plug the correct sequence into the already-developed platform to create a new vaccine.

But wait, there's more. The CNN story is about Fauci's interest in genetic vaccine platforms. What about Daszak?

In February 2016, Daszak participated in a working group on Rapid Medical Countermeasure Response to Infectious Diseases: Enabling Sustainable Capabilities Through Ongoing Public- and Private-Sector Partnerships.[372]

....

371 Scutti, "World Health Organization gets ready for 'Disease X'."

372 Rapid Medical Countermeasure Response to Infectious Diseases: Enabling Sustainable Capabilities Through Ongoing Public- and Private-Sector Partnerships: Workshop Summary, "Developing MCMs for Coronaviruses."

The summary of the workshop bemoans the difficulty of developing countermeasures when nobody is that interested in them until a pandemic strikes, at which point it's too late. And who is doing the bemoaning? You guessed it:

> Daszak reiterated that, until an infectious disease crisis is very real, present, and at an emergency threshold, it is often largely ignored. To sustain the funding base beyond the crisis, he said, we need to increase public understanding of the need for MCMs such as a pan-influenza or pan-coronavirus vaccine. A key driver is the media, and the economics follow the hype. We need to use that hype to our advantage to get to the real issues. Investors will respond if they see profit at the end of process, Daszak stated.

Just to make it even more clear that Daszak and EcoHealth Alliance are active participants in the global biodefense public-private partnership, we also know that EcoHealth is mostly funded by the State Department and Pentagon.

In an extensive expose on Peter Daszak and EcoHealth Alliance, *The Intercept* reported in December 2021:

> EcoHealth Alliance's funding from the U.S. government, which Daszak has said makes up some 80 percent of its budget, has also grown in recent years. Since 2002, according to an Intercept analysis of public records, the organization has received more than $118 million in grants and contracts from federal agencies, $42 million of which comes from the Department of Defense. Much of that money has been awarded through programs focused not on health or ecology, however, but on the prevention of biowarfare, bioterrorism, and other misuses of pathogens.[373]

....

373 Lerner, "The Virus Hunters: How the Pursuit of Unknown Viruses Risks Triggering the Next Pandemic."

Here's what nearly two decades of government funding for EcoHealth Alliance looks like (graph from *Intercept* article):

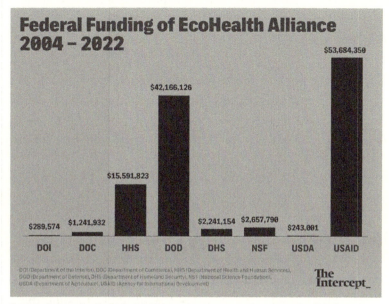

Federal Funding of EcoHealth Alliance 2004 – 2022

$289,574	$1,241,932	$15,591,823	$42,166,126	$2,241,154	$2,657,790	$243,001	$53,684,350
DOI	DOC	HHS	DOD	DHS	NSF	USDA	USAID

DOI (Department of the Interior), DOC (Department of Commerce), HHS (Department of Health and Human Services), DOD (Department of Defense), DHS (Department of Homeland Security), NSF (National Science Foundation), USDA (Department of Agriculture), USAID (Agency for International Development)

The Intercept_

Total funding received by EcoHealth Alliance through grants and contracts from U.S. federal agencies since 2002. The National Institute of Allergy and Infectious Diseases is a division of the Department of Health and Human Services and its grants are represented under HHS. Graphic: Soohee Cho/The Intercept

As RFK, Jr. wrote, based on this information, in *The Wuhan Cover-Up*:

By far, Daszak's largest funding pool was the CIA surrogate, the United States Agency for International Development (USAID). Through USAID, the CIA funneled nearly $65 million in PREDICT funding to EcoHealth between 2009 and 2020.
(p. 228, Kindle Edition)[374]

Yet another article examining Daszak's military/biodefense ties appeared in *Independent Scientist News*[375] in December 2020, reporting that most

---

374 Kennedy, *The Wuhan Cover-Up*.

375 Husseini, "Peter Daszak's EcoHealth Alliance Has Hidden Almost $40 Million In Pentagon Funding And Militarized Pandemic Science."

of EcoHealth Alliance's Pentagon funding "was from the Defense Threat Reduction Agency (DTRA), which is a branch of the DOD which states it is tasked to "counter and deter weapons of mass destruction and improvised threat networks."[376]

Furthermore,

> The military links of the EcoHealth Alliance are not limited to money and mindset. One noteworthy 'policy advisor' to the EcoHealth Alliance is David Franz. Franz is former commander of Fort Detrick, which is the principal U.S. government biowarfare/biodefense facility.

The ISN article also provides a handy spreadsheet detailing EcoHealth funding.[377]

CONCLUSION

If Congressional investigators are serious about uncovering the origins of the Covid pandemic and Peter Daszak's ties to it, they should ask the following questions. The answers are key to understanding the entire global biodefense public-private partnership:

Non-public health funding sources and projects

- Most of the government funding for EcoHealth Alliance comes not from public health agencies but from USAID (State Department/ CIA) and the Pentagon. What projects are these non-public health agencies funding? Are these projects related to biodefense/ biowarfare research?
- Is the USAID and Pentagon-funded virus research conducted by EcoHealth and/or its partners intended primarily to prepare for naturally occurring pandemics or for potential biowarfare/bioterrorism attacks?

....

376 Defense Threat Reduction Agency, Landing page.

377 *Independent Science News*, "Ecohealth Funding as of 01/01/2020."

- Do the USAID and Pentagon-funded projects conducted by EcoHealth and/or its partners involve creating pandemic potential pathogens as part of biodefense/biowarfare research?
- Do you know or suspect that SARS-CoV-2 was an engineered virus created as part of a USAID and Pentagon-funded biowarfare/biodefense project?
- Do the USAID and Pentagon-funded projects conducted by EcoHealth and/or its partners involve work on medical counter-measures against potential biowarfare/bioterrorism agents?

Disease X op-ed

- On February 27, 2020, before the Covid pandemic had been declared and before anyone in the U.S. had died of Covid-19, you wrote an op-ed for *The New York Times*[378] stating that the novel coronavirus was "Disease X." You explained that the term Disease X was coined by you and a bunch of experts at the World Health Organization in 2018. Did you think SARS-CoV-2 was a known pathogen that had "changed its epidemiological characteristics" by "increasing its transmissibility or severity"? If yes, what made you think that?
- Did you think SARS-CoV-2 was a potential bioweapon that had been developed using funds from USAID and DOD by EcoHealth Alliance and/or its research partners in China or elsewhere?
- *The New York Times* has subsequently erased your Disease X op-ed from their online 2/27/2020 issue. You can only find it through the direct link. Why do you think they have made it all but impossible for anyone who doesn't already know about the article to find it? Do you regret having written it?

....

378 Daszak, "We Knew Disease X Was Coming. It's Here Now."

Linking Disease X to genetic vaccine platforms

- In the *NYT* op-ed, you provided a link from the term "Disease X" to a 2018 CNN article[379] in which Dr. Anthony Fauci says that, in order to combat such dangerous as-yet-nonexistent pathogens, the WHO recognizes that it must "nimbly move" and that this involves creating "platform technologies." Fauci goes on to say that "scientists develop customizable recipes for creating vaccines. Then, when an outbreak happens, they can sequence the unique genetics of the virus causing the disease, and plug the correct sequence into the already-developed platform to create a new vaccine."

  That sounds an awful lot like the mRNA platform used for the Covid countermeasures that came to be known as the "mRNA vaccines."

  Why did you link to that particular article from your op-ed about disease X? Were you suggesting that the solution to the pandemic that you appeared to be predicting would be a genetic platform in which the "correct sequence" could be plugged to create vaccines?

- Were you already aware of the Covid mRNA vaccines being developed at the time of your op-ed (February 27, 2020) by Moderna and BioNTech/Pfizer, long before the official launch of Operation Warp Speed (May 2020)?

- Is it true that the Pentagon considered the mRNA platforms to be the preferred countermeasures against Covid-19, and that these were always intended to reach full funding and development, starting all the way back in January 2020?

- Was the USAID and Pentagon-funded research conducted by EcoHealth and/or its partners related to the development of such mRNA vaccines? If so, how?

....

379 Scutti, "World Health Organization gets ready for 'Disease X'."

The need for a crisis to justify funding and development of genetic vaccine platforms

- In 2016, you participated in an Institute of Medicine working group on Rapid Medical Countermeasure Response to Infectious Diseases.[380] It sounds in that report like you're saying that we need the media to hype up a crisis so that investors will want to fund the type of pan-coronavirus vaccine that is exactly the genetic platform you highlighted in your op-ed, and also exactly the platform that emerged into public awareness shortly after your op-ed, and became known as the Covid mRNA vaccines.
  - » Can you explain this uncanny overlap between your description of what was needed to get such platforms developed in 2016 and what actually happened in 2020?
- Did the USAID and Pentagon-funded research on coronaviruses conducted by EcoHealth Alliance and/or its partners support the development of such platforms? If so, how?
- Were you aware of a plan to use the emergence of SARS-CoV-2 as a trigger for the media hype, public-private funding, and massive mRNA vaccine development and deployment in early 2020 – exactly as you described them in 2016?
- If you were aware of such a plan, who was involved in it, and what was your role?

....

380 Rapid Medical Countermeasure Response to Infectious Diseases: Enabling Sustainable Capabilities Through Ongoing Public- and Private-Sector Partnerships: Workshop Summary, "Developing MCMs for Coronaviruses."

QUESTIONS FOR FUTURE
INVESTIGATIONS

In this chapter, I provide lists of questions for further investigation. The global Covid coup, as discussed in this book, was arguably an inevitable result of the rise of the gargantuan biodefense global public-private partnership (see Chapter 1). However, the role of the military/intelligence, academic/scientific, and global governance actors in the pandemic remains almost entirely outside of the public discourse about Covid.

If we do not expose what happened, it will necessarily happen again – maybe not a global emergency involving a virus, but one involving a "climate disaster" or "cyber pandemic" or a similarly vague but terrifying "catastrophe."

My hope is that the information and research in this book will prompt additional research into all of the following questions:

Who actually determined the U.S. government's Covid response policy?

We know from official government documents (see Chapter 3) that it was the National Security Council (NSC), NOT the public health agencies. But who exactly on the NSC was in charge? Who wrote the policy?

What was the U.S. government's official Covid response policy?

Again, we know it was devised by someone or a group of someones on the NSC, but where is the policy document and what does it say?

Why the secrecy?

On March 11, 2020, Reuters reported[381] that "The White House has ordered federal health officials to treat top-level coronavirus meetings as classified." Reuters sources said "the National Security Council (NSC), which advises the president on security issues, ordered the classification."

Furthermore, government officials said "dozens of classified discussions about such topics as the scope of infections, quarantines, and travel restrictions have been held since mid-January" and they were held "in a secure area called a 'Sensitive Compartmentalized Information Facility,' or SCIF."

Reuters noted that:

SCIFs are usually reserved for intelligence and military operations. Ordinary cell phones and computers can't be brought into the chambers. HHS has SCIFs because theoretically it would play a major role in biowarfare or chemical attacks.

- Why were Covid meetings held in a secure SCIF (see below) normally reserved for intelligence and military operations?
- Why were these meetings classified?
- Where are the documents pertaining to what was discussed/decided at these meetings? Why are they not declassified and shared with the public?

Regarding Lead Federal Agency (LFA) for Pandemic Response:

On March 13, 2020, the same day as the official date of the *PanCAP-A* (see Chapter 3.5), President Trump declared a nationwide emergency under the Stafford Act.

President Trump, in his letter invoking the Stafford Act stated that:

381 Roston and Taylor, "Exclusive: White House told federal health agency to classify coronavirus deliberations - sources."

In accordance with this determination, the Federal Emergency Management Agency may provide, as appropriate, assistance pursuant to section 502 and 503 of the Stafford Act for emergency protective measures not authorized under other Federal statutes. Administrator Gaynor shall coordinate and direct other Federal agencies in providing needed assistance under the Stafford Act, subject to the Department of Health and Human Services' role as the lead Federal agency for the Federal Government's response to COVID-19.[382]

Yet five days later, on March 18, 2020, FEMA was directed by the White House to take over as Lead Federal Agency (LFA) for the government's Covid response, a role it was not prepared for and had never held before. HHS, the agency named in every pandemic preparedness document as LFA was removed from that position.

- What was the reason for this unexpected, unprecedented removal of HHS from its role as LFA?
- How did this change affect the role of HHS in the management of the pandemic?
- How did this change affect the overall U.S. government response to the pandemic?
- On what basis was FEMA given the LFA role?

....

382 The White House, Press Release, "Letter from President Donald J. Trump on Emergency Determination Under the Stafford Act," March 13, 2020.

Questions for President Donald Trump and/or members of his first administration

Why did you agree to spend trillions of dollars to keep everything shut down?

- It was shocking when you seemed to pivot 180 degrees[383] in just a few days, from saying that Covid would not be worse than a bad flu season, to announcing that we would throw everything we had at it, locking down the whole country — a devastating step that had never been taken before, for any reason, including war. It was especially surprising that you agreed to the economic shutdown. What made you change your mind?

Should you have allowed the security state to take over?

- A lot of information has come out[384] suggesting that you changed your mind because your National Security Council, and related military and intelligence leaders, told you the virus was a potential bioweapon that leaked from a Chinese lab. Is that what you were told? Did they tell you millions of people would die and you would be responsible, if you didn't follow their plan?
- In a *Time Magazine* article[385] you were quoted saying "I can't tell you that" when you were asked about why you thought the virus came from a lab in Wuhan. You said, "I'm not allowed to tell you that." Who was not allowing you to speak openly about the possibility that it was a lab leak? Can you speak openly about it now?
- Who made the decision in the middle of March 2020 to invoke the Stafford Act in all 50 states at the same time (which had never been done before), and to put FEMA in charge as the Lead Federal

383 Tucker, "How They Convinced Trump to Lockdown."

384 Ibid

385 Elliott, "How Distrust of Donald Trump Muddled the COVID-19 'Lab Leak' Debate."

Agency for pandemic response, when FEMA had no warning and no experience in this area at all? Who decided to remove HHS from the role of Lead Federal Agency, which it was supposed to have according to every public health pandemic planning document before Covid? Did you make those decisions or did the NSC or other military or intelligence advisors tell you to take those steps?

Who was actually in charge?

- When you brought Scott Atlas in,[386] he advised you to open the country back up immediately. It seems like you really wanted someone in the White House with an opinion that was different from the one you were hearing in favor of lockdowns. But, for some reason, there was enormous resistance to bringing any experts in. There was even supposed to be a meeting at the end of March (long before Atlas arrived) with top epidemiologists that mysteriously got canceled.[387] Why did you have so little control over who advised you about the pandemic? Why didn't you follow the advice of Scott Atlas if, as he reported in his book, you pretty much agreed with him that the lockdowns were disastrous?

- Most people think Anthony Fauci was in charge of the pandemic response. But in his book, Dr. Atlas reports that you said the main problem wasn't Fauci, it was Deborah Birx (See Chapters 3.1-3.4). Is that because Birx was in charge of coordinating the NSC/DHS response, and Fauci was just a front to make it seem like a public health response?

- A few months into the lockdowns, you sounded as if you had lost control of the situation, like in the tweet from May 18th, 2020 when you wrote in all caps: REOPEN OUR COUNTRY! You'd think if anyone could have ended the lockdowns, it would have

....

386 Tucker, "A President Betrayed by Bureaucrats: Scott Atlas's Masterpiece on the Covid Disaster."

387 Hartmann, "The Most Important Meeting in the History of the World That Never Happened."

been the President. But you seemed to feel helpless to reverse what was happening. Is that because there had been a sort of silent coup of the NSC and Department and Homeland Security?[388]

Was it a biodefense or a public health response?

- If the answers to all the previous questions are classified, that would confirm that the response to Covid involved secret machinations of national security entities,[389] or what you often refer to as the Deep State. Can you at least confirm that much?

Did the Deep State effectively stage a coup against your administration?

- In March 2023, you said: "Either the Deep State Destroys America, or we destroy the Deep State."[390] Were you just mad at the justice department for trying to prosecute you, or were you frustrated because the National Security Council, DHS, and DoD seized control of the Covid response and you feel they did not behave in the best interests of all Americans?
- Here's my guess as to what the Deep State told you about Covid: "We, your biowarfare and bioterrorism experts, are hereby informing you that the novel coronavirus is a potential bioweapon that unfortunately leaked from a bioweapons lab into the civilian population in China. It sounds bad, but luckily we've spent many years planning for just such an eventuality. If you don't do what we say, millions will die and you will be blamed. If you follow our plan, you might very well become the President who takes credit for a scientific miracle that will rid the world of pandemics forever." Is this a fair representation of what you were told?

388 Senger, "Was the Covid Response a Coup by the Intelligence Community?"

389 Lerman, "What to Ask a Covid Task Force Member Under Oath."

390 Allen, "Awaiting possible indictment, Trump rallies in Waco and vows to 'destroy the deep state.'"

Did you participate in censorship and propaganda?

- Were you aware of the massive censorship[391] and propaganda[392] that were happening to make people accept the lockdowns and vaccines? Do you feel like you were part of that campaign to convince people? Or do you feel like you were somehow forced to participate in it?
- On March 7, 2020, Tucker Carlson came to warn you[393] that "someone who works in the U.S. government, a nonpolitical person with access to a lot of intelligence" told him the virus would kill millions of people if you didn't lock down immediately and wait for vaccines. Do you know who warned Tucker and, most likely, urged him to warn you?

Did you engage in international coordination of the response?

- Were you in touch with leaders of other allied countries to coordinate the response to the pandemic? It's pretty astonishing how most of our closest allies ended up doing exactly the same thing at the same time (See Chapter 3.9). If you were not the one who was coordinating with foreign leaders, were you aware of that type of coordination going on – especially with the UK, Canada, Australia, New Zealand, Israel, Germany, and other NATO allies?

What's your position on the mRNA injections?

- Were you told by your biodefense team that mRNA technology was a miraculous platform that would end the threat of pandemics, among other amazing accomplishments?
- You have repeatedly expressed great pride in the "success" of Operation Warp Speed, which produced mRNA shots that were

....

391 Kheriaty, "The Censorship Hegemon Must Be Stopped."

392 Malone, "Propaganda and the U.S. Government."

393 Tucker, "This Was Tucker Carlson's 'Greatest Public Mistake'."

supposed to prevent Covid infection (as stated explicitly in the contracts signed by the DoD and the pharma companies under your administration – see Chapter 5.1). The injections were actually administered only once Biden became President, so one could argue that he was responsible for whatever happened after that. Would you agree that the Covid mRNA vaccines failed to accomplish what they were supposed to?

- When it became obvious that they prevented neither infection nor transmission, and when evidence emerged of extensive harm from side effects,[394] including death[395] — did you change your mind?

Questions for Anthony Fauci and/or Covid Task Force members

Who was in Charge of Government Communications about Covid?

According to the U.S. Government's COVID-19 Response Plan, starting on February 28, 2020, "all federal communication and messaging" about the pandemic had to go through the Office of the Vice President, which housed the Task Force, which was led by the National Security Council.

- Who on the Task Force was in charge of crafting public communications about the pandemic?
- Who on the Task Force was in charge of efforts to censor messaging that questioned or contradicted Task Force/NSC policy?
- Who outside the Task Force was in charge of designing and enforcing the censorship efforts on behalf of the Task Force/NSC?

....

394 Barnett, "Insights from the Hermit Kingdom's 2022 Vaccine Safety Data."

395 Elijah, "The Veil of Silence over Excess Deaths."

Why was the CDC Forbidden from Communicating about the Pandemic?

Although it was supposed to play a leadership role[396] in pandemic communications, starting on February 28, 2020, the CDC was actually "not permitted to conduct public briefings," according to a Senate report.[397]

It sounds like the agency that was supposed to be in charge of communicating with the public about the pandemic was itself being CENSORED by the Task Force/NSC.

- Who forbade the CDC from conducting public briefings about the pandemic?
- Why were CDC communications with the public completely shut down?
- Was this part of the overall efforts by the Task Force/NSC to censor any messaging that contradicted their policy?

Why was the Intelligence Community so Heavily Involved in Covid Censorship?

Many deeply and carefully investigated reports show extensive involvement of military/intelligence agencies and personnel in Covid censorship efforts.

Here are just a few examples:

How Twitter Rigged the Covid Debate,[398] by David Zweig

Pentagon Was Involved in Domestic Censorship Scheme,[399] by Alex Gutentag

....

396 Lerman, "CDC Was NOT in Charge of Covid Communications. The National Security Council Was."

397 U.S. Senate Committee on Homeland Security & Governmental Affairs, *Historically Unprepared: Examination of the Federal Government's Pandemic Preparedness and Initial COVID-19 Response,* December 2022

398 Zweig (@davidzweig), "The Twitter Files: How Twitter Rigged The Covid Debate."

399 Gutentag, "Pentagon Was Involved In Domestic Censorship Scheme, New CTIL Whistleblower Files Show."

The Virality Project Was a Government Front to Coordinate Censorship,[400] by Andrew Lowenthal and Alex Gutentag

- Were members of the Task Force coordinating with the FBI, CIA, DHS, CISA, or any other intelligence entity to censor messaging that questioned or contradicted Task Force/NSC policy?
- Why were intelligence agencies involved in censoring Covid messaging?

Were International NGOs and the WHO Involved in the Censorship of American Citizens?

Here's one of the earliest known instances of Covid censorship from all the way back in February 2020, in which the following international cast participated:

- Anthony Fauci of the U.S. NIAID and Francis Collins of the U.S. NIH
- Jeremy Farrar, then head of the British Wellcome Trust (the wealthiest nonprofit in the UK[401] that prospered during Covid[402] and gave money to EcoHealth Alliance,[403] among other[404] Covid-related orgs) now Chief Scientist at the WHO[405]

400 Lowenthal, "The Virality Project was a government front to coordinate censorship."

401 Gordon, "Wellcome Trust Saw 34.5% Returns for Fiscal Year 2020-2021. Here Was Its Strategy."

402 Moss, "Wellcome Trust 'prospers' under COVID-19 fallout with 12.3% return."

403 Lerman, "Peter Daszak Gets DOD and CIA Funding. Why Don't They Ask About That?"

404 Coalition for Epidemic Preparedness Innovations, "Bill & Melinda Gates Foundation and Wellcome pledge $300 million to CEPI to fight COVID-19 and combat threat of future pandemics."

405 World Health Organization, "World Health Organization names Sir Jeremy Farrar as Chief Scientist, Dr Amelia Latu Afuhaamango Tuipulotu as Chief Nursing Officer."

- Tedros Ghebreyesus,[406] head of the World Health Organization (WHO), and Bernhard Schwartlander, the WHO representative in China (about whom little info is available online – and who requires more investigation).

As reported by U.S. Right To Know:[407]

on Sunday, February 2, 2020, at 11:28AM, Farrar flagged a ZeroHedge article [now archived][408] in an email to Fauci and Collins, raising the possibility of virus=bioweapon. In the email, he mentioned that the WHO leaders were in the process of making an important decision.

From: Jeremy Farrar   (b) (6)
Sent: Sunday, February 2, 2020 11:28 AM
To: Fauci, Anthony (NIH/NIAID) [E]   (b) (6); Collins, Francis (NIH/OD) [E]
     (b) (6)
Cc: Tabak, Lawrence (NIH/OD) [E]   (b) (6)>
Subject: Re: Teleconference

Tedros and Bernhard have apparently gone into conclave....they need to decide today in my view. If they do prevaricate, I would appreciate a call with you later tonight or tomorrow to think how we might take forward.

Meanwhile....

https://www.zerohedge.com/geopolitical/coronavirus-contains-hiv-insertions-stoking-fears-over-artificially-created-bioweapon

---

Just two and a half hours later, at approximately 1:57PM ZeroHedge was suspended on Twitter.[409]

----

406 Amhara Professionals Union, "Calling your attention regarding Dr. Tedros Adhanom Ghebreyesus, who is one of the finalists for the assignment of WHO Director General. Dr. Ghebreyesus is an individual suspected of a crime against Humanity in his home country."

407 Kopp, "Timeline: The proximal origin of SARS-CoV-2."

408 Durden, "Coronavirus Contains "HIV Insertions", Stoking Fears Over Artificially Created Bioweapon."

409 Kopp, "Timeline: The proximal origin of SARS-CoV-2."

- Was the correspondence between Fauci and Farrar, involving the leaders of the World Health Organization, in any way related to the suspension of ZeroHedge on Twitter?
- If so, who was responsible for conveying the message to Twitter about the suspension?
- Were international organizations like the WHO, and NGOs including the Wellcome Trust, involved in Covid censorship activities in coordination with U.S. officials/agencies?

I hope this book will engender many more questions. And I hope someday we will get answers.

ABOUT BROWNSTONE INSTITUTE

Brownstone Institute, established May 2021, is a publisher and research institute that places the highest value on the voluntary interaction of individuals and groups while minimizing the use of violence and force, including that which is exercised by public authority.

INDEX

Published by Brownstone Institute
Austin, Texas

Made in the USA
Coppell, TX
12 May 2025

49230300R00173